The White Mouse

JACK DUARTE

For information, address Cloud 9 Press,
PO Box 385, Lexington, KY 40588.
ISBN: 978-0-9894367-1 - 7

Cover by Chris Inman, Visual Riot
Interior Design by Chip Holtzhauer
E-pub Design by Mark Vorenkamp

Also by Jack DuArte

The Resistance (Revised)

SINGAPORE (Revised)

Spitfire

MALTA

Dedication

To the memories of Nancy Wake Fiocca, Violette Szabo
and all the other Special Operations Executive agents
who fought against Axis oppression.

And, to my dear friends John Hernandez, Lisa Sins Hart,
Karen Elliott, Karl Forester, and Rex Bailey, all of whom
are battling various illnesses.

Acknowledgements

In Great Britain:
David Manson, Ashley House

In France:
Eugenie Cantier

In the United States:
Rex Bailey

To My Editors:
Richard Francis for his time and effort.
To Susan DuArte for her exactness and complete
attention to detail. To John Duarte for his exceptional
insight into the flow and substance of this novel.

Forword

The daily *Société Nationale des Chemins de fer Français* (SNCF) train from Perpignan and the Pyrénées puffed steadily against an ominous grey and black background as it neared the stone outline of the new multi-leveled Toulouse main railway station. As the engineer slowly eased the control of the 230B steam-powered #585's engine, his attention was diverted to a group of uniformed men waiting at the end of the station platform. One of them waved a red flag in a downward movement to signal the train to come to a complete stop.

The engineer contemplated. *The stupid Vichy police again. This time they will board the train before we even enter the station. What difference would it have been for them to wait for us to stop inside the station? Their typical idiotic flair for the dramatic. Oh, well, I am just an engineer...*

The train came to a complete stop and the group hurried to board the coaches. It was important to the Vichy policemen and Milice operatives that no one aboard the train be allowed the chance to escape. Several trucks appeared around the station's rear and came up to a spot just abreast of the lead carriage.

On board the train, the somewhat abrupt stop did not go unnoticed. In the lone first class coach that was lined with lace curtains and operable electric lights, Nancy Wake Fiocca looked out her window at the unfolding turn of events. Nattily dressed in a dark blue suit that would be considered a perfect traveling dress by most French women, she surveyed the scene in front of her. Obviously the Vichy police were looking for someone who had something to hide, and she certainly was well-qualified in that regard. As she weighed her options, she realized she had only a few moments to act. She remembered that she had worn flat shoes rather than heels, a fact that was favorable. An instant later she decided to make a quick run for it. Nancy jumped off the train and headed for the last of the waiting trucks, athletically leap-frogging the tailboard. As she rounded a corner, a group of angry, shouting students holding protest cards demanding more classes and a looser school environment, presented a formidable barrier. She tried to make her way through the melee, but the crowd was too thick.

An instant later, the sweaty hand of a Vichy policeman grabbed her collar and roughly pulled her away from the crowd.

"Sorry, Mademoiselle, you must come with me," he muttered in a gruff tone. "We have some questions for you and the others on the train. You will be taken to the gendarmerie with the others."

When the trucks were filled with all the passengers, they slowly lumbered to the main police station on the boulevard de l'Embrochure a mere five minutes away. Upon arrival, the entire group of around eighty passengers was placed in two large rooms and told to wait.

Nancy pondered her situation. As the wife of a wealthy Marseilles businessman, she should not have much of a problem explaining her presence on the train. But, as a secret operative of the French Resistance attempting to escape France, the Australian-raised brunette knew she was snared in a most dreadful setting.

No need to get all upset. I didn't see the policeman who caught me say anything to anyone else about my attempted escape. I pray he thought I was just scared and ran at the thought of facing the police. I must hope for the best and put on a good show. After all, I am dressed well beyond the average Frenchwoman and that will help. I also have a current carte d'identite that is genuine, so I just need to come up with a story that makes some sense. Bloody unlucky for me it is. Something must have happened to put the Vichy police on edge. They don't usually stop trains before they reach the station. That was odd…

About an hour later, a number of the detainees were escorted out of the room for questioning. Nancy's turn came about fifteen minutes later when a small, pock-marked man entered the room and signaled in her direction. He nodded for her to come with him.

He held the back of her arm and followed closely behind. At a doorway on the right, he beckoned for her to enter. The man turned the handle and opened the door, revealing another larger man in the standard Franc-Garde policeman's uniform. His dark blue jacket covered a white button-down, collared shirt and a thin black tie. The Vichy insignia, a silver circle with a looping 'V', which crossed down into it, stood out against the dark blue coat. The man sat behind a table beneath a suspended light, the only illumination inside the smallish room. The oval-faced officer puffed on his Gitane as the small man roughly pushed Nancy toward a chair facing him. Nancy looked sordidly at her captor and took the chair.

"What is this all about?" she demanded with authority. "Why am I being detained? You have no right…"

"Shut up," the seated man interrupted. "I am the one who asks the questions here."

"But, there must be some mistake. I…"

"I told you to shut up," he repeated. He reached over the table and slapped her hard on the face. "Next time I won't be so gentle."

Nancy recoiled, feeling genuine pain on her left cheek. *The prick, he actually hit me.*

"What were you doing on the train from Perpignan? Tell me the truth or it will be harder for you."

Nancy considered her plight and began the story she had formulated while waiting for the interrogation.

"My husband and I were on a holiday in the mountains," she began as earnestly as possible. "We had a dreadful fight and he left me. I don't know where he went. I waited a day and then decided to return to Marseille where we live. You can check with the authorities in Marseille to insure my story is true. Go on, check it out, then release me," she demanded.

"And you know nothing about the explosion at the cinema?" he replied, looking directly into her face.

"What explosion? I was in Perpignan for the last four days. I don't even know about any explosion. Are you insane accusing me of such a thing? I want to talk to your superior. We'll get to the bottom of all this."

The tall, attractive young woman's verbal attack took the seasoned officer back a bit. *Maybe she is telling the truth, she is certainly adamant enough about it all. Perhaps I should give her a chance to cool off in the jail... think about her circumstances...*

The Vichy policeman looked at Nancy and gestured to his associate.

"Take her out and put her in a cell. And, be careful, Marcel. She seems to have a lot of spunk."

The second policeman nodded, then grabbed Nancy's elbow and jerked her to her feet. He pushed her out into the hallway and down a narrow corridor to where a series of individual cells were located. Finding an unoccupied one, he opened the cell door and gestured her inside.

Nancy looked around the grubby cell that was complete with a soiled mattress. The place was void of anything else.

Well, I've done it now. Fine mess I'm in. I've gotten myself captured and placed in this lousy cell. I guess I'll just have to wait it out. Might as well try and rest a bit, no telling what will happen next. She removed her jacket and placed it as a pillow on which to place her head. There was no way she was going to let her face touch the soiled and greasy mattress. No way in hell.

◆　◆　◆

After a disconcerting, and oft-interrupted lie-down that scarcely resembled sleep, Nancy awoke to a soundless and almost totally black environment. She looked at her watch and realized she had been in the cell for more than six hours. Just before midnight, another Vichy officer came and removed her from the cell. He said nothing, but wasn't nearly as rough and offensive as the first officer. He marched her back to the original interrogation room where the same large police-man from earlier was seated. His uniform coat was missing and his collar was now unbuttoned. He looked up as she entered the room.

"Have you changed your mind and decided to tell me the truth?" the Garde officer spoke first. "You must realize that it will go much easier for you if you do."

"I've already told you I know nothing about any bombing. Have you checked my story in Marseille?" she again enquired as forcefully as she was capable of doing.

"No one has ever heard of you in Marseille. Lies. Nothing but lies. You are lying to save yourself," the policeman replied, unconvincingly.

"I don't believe you even took the time to check," Nancy responded bravely. "If you had you would be setting me free."

"*T'es une pute*" was the policeman's agitated reply. "A prostitute is what you are." He slapped her hard across her right cheek. The second policeman neared and grabbed her arms. The two officers pushed and shoved the helpless woman who attempted to push and shove back to little avail. Finally, the order was given to take her away. She was led down a different corridor from before and forcibly thrown into another room. The room reeked of a foul, earthy smell. Nancy gathered herself and sat up.

She had been thrown into a stinking toilet room with a hole in the floor. It would be her new home for the foreseeable future. She looked around and consid-ered her circumstances. For some reason her mind drifted back to Australia and her youth. She remembered her mother and the time she ran away from home. At that time, Nancy became a nurse and learned how to help people in need. Now *she* was the one in need. Would there be someone to help her?

◆ ◆ ◆

That evening, another gendarme entered the room. Nancy had noticed him earlier when entering the station, but up to now, he had not had a hand in her interrogation. He entered and placed his finger across his mouth for her to remain silent.

"Come with me," he said softly, almost whispering. "They've gone home for the night."

The man's calm demeanor reassured Nancy. She followed him into a small interior office. He pointed to a table in the middle of the room. "There is some coffee and a little something to eat."

Nancy looked at him and rushed toward the coffee. "I haven't had anything to eat or drink since I came here," she confessed. "I am on the verge of starving."

"Eat what you can and then you can rest on the table when you finish. I will leave my greatcoat to cover you. I will return before the others arrive in the morning and take you back to *la chiotte*."

Nancy regarded the man and shook her head in appreciation. Under any circumstances, the prospect of spending the night on a desk with a coat for warmth certainly beat the alternative of lying on a cold concrete floor next to a stinking hole in the floor.

Maybe there is some hope after all, she resolved. *If my benefactor isn't in the Resistance himself, at least he is a Frenchman who hasn't lost all his senses. I must simply toughen myself to this situation and outlast the bastards. They are looking for someone to blame for the blasted bombing and I happen to be available. This must all run its course, it just must.* Exhausted and weak from her ordeal, she quickly fell asleep. The hardness of her bed made no difference and Nancy slept soundly for the first time since she left Perpignan.

◆ ◆ ◆

The same dreary charade lasted for the next four days, with Nancy being grilled by day and left in the stinking toilet room at night. The same gendarme came each evening and rescued her from her pitiful chamber. Each night he provided food and coffee for her to recharge herself. By now, her blue suit was torn and dirty and smelled from the time she spent in *la chiotte*.

Time passed by slowly and Nancy found herself delving back into her memory to help overcome the putrid smell and the basic inopportune events of her arrest.

More than once she returned to her childhood. She could clearly remember the story her mother often told. At Nancy's birth, the midwife assisting noticed a spot on the top of Nancy's head and pronounced it a sign of good luck. Nancy's mother believed the woman and repeated it often to her daughter. Nancy grew up believing the mark would aid her throughout her life. At present, she doubted the mark for the first time in many years. *What's to come of all this? I've been here for two days and nothing has happened. How long will this last? Will my lucky spot get me out of this mess?* She resolved to be positive about the situation and finally managed to doze off to sleep.

For reasons she could not conceive, Nancy had come to the conclusion that the Vichy police *actually believed* she was a prostitute and that she had some involvement in the cinema bombing. Each day she was roughed up and yelled at constantly, but she decided to hold her ground on that matter. Giving in to them was never an option, and she determined to remain firm at all costs.

On the fifth day, Nancy was again pulled into the interrogation room. She looked up and saw an additional face in the room. The face was part of a well-dressed, tall man in a business suit standing between two Vichy policemen. She looked more closely and saw the face that was actually *smiling* at her.

It can't be. O'Leary here? I must be hallucinating. Why would the head of the local French Resistance be smiling at me across the desk? Am I going crazy?

O'Leary continued grinning as several scenarios crossed Nancy's flustered mind.

Why is he here? I must not show any recognition for him. That would be quite unwise for both of us. Then a thought entered her mind. *He must be here as a free French citizen, not in the cause of the Resistance. The policemen are actually showing respect for him, or so it seems.*

O'Leary mumbled something to the policemen who both laughed. He approached Nancy, kissed her on each cheek and whispered to her to start looking as if she was at least somewhat *fond* of him. He had just told the Vichy officers that Nancy was his mistress and it was all a big mistake.

Thirty minutes later, the pair walked hand in hand out of the police station. Still a bit wobbly from her ordeal, Nancy could not believe her sudden turn of fate.

"I told the police that you were a friend of Pierre Laval, the chief minister of Vichy," O'Leary confessed. "Good thing he was on a holiday or something. I also told them you were my mistress."

Nancy glanced up at him but quickly smiled. "Good show, Pat. It was downright disgusting in there. They thought I was a prostitute. A prostitute, me? With these nice clothes? Can you believe it?"

Pat O'Leary patted her arm in encouragement. "You are safe now," he assured her. Unconvinced, Nancy glanced behind her back fully expecting a horde of gendarmes to come dashing from the station intent on undoing their mistake. She saw nothing and squeezed O'Leary's arm in thanks. She was free again, but this episode had left a distinct mark on her psyche. Nancy Fiocca was determined to do something about it. She touched her head's lucky spot, a salute to her sudden turn of fortune. The semblance of a plan was already starting to form in her weary mind.

Chapter One

More than a year had passed since United States Army Captain Brian Adams Russell had joined the forces of Great Britain's Special Operations Executive or SOE as everyone in the know called the organization. His own section, F, was so designated due to the unit's efforts to aid the French Resistance and the Free French Forces of General Charles de Gaulle.

Russell's presence in the SOE-F was no accident. The Massachusetts-born, Yale-educated student and later graduate of the Sorbonne was an important cog in the clandestine wartime machinery. The SOE-F was the main troublemaker for the Germans occupying France. His fluency in French and true feelings for French culture and the French people made him an invaluable component of the important operation.

What's more, his first important mission that involved saving some of the Louvre's masterpieces from the Gestapo had earned Russell plaudits from his superiors and everyone involved. Since that time, his boss at F, Colonel Maurice Buckmaster, had seen fit to give Russell additional responsibility and had even parachuted him back into France on an important courier mission. That job had proven uneventful and Russell had again returned to England.

His new position had entailed the task of interpreting the huge amounts of intelligence information that SOE-F received on a daily basis from their agents in France. The reports were decoded then sent to Buckmaster's assistant Vera Atkins. Atkins assigned a level of importance to each message and then forwarded them for intelligence interpretation. In that manner, Russell received only the messages that Atkins felt were most important to F's mission.

The fact that his duties consumed practically all of his conscious time was perfectly okay with Captain Brian Russell. He enjoyed little social life except for an occasional drink with friends or an infrequent sip from Colonel Buckmaster's private stash of aged Scotch that his boss kept in an inconspicuous cabinet in his office.

Brian Russell had never gotten over the unexpected parting at the *Pont d' Espagne* with Christine Allard that happened almost two years before. The incredible setting high in the Pyrénées had surfaced in his mind numerous times since it occurred. He was truly in love with the striking French Resistance partisan who had chosen to return to her homeland's continuing fight rather than accompany Russell to freedom in Spain.

Although he knew it was virtually impossible, Russell had tried to uncover information as to her location through the F's intelligence sources. But, these infrequent contacts were spotty at best, and had produced no viable results. The location and whereabouts of the beautiful French woman, whose code name was Jeanne, remained veiled and Russell had long since despaired of ever finding her again. He immersed himself in his work and reinforced his desire to help bring the war to an end. Even the fact that his captaincy in the US Army had been changed to permanent status only cheered him for a short while. After all, little changed in Russell's daily routine except for the paperwork involved in the promotion. He had held the provisional rank of captain for more than a year and a half.

The prearranged meeting on the second floor of the remarkable villa located at 425 rue Paradis in Marseille brought together the Gestapo's two top leaders in that part of France. SS Oberstumbannfuhrer Ernst Dunker greeted his subordinate, SS Sturmbannfuhrer Rolf Muhler, with a casual wave of his Lord Salisbury Turkish cigarette that he had been able to buy on the black market. He had noted a few moments earlier that his supply of these hearty fags was rapidly dwindling and that he would have to make another foray into Marseille's seedy Vieux Port section to secure more.

The SS Colonel motioned for Muhler to have a seat across from his desk as he drew the final flavors and extinguished the cigarette.

"Muhler, I wanted to talk to you about the French agent that has been giving us so much trouble of late. I suspect there is nothing new to report, is there?"

"Not really, Herr Oberstumbannfuhrer," Muhler replied cautiously. It was the second meeting about the elusive agent in the past week, and he was worried his superior was ready to take some retributive action against him in this case. Dunker's shady past as a gangster in Berlin was widely known throughout the Gestapo and Muhler was prepared to give his superior in the Marseille Gestapo a wide berth in any confrontation. "You are aware of the attempts we have made to capture her. She seems to have a sixth sense about the traps we set. Either that or she's the luckiest woman in southern France right now."

"Lucky and smart. You forgot to add smart to your description," Dunker added frivolously.

"Yes, smart too. She is certainly that."

"She is as clever as a mouse, you might say. A *white* mouse at that."

"I guess so. The name seems to fit her."

"I want to make a point of calling her that from now on. It might help us catch her. And, I want to offer a reward. Let's start with one million francs for information leading to her capture. There are enough Vichy sympathizers around to find someone who will turn her in. I'll be surprised if we don't get some information right away. A little money goes a long way in these matters."

"I'll see to it right away, Herr Oberstumbannfuhrer. It will be my pleasure," offered Muhler, suddenly pleased with the turn of events. *At least he isn't blaming me for our inability to capture the woman. This could certainly have been worse.*

"And, Muhler," Dunker added. "Put the White Mouse on our most sought after list, but not too high. There are others who are more important at this time."

Muhler nodded his understanding and stood up. He turned and walked to the door. He had reached the door when he heard a nearly inaudible, "Heil Hitler" from behind the desk. He muttered his own "Heil Hitler" as he departed the room. It was then he noticed his collar was moist with sweat. He walked quickly down the corridor and returned to his own office on the bottom floor of the villa.

After resting a few days from her gruesome ordeal in the apartment of a Resistance sympathizer in Toulouse, Nancy Fiocca made her way back to Marseille. She made it a point to stay clear of the railroad system, suddenly uninviting to her frazzled nerves. She accepted a ride on a furniture delivery truck that seemed to make stops in every possible place between Toulouse and Marseille. These included Castres, Montpelier, Nimes, Aries and Nancy's personal favorite, the charming locale that comprised Aix-en-Provence.

By the end of the trip, Nancy was close friends with the driver, a Resistance member who often hid certain illegal items from the ever-watchful eyes of the Franc Garde and the Milice. He regaled her with stories of ineptitude and incompetence on the part of the Vichy police and of his ability to keep his secret cargoes from their examination.

As she passed the splendid *plane* tree elegance of the Cours Mirabeau in Aix-en-Province, Nancy thought of the pleasant time she and her husband Henri enjoyed before the war. The couple had strolled down the wide street and enjoyed pastis at the famous Les Deux Garçons Café. It was a warm afternoon. The *pastis* energized them, making their time together even more memorable.

The Fioccas had returned to Aix as often as possible and had never failed to enjoy the pleasures of the picturesque surroundings. As the trees and cafes passed behind the furniture truck, Nancy wondered if she would ever be able to enjoy such pleasantries with her husband again. While their home in Marseille was comfortable and inviting, Nancy took special pride in the fact that both she and Henri shared the love of a nice home and restful surroundings. They often cuddled together on a large sofa with their dog that almost enveloped them. Frequently they had gone to sleep in each other's arms.

The Fioccas had returned to Aix as often as possible and had never failed to enjoy the pleasures of the picturesque surroundings. As the trees and cafes passed behind the furniture truck, Nancy wondered if she would ever be able to enjoy such pleasantries with her husband again. While their home in Marseille was comfortable and inviting, Nancy took special pride in the fact that both she and Henri shared the love of a nice home and restful surroundings. They often cuddled together on a large sofa with their dog that almost enveloped them. Frequently they had gone to sleep in each other's arms.

Early that morning, the truck took her to the apartment Nancy and Henri Fiocca shared that was located on a hill overlooking Marseille. She thanked him profusely and offered to pay him for his trouble.

"Oh no, Madame. I could never take even one franc in the work of the Resistance. The work is sacred to me and to many other Frenchmen."

"Well then, *merci beaucoup, mon ami,*" Nancy replied in perfect French. "*Que Dieu soit avec sous.*"

The driver nodded and put his truck into gear. The old Citroën U-23 lurched forward and began to descend the hill. Nancy watched his progress and finally entered the building that housed the Fiocca's spacious apartment. She took out her key and opened the front door.

Henri Fiocca emerged, fastening his silk bathrobe as he greeted her. "Nonceeee, where have you been? I have been worried that you had come to some harm. I called around but no one has heard from you? I was truly worried."

"This time you had good reason my darling Henri. I tried to get to Spain over the Pyrénées as you suggested, but the weather was so foul that I finally gave up. I took a train from Perpignan to get back here, but there was trouble in Toulouse." She began to tear up and stopped talking.

Henri took his wife and squeezed her gently. It was one of the first times since they had met that he had actually witnessed her crying.

"Nonc-eeee, sit right down and tell me all about it. I will get you some fresh coffee. I have just brewed a new pot." He handed her a handkerchief and walked away. Nancy took a place on their large beige sofa and wiped her eyes. *I must really be exhausted if I cry this easily. Get yourself together, old girl. The worst is behind you now. Henri is a tough old sod, but this will be hard for even him to absorb.*

Henri Fiocca returned a few moments later with a steaming cup of coffee. The coffee was a rarity in occupied France, but readily available on the black market. Nancy Fiocca had been sure to purchase as much as she could find, and kept a good supply for all the frequent visitors that appeared through her escape network. She saw early on that a cup of fresh coffee went a long way in reassuring the tired airmen and Jewish escapees that came and went.

He took her hand and spoke directly into her eyes. "Now, you must tell me everything that has happened. Don't leave out a thing. It will be good for you to get it all out."

Nancy looked back into his sympathetic eyes and winced.

"I have a feeling you will not enjoy hearing about this, Henri. Some of it is downright sordid. But, I will try and remember everything that happened."

The war was well into its third year and Violette Szabo was proud to be a very tiny part of it. As a member of the Auxiliary Territorial Service she was delighted to be a female member of the formerly volunteer organization that provided non-combative roles for Great Britain's women. Her sisters in the ATS drove cars and lorries, cooked, operated searchlights and even became part of anti-aircraft batteries. In short, these women did everything that was necessary to keep England's was machine operating at its highest level.

Violette was pleased that the ATS included among its members Princess Elizabeth who trained as a lorry driver and Mary Spencer-Churchill, the prime minister's youngest daughter, who served in the mixed field battery units. While she longed for more robust duties, Violette was perfectly happy to serve wherever her country needed her.

The attractive young French woman was born in Paris, to a French mother and English father. The Bushell family moved to Brixton where Violette attended school. She met her husband Etienne on Bastille Day, 1940. They were married during a lull in the Battle of Britain after a short 42-day courtship.

Etienne Szabo was a French Legionnaire officer and was soon sent to join to the Free French Forces serving in North Africa. Back in London, Violette was already pregnant with the couple's first child that was expected in late fall of 1942.

As summer ended, her now advanced pregnancy limited her ability to work. But Violette never missed the chance to contribute to the ATS. She accepted the most menial of tasks without hesitation, and always carried a positive attitude around her workplace.

She was bolstered by Etienne's infrequent letters from the battlefront, and wrote him several times a week to keep him up to date on events in London. When the time for the baby's birth finally occurred, she presented her husband with a healthy baby girl whom she named Tania. The birth brought her a hiatus from her ATS duties, and Violette Szabo took great delight in the role of new mother.

Tania was a joyful baby, slept at a level way above most newborns, and generally filled Violette's life with great happiness. Even in war-torn London, Violette managed to get her baby into fresh air and cheery surroundings. After several months, she enquired as to the possibility of bringing Tania to work with her and was elated when the permission finally came.

From that time one, Mrs. Szabo and baby were never apart. Even when forced into bomb shelters, Tania was always at Violette's side.

Tania's first birthday party was underway at her parents flat just off Marsh Wall when a knock on the door caused a pause in the proceedings. Violette's mother answered the door and was greeted by a uniformed member of the Telegraph Delivery Service. Her face dropped as she recognized the uniform.

"Telegram for Mrs. Szabo," the young man announced.

Mrs. Bushell reached for the envelope without saying a word. The delivery man tipped his hat and was gone.

As she returned to the party, Violette noticed the look on her mother's worried face. She picked Tania up and held her softly in her arms. The baby relaxed and Violette took the telegram and carefully opened the document.

She read the contents and started to cry softly.

The telegram read:

```
MRS.VIOLETTE SZABO
16 BURNLEY ROAD
LONDON

REGRET TO REPORT THAT YOUR HUSBAND, ADJ-CHEF
ETIENNE SZABO, 13TH DBLE, WAS KILLED BY ENEMY AC-
TION AT EL HIMEIMAT, EGYPT ON 24 OCTOBER 1942.
= WAR OFFICE
```

Violette was crushed by the news that her husband had not lived to see his daughter. She was also aware of a deep feeling within her that would cause her much duress during the following months. She had no idea how that feeling would develop into a passion that would change her life forever.

SS Sturmbannfuhrer Rolf Muhler was cautiously optimistic when one of his top operatives in Marseille brought a plan to him that would definitely corner the White Mouse for once and for all. The plan was simple enough and involved another Milice agent that had managed to infiltrate a section of the French Resistance's escape network for Allied airmen and soldiers.

The Milice agent was named Briac. He lived in a small town outside Marseille called Cassis, an area that was well regarded for its local wines. It was Briac's job to secure papers for Jews passing through the area and even for downed allied airmen who were able to speak French.

Briac's plan was to wait until a large number of escapes had gathered, all waiting to head south. One of the escapees would claim to have some important military information concerning German troop movements, and would refuse to pass on the news to anyone except the head of the escape network. Even though the plan reeked of a potential trap, Briac would provide just enough inside information to make the ploy plausible. Once the news filtered back to the escape network's leaders, the White Mouse would certainly be consulted. Only she, Briac believed, would be willing to venture out to assist in obtaining the information.

Muhler finally agreed to the plan, even though it seemed a bit far-fetched to him. If the White Mouse failed to nibble at the bait and refused to come to Briac's meeting, the whole plan would quickly fall apart.

There was, however, the possibility that the wanted woman would appear. It was enough to have Muhler detail a large number of men to assist in the plan. He also decided to have most of the Gestapo men dress in French clothing rather than their dreaded trench coats and hats. He would give this plan every chance to succeed, and if he was lucky, The White Mouse would be his.

Briac chose an address, 20 rue Saint-Clair, for the meeting. Near the harbor, there were only two possible entranceways, one leading toward the docks and the other up a series of stairs toward the Avenue de la Viguerie. The assigned time was 9:30 in the evening, well after darkness had fallen.

When the information reached Nancy Fiocca, she immediately saw the problems involved. She knew a price had been placed on her head and was aware that the Germans and their Milice cronies were willing to do anything to get their hands on her. Still, the thought of fresh military information on German troop movements was very inviting.

She decided on a plan of her own. On the day prior to the proposed meeting, Nancy sent word to another Resistance leader in Cassis, a man whose code name was Cassien.

"I want you to find a young woman around the age of twenty-five, perhaps someone you are not too fond of. Please provide her with a basket of baguettes and fruit. She should take the basket at exactly 9:30 on the next evening to a house at 20 rue Saint-Clair in Cassis. I will be somewhere around that address. If nothing happens when the baguettes are delivered, I will then approach the building. Is all this possible?"

"Certainly, I don't see a problem. I already have someone in mind for the job."

The following day arrived and everything was set in place. When the young woman knocked on the door, she was met by a swarm of unidentified men, some brandishing revolvers in the moonlight. The frightened woman was taken away in a car escorted by a number of the armed men.

From a nearby location, Nancy witnessed the entire scene. *Another trap... good thing I was cautious about this one. The young woman is in no real danger; the fools will soon realize they've been duped. They will question her for a while and then let her go. The Gestapo is really going out of their way to trap me. It might be time for me to get my little Australian arse out of this place. Henri has been after me to leave. I guess this time he is right.*

Chapter Two

Brussels-born Denis Rake had experienced an undistinguished career in musical comedies in London's West End for nearly fifteen years. Just prior to be beginning of the war, he left the cast of Ivor Novello's *The Dancing Years* to start his duties with the Royal Army Service Corps. His principal function at the time was that of translator. He became part of the British Expeditionary Force, and was posted to the Southern French City of Bordeaux. Rake was later aboard the Cunard liner *Lancastria* that was bombed and sank off the harbor of Saint-Nazaire by a German Ju88 aircraft. He was picked up by another vessel and eventually reached England.

Rake possessed a tremendous enthusiasm for hazardous assignments and survived another sinking while serving aboard a French minesweeper. An unashamed homosexual, Rake proved himself through these chilling assignments that often tested the limits of his courage.

A chance pub encounter where Denis Rake heard chatter about a secret organization working behind enemy lines perked his interest. He quickly enquired at the War Office about such an organization and was interviewed by Lewis Gielgud, the recruiter for SOE's F Section. Rake's French skills impressed his commanders, even though he was effeminate and relied on sedatives to help him sleep. He quickly learned the complexities of a radio operator.

His first mission was aboard a trawler that dropped him at Juan-les-Pins, where he sought safety with a Resistance contact in Antibes. He then met American SOE agent Virginia Hall in Lyon, where he briefly transmitted for both the SPRUCE and PRUNUS underground networks. When advised that the police had a description of him, Rake decided to flee to Paris. Detained and arrested entering the occupied zone, he bravely bribed one of the guards and made it to the French capital.

Fearing capture at any moment, he entered into an affair with an unsuspecting

German Officer. He also utilized his theatrical talents by preforming as a Belgian drag queen in such clubs as *Le Grand Ecart* and *Chez Ma Tante*. His natural demeanor and the quality of his performances made it utterly impossible for anyone to suspect he was a British spy.

Later, he was arrested again and sent to the prison at Castres where he became seriously ill. After months of solitary confinement, he was moved to another POW camp at Chambaran, just south of Lyon. Rake eventually managed to escape and crossed into Spain through the Pyrénées. He eventually made it back to England.

Thoroughly exhausted and totally unable to cope, Denis Rake suffered a nervous breakdown. When he returned to duty, he became part of the agents' 'finishing school' on the Beaulieu Estate, a duty he thoroughly enjoyed. But his desire for action and danger never subsided. He knew that one day he would get another chance to fight the Germans he so severely hated. He firmly believed that it was only a matter of time.

Although she had only met SOE Agent Denis Rake in passing, Baltimore-born Virginia Hall served as an important cog in the French Resistance's efforts to thwart Vichy France's wartime activities.

After attending Radcliff and Barnard Colleges, Hall continued her education in Europe. With aspirations of joining the Foreign Service of the United States, she accidentally shot herself in the leg while hunting in Turkey. Her leg was later amputated from the knee down, and replaced with a wooden appendage that she immediately named 'Cuthbert.' The loss of her leg excluded her from any sort of diplomatic career. She returned to the States to attend graduate school at Washington's American University.

The stately brunette with high cheekbones and short, cropped hair, was in Paris when the war started. Hall made her way to England and became an early volunteer for the newly-formed Special Operations Executive. Her previous experience and contacts in unoccupied Vichy found her back in France in August of 1941. She was given a cover as a correspondent for the *New York Post* during her time there.

When Germany suddenly decided to seize the remainder of France in 1942, Virginia Hall was lucky to make it out of France and into Spain. Known to the Germans as 'the limping lady,' she had recently been placed on the most wanted list. Even with the incredible prospect of climbing the Pyrénées on a wooden leg, the hearty American made the trek without complaint.

While she was safe for the present, Virginia was adamant about returning to France and actively participating in the war. She was sure that she would be given another chance. She just prayed she wouldn't have to wait too long.

Parachute training was the next course scheduled for all new SOE agents. They were sent to RAFS Ringway that was located about eight miles south of the City of Manchester, Cheshire. For Violette Szabo, it was another adventure into the world of her late husband Etienne, a career military officer.

The base was homed by the Parachute Training School and consisted of two main hangars and associated staff buildings and barracks. RAFS Ringway was also domicile to the British Airborne Commandos and the fiery red berets that they always proudly displayed.

The SOE decided to board its agents away from the regular soldiers in training to be parachutists. An older Edwardian mansion located on the outskirts of the airfield was selected to house the steady flow of male and female agents scheduled to be dropped in one European country or another. SOE-F was the chief supplier of agents to the parachute school and practically the only agency that used female agents on a continuing basis.

Violette and her sister female agents were treated exactly as if they were men. From the first classes at Parachute Training School that discussed their jumping, Violette was pleased to be treated as an equal.

Royal Air Force Flight Sergeant Bill Brereton was the instructor explaining the use of static line parachutes. "These chutes," he pointed at a heap of chutes on a nearby table, "are the very latest in design. The chute's official name is the GQX-type after the chap who invented it, a Mister Raymond Quilter.

The chute is a 28-foot Irvin-type in a GQ packing bag that employs a unique method of operation. Here, the rigging lines of the parachute are *withdrawn* from the bag *before* the canopy. Thus, the parachutist now hooks his or her static-line, which extends from inside the bag, to a strop attached to a bar running along the inside of the roof of the fuselage of the airplane. The static-line then, together with the weight of the parachutist, breaks open the bag once the length of the line was fully extended after the parachutist's exit from the aircraft. This further enables the rigging lines from the parachute to be withdrawn first and to be fully extended

13

before the canopy filled with air."

Flight Sergeant Brereton looked among the faces to see if anyone in the class had really grasped his explanation. He settled on Violette Szabo, whose radiant face and nod of approval meant she understood the new method's effects. He continued, "This method has the added advantage of *delaying* the opening until the parachute is well clear of the aircraft. If you manage to keep your body upright on exit you are more likely to ensure an unimpeded opening of the rigging lines and canopy. The effect of the aircraft's slipstream on the jumper is modified by the drag of the static-line and, if a good exit is achieved, the canopy is fully developed before much vertical height is lost."

He looked around the class again and saw that some of the other agents had finally surmised the meaning of his statement. A raised hand from the middle of the classroom caught his attention. The hand belonged to the beautiful young woman in the second row who had first caught his attention.

"Yes, a question?"

"Yes, flight sergeant. I was just wondering when we get to make our first jump," Violette Szabo asked innocently.

"Soon, young lady," Brereton replied pleasantly. "Quite soon, actually. If the weather holds, some of you will get your first chance to jump as early as tomorrow afternoon. Others will have to wait until the following day, I'm afraid. Now, I want you all to come forward and examine one of these chutes for yourselves. You will someday consider them your most important friend, a friend you simply cannot live without."

The class groaned at the flight sergeant's dry pun, and quickly moved toward the table that held the parachutes. Violette Szabo was the first new agent to put her hand on a GQX. She examined it carefully and nodded her head again. She was already concentrating on what it would be like to make her first jump.

When informed of his subordinate's unsuccessful scheme to trap the White Mouse, SS Obersturmbannfuhrer Ernst Dunker just shook his head in disgust. He looked at his fellow SS officer and cocked his head.

"She is too smart for you, Muhler. You must face the facts. The White Mouse is

14

still free and continues to be a major thorn in our side."

SS Sturmbannfuhrer Rolf Muhler sat silently, refusing to meet Dunker's derisive glare. He remained silent, his slumped posture that of a mentally-battered man.

"For some reason, this woman has the power to see into our plans," Dunker continued. "I must admit, I have never seen anything like it since I joined the Gestapo. It's more than a sixth sense, it borders on the supernatural."

Muhler shook his head in agreement, but continued his silence.

"I don't know if there are many more tricks we can employ. If I am correct, we have tried to trap her on five different occasions. Of course, all have failed."

"Six if you count Cassis," Muhler corrected his superior flatly. "This time I really thought we had a chance of catching her."

"Increase the reward to five million francs, Sturmbannfuhrer. And, place her at the top of our most wanted list. Let's see if the added exposure will ferret her out."

Dunker waited to see Muhler's response to his facetiousness, but was disappointed when he received no response. Muhler wasn't even aware of his superior's play on words, another frustration for the SS Colonel.

"No more traps for a while, Muhler. We will now wait her out. After all, she really can't be all that smart or she would be working *for* us. Don't you agree?"

"Jawohl, Herr Oberstrumbannfuhrer," Muhler concurred. "That would make much more sense. Then I could concentrate on other matters."

Dunker abruptly arose and left the room. This time there was not even a whispered "Heil Hitler" as he departed.

Henri Fiocca stared with a worried look on his face as his wife related her latest escape from the Gestapo trap in Cassis. When she finished, he lifted his Armagnac and took a small sip.

"Nonc-eeee," he began earnestly, "I think you will agree the time has come to do something about all of this. So far, Cherie, you have been quite lucky. I know you agree."

Nancy looked into the tall man's caring eyes and shook her head. "Yes, Henri, I have been quite fortunate. But, you must agree, there has always been work to be done."

"Yes, but you must be realistic. We have heard reports that there is a price on your head and for that very reason we must be alert. There are too many holes in the Resistance network and it seems there are more informers by the day. We have already seen more than a thousand people pass through our escape network. You have done your part and much more. It is time for you to leave Marseille."

Nancy Fiocca knew her husband was right, and the time had come.

"You want me to go back to England, don't you?" she asked plaintively.

"It's the only possible alternative, Nonc-eeee." For your own good. You will be no benefit to the war effort if you are captured or dead."

"Well then, I'll leave right away. No point in wasting time, is there?"

"No, my darling. It's the only smart thing to do."

"I guess I'll try the Pyrénées again, I really don't have any other option."

"Since we set up the escape route, I guess we should have the right to use it ourselves," Henri added.

"You mean you are going with me?" Nancy probed, suddenly enthused.

"No, Nonc-eeee. I simply can't come with you. I didn't mean to upset you. I would love to come with you if the situation was different. The fact is I have too much to lose here in Marseille. My family's shipping business goes back many generations and our other businesses must continue to operate. Since I am the head of everything we own, I feel I must be here to insure it is done properly. I wish there was an alternative, but I have thought about it for a long time and I see no other way."

"What if the Gestapo or Milice trace me back to you? What will you do then?

"I will cross that problem when and if it occurs. So far, there had been no indication that they even suspect I am involved."

16

"With all that money they are offering, it would be inviting to some of our acquaintances to turn you in. After all, a good number of people know about our activities."

"I have only supported you with money, Nonc-eeee. I've never even been on one of your escapades."

"I know, I know. But if anything ever happened to you, I don't know what I would do."

"You would survive, my dear wife. You are a strong woman, the strongest I have ever been around. Your strength is one of your greatest virtues. And, you hate the Nazis and the Vichy goons as much as I do, maybe even more.

You must return to England and do the job you were intended to do. It will all work out in the end."

"But, you will be the one in constant danger, Henri."

"That I cannot help. I promise I will always be cautious about my affairs."

"Speaking of *affairs,* I want you to promise me something."

Henri looked up, suddenly curious.

"If I am gone for a long time, I know you will have affairs and I think it will be okay. But, I just want you to know that the same conditions will apply to me. If I consider it necessary or useful, I don't want to feel guilty about sleeping with someone."

"You have become more French than English, Nonc-eeee. You know that?"

"Whatever you say. I just wanted it all understood."

"I agree, *Mon Cherie.*" He took her hand and kissed it gently.

Nancy looked down at her terrier Picon, who was always by her side. "I am going to miss you terribly, little one. But your father will take care of you while I am away." The little dog seemed to nod his blessing, but eventually put his head back on the floor.

When Nancy finally left, Picon followed her as she walked away, howling loudly every step of the way. Nancy tried to coax the animal back to where Henri stood at the doorway, but Picon would have not of it. He continued to follow her until she yelled at him to leave. Deflated, Picon dropped his ears and made his way back to Henri. He was dejectedly aware that his mother had just left.

US Army Captain Brian Russell made his way through the wide corridors of 1 Dorset Square, the current offices of SOE-F. The location was one of the finest in London, and in close proximity to Regents Park and within a long walk of Whitehall and other London fixtures. It was also a mere six blocks from the SOE's main headquarters at 64 Baker Street should the need arise for sudden or impromptu meetings.

Russell was shown into Vera Atkins' small office as soon as he arrived. This was in keeping with Miss Atkins' strict policy of organization where little time was wasted on either idle chatter or inconsequential actions. She was prompt to the second and expected all her appointments to be the same. It was Russell's first official visit to her office even though he had known her for months and had spoken to her on numerous occasions around the campus.

"Captain Russell, it is certainly nice to see you on such a fine morning," she announced cheerfully. "So nice of you to be prompt."

"I know the drill," Adams replied with equal cheer. "Time lost is time never recovered, or something like that."

"Yes, *something* like that."

She motioned for Russell to sit down and the young officer complied.

"Brian...is it okay that I call you Brian?" she asked.

"Fine with me. Okay if I call you Vera?"

"Actually, everyone around here calls me Miss Atkins. I believe that would be more proper."

"Whatever," Russell replied. I was just joking a bit anyway."

"I see. Well, let's get right down to business. I have something I want to discuss with you."

Brian Russell listened attentively as the pleasant looking woman began. Her hair was fashioned into a chignon, a French style that many young British women preferred.

"I have been discussing with Colonel Buckmaster the possibility of using your talents in another area, Brian. As you know, we have developed a fairly sophisticated training schedule for our new agents. Each of them speaks fluent French and many are also good in Italian and even German. These agents are put through an initial training at our country house where they have no contact with the outside world. They next go through a commando course in the Scottish Highlands that is followed by a survival course in Hampshire. They even go through parachute training at a place near Manchester."

"I am familiar with all that, Miss Atkins. I'm just not sure how it affects me."

"One of the things we have been lacking is actual course time with experienced field agents. We want these new people to have the benefit of experienced hands. Yours, for example."

"So, I am to give these new agents the benefit of my deep familiarity with the German and Vichy French operating systems," Russell said half-jokingly.

"I do wish you would take all this seriously Captain Russell," Atkins replied stiffly, "these are most serious times."

Russell regarded the serious-minded Brit and thought to himself. *Good Lord, I am beginning to believe that some of these people are completely humorless. I can't even attempt to keep it light. Oh, well, I Guess if all this was happening in the US I might have a different attitude. After all, it seems as if half of London has been either destroyed or bombed. No telling what each of these people has endured. I'll just keep my humor to myself from now on.*

"...and your part will be to give some firsthand accounts of how our enemies' systems work. How the Germans think about certain things and what the best way to approach certain situations in the field would be. Do the Germans and Milice think alike and how that dissimilarity might be used against the bastards? This sort of information could prove invaluable to these new agents and possibly save their lives if they were ever forced into a corner."

Captain Brian Russell acknowledged Atkins' words even though he was deep in thought. He had already begun to process the implication of her words and how it might be applied to certain situations he had already experienced. *I do have some-*

thing meaningful to contribute and it certainly might help some of these new people. I must make amends for my shortsighted poke when we started and get back on Vera's good side. I think I know just how to do it. I'll just…

Almost two days to the month after she had left Henri in Marseille to attempt an escape through the Pyrénées into Spain, Nancy Fiocca was ready to leave Nice. In the seaside city, she stayed with a dear old friend, Mme Sainson. Mme Sainson had been an important cog in the initial escape route and Nancy was fortunate that she was now able to utilize the route that she had helped set up in person. The older woman was also the most colorful person that Nancy Fiocca had ever encountered. Her code name was Delilah and she was already a legend in Resistance circles. She took great delight in taking touristy photos of many of her escaping airmen with numerous members of Mussolini's occupation army in the background.

The weather finally relented and guides were beginning to escort individuals and groups to Spain who were all in dire need of leaving *La Belle France.*

Since Nancy had tried to escape this way on several prior occasions, she was aware of the myriad of problems before her. There were several others at Mme Sainson's apartment awaiting escape, so it was decided that they all travel in a group. The entire party, Resistance member Bernard Gohan, a British officer from New Zealand, and two American airmen boarded a train with Nancy from Nice to Perpignan with freshly forged identification passes.

In Perpignan, the group was forced to add two more French girls who desperately needed to leave the country. Even though the group had grown to a number that Nancy decided was too bulky, she decided to trudge ahead. *Seven people in one place are bound to attract attention, and I'm not at all sure the girls will be able to keep up. Blast it, I'm not going to back down now. These horrible mountains will not get the best of me, I simply won't allow it. If it gets too tough up there, we will just have to leave them to fend for themselves. This is, after all, war!!!*

The other pressing matter was finding guides for the journey. Due to some problems within the escape network itself, some informants were causing lapses in information. Thus, Nancy did not have the use of the Resistance's current passwords. She did, however, have the address of one of the guides.

She approached the house with caution, having visited it once in the company of Patrick O'Leary.

As the door opened, she confronted the startled man.

"Monsieur, I am Nancy Fiocca, and I know that you are in charge of guides to go over the mountains. I had a hand in starting this escape network some time ago. I know our leader O'Leary quite well, and I hope you do also. I desperately need to go to Spain and I now need your help. I've had enough trouble getting this far, so don't give me any crap."

The besieged man had no choice but to break into a smile. He was amused by Nancy's natural audacity and quickly invited her in for a drink. In a short time, the entire trip was planned. The group would make the first part of the journey, some 15 miles from Perpignan, in a coal truck hidden underneath piles of coal. It was early May and the truck managed to pass through a number of checkpoints and eventually dropped them at a spot where they would walk the remainder of the way. At that point, the group was twenty miles from Spain.

Around sunset, the group's two guides came into view. The head guide was a Spaniard, code name Jean. He started by making each person take off their shoes and put on a pair of rope espadrilles instead. Jean was a tall, dark man, and very thin, perfectly suited for the deep forest. Wanted by the Gestapo in France and the police in Spain for murder, Jean was blasé about the attention shown him by both sides. An expert in the art of tracking, Jean had guided numerous escapees on the difficult journey.

His companion was an attractive woman named Pilar who was accompanied by her mongrel dog. The group began their walk and continued without saying a word. The air became thinner and the snow began to accumulate along the route. The rise in elevation actually worked in their favor since the sniffer dogs the Germans used were less reliable at high altitudes.

When the question of how much farther they had to go was asked, Jean answered "*Una montana mas*" in a thick Catalan accent.

Eventually Nancy was able to pry from Jean the fact that he was the seventh generation of his family to be involved in smuggling. However, he admitted that he was the only one who actually smuggled people *out* of France.

One of the Americans began complaining and Nancy put him right in his place. Another French girl complained that she was totally exhausted in an attempt for sympathy. Nancy chose the perfect moment and forced the French girl to trip causing her to fall into a pool of cold water. The unfortunate girl now had little choice but to go on and complete the trip.

At around 12,000 feet, they crossed a point where both Spain and France were outlined for many miles by numerous waves of white-capped mountains. At last, the weary band could agree on something. They were finally on their way *down*.

The group had walked without really stopping for nearly forty-eight hours. They were grimy and absolutely wretched from their difficult journey. More importantly, they were all alive and safe in Spain.

Edward Travis assumed his new duties as director at Great Britain's secret code breaking center at Bletchley Park in Buckinghamshire with little fanfare. Originally known as Station X, the regally proportioned master house and its added facilities was home to hundreds of encryption experts and intellectuals who made up the staff. Early on, Travis had attempted to bring his atypical workforce closer together in their efforts to outwit their German enemies' similar code breaking attempts.

Travis had inherited a brilliant, yet somewhat divided group of intelligentsias. Constant bickering and intense rivalry among different factions tended to undermine the Park's ability to stay ahead of its Axis rivals.

It was true that Germany's heralded Enigma machine had been cracked in 1937 by Polish mathematicians who supplied the key ingredients to the Enigma equation. More recently, German Abwehr head, Admiral Karl Donitz, had ordered additional security measures added to his Enigma machines to protect their security. It was up to the experts at Bletchley Park to overcome these countermeasures and maintain the Allies' code superiority over their enemies.

Travis found his warm personality and attention to administrative detail made an immediate impression on his men and women. Morale quickly improved and a number of advances were immediately apparent. The daily business of decoding German and Italian messages and routing them to their specific intelligence destinations within Great Britain returned to close to normal.

Travis' efforts also brought about a much better working relationship with other intelligence agencies. Interaction between The Park and other British and allied services were greatly improved. Included in this group was the Special Operations Executive who utilized Bletchley Park's think tank in a number of its covert activities.

The list of new applicants for the SOE had just been delivered to the office of Colonel Maurice Buckmaster, SOE-F's competent head man. Buckmaster was pleased to see the list was three pages long. If SOE's mission was to be fulfilled, immediate training of a number of these potential agents would have to begin. He had heard the rumor circulating about the upper tiers of Allied leadership in mid-1943 that a large offensive action was already being planned for the following year. Buckmaster correctly surmised that the landings would be directed against one or more areas in France, and that his SOE-F would bear the responsibility for much of the clandestine and even overt activity that would accompany such an attack.

Educated at Eaton College, Buckmaster became a reporter for the French newspaper *Le Matin*. When the war started, he returned to England where he became part of the British Expeditionary Force that attempted to hold positions in France. He was part of the famous retreat at Dunkirk and was next attached to 50 (Northumbrian) Infantry Division as an IO (information officer). Buckmaster joined the SOE in March of 1941 and was made head of F Section that same September.

While not incredibly intelligent, Buckmaster was personable and skilled at the administrative aspects of his job. Buckmaster took keen interest in his agents and their missions in the field. He took great delight in their accomplishments and was visibly upset when any of his agents was reported missing or killed.

A name on the new agents list caught his attention. He studied the name for a moment and called for his assistant, Vera Atkins, to come into his office.

"Come right in," he spoke evenly as she entered the room. "Have you had a chance to go over the new list?"

"Yes, colonel," She answered. "And I bet I know what you want to see me about."

"I'm sure you do, Vera. Her name sort of stands out, doesn't it?"

"Yes, sir, it does. But I knew she was coming, at least I thought she was."

"What do you mean?"

"Well, when she was being interviewed, Lewis Gielgud phoned me to say she was available. Naturally, I jumped at the chance to have her work with us."

"You never cease to amaze me, Vera. Think of it, The White Mouse right here with us in F Section. This woman has caused the Gestapo more trouble than anyone in Southern France. She has the highest price on her head of anyone in the Resistance. The very thought of it gives me a chill."

"Righto, colonel," Vera Atkins beamed. "I agree. She will be a great asset."

"But, Vera," Buckmaster considered. "We must be quite careful in how we handle her once she arrives. We must insure that she receives no special treatment from the staff. She must be just another agent. That's for her own good as well as ours."

"I agree, sir. I'll see that she is treated as just another agent."

"Good. Now, when is she to arrive?"

"Day after tomorrow. Most of the new people should be here by 1000 hours. I've scheduled a meeting for all new agents just before lunch."

"I want to talk to her after she's settled in. It will be helpful to get to know her a little bit."

"Certainly, colonel," Vera replied with a smile. "I had an idea you might. Should I send her here right away?"

"No, no. Wouldn't want to make a fuss, would we?"

"No, sir. I'll wait until she has some free time. Wouldn't want to single her out, would we?"

Buckmaster sighed as her words hung in the office. At length he also broke into a smile. *It's nice having the French Resistance's most wanted agent right here in our midst. She will bring more authenticity to what we are doing and an air of practicality to our work. It will be interesting to see how she fits in with everything.*

He paused for a moment, but eventually returned to the list he was holding in his hand.

Chapter Three

Among those in attendance for the initial meeting of the newly arrived agents were US Army Captain Brian Adams Russell and Vera Atkins. While Atkins sat behind a podium, Russell sat among a group of instructors on one side of a large open room. The setting was an old country house that was formerly Wanborough Manor in Guildford, Surrey. The location in southern England was but one of a number of such locations given over to the SOE to harbor their various training needs. It was also known by everyone who served there as "The Mad House."

While drafty and usually in need of modernizing, these wonderful old homes provided the degree of obscurity and naturalness that was necessary for SOE-F's main mission.

The major in charge of the training school welcomed everyone formally and then introduced the group of instructors *en masse* to the new arrivals. He then labored through a lengthy opening statement that Russell found too long and quite boring. The new agents, however, were almost mesmerized by the officer's words and hardly seemed to take a breath during the half-hour talk.

Russell took the time to study some of the faces in the group and tried to imagine the circumstances that brought these enthusiastic people together. There were men and women, young and middle-aged and some who actually looked French. This latter observation involved hair styles and clothing and the hair coloring on some of the women. Russell saw the distinctive dark red/black that many French women preferred was a feature on at least two of the women.

I know that they must all be fluent in French, that's a given. But what else makes them so valuable as agents for SOE–F? If they have recently lived in France, that would be a great help. And if they thoroughly despised the Nazis and what they stand for, that would also be good. But what else? Russell searched his mind but came up blank on any additional clues. He sat back and listened as the major concluded his opening remarks.

The group was next broken into smaller units with the prospect of a lunch soon thereafter. As she left the area behind the podium, Vera Atkins passed next to Russell.

"Thank you for the vase and flower, Brian," she said quietly. "It was totally unexpected."

"I just wanted to make up for the fact that you think I don't view things seriously," Russell replied. "It was just a little token."

"So noted. It was very nice of you to bother. Really."

"Well, that's that. Are you staying for lunch?"

"No time for that. I have to be back in London as soon as possible. There are many things to do before this afternoon is over."

"I wish I could head back to London with you. I feel I could be doing more there."

"You will be doing important things here, Brian. In some ways, your input might be more important to these new agents than anything they are taught. I believe you will be responsible for saving some lives."

"If you say so," Russell responded, unconvinced. "But I will do what I am asked if it really helps out."

"Good for you Brian. I'm sure you will do well."

"See you around, sometime."

"Goodbye, Brian. I'll be in touch."

Russell waived as Vera departed, and turned toward the mess hall. A good lunch would do wonders for his unusually middling attitude.

As soon as she reached the SOE-F office at 1 Dorset Square in London, Vera

Atkins was summoned into the office of Colonel Maurice Buckmaster. The colonel looked up from his desk where a number of papers were spread out.

"Glad you are back Vera. Did everything go well?"

"Just as expected," she returned. "We have an excellent lot to work with and they seem quite eager to get down to work. I couldn't take my eyes off Nancy Fiocca, but she never suspected I was looking. No one paid her any particular attention; I don't believe any of them even know about her work in France."

"Nor should they, after all most of her work is still classified. Did you actually speak to her?"

"Only once, for just a second. I welcomed her to SOE–F and she replied that she was delighted to be here. I felt she really meant it."

"That would be in keeping with the reports we have received. A real team player and all that rot."

"She seems too good to be true. It's a shame she will no longer be able to operate in Marseille."

"That's why I wanted to see you Vera. I've been thinking about that very thing."

"I don't understand, colonel. What have you in mind?"

"I want to see if it is possible for us to continue the activities of The White Mouse around Marseille even if she is no longer there. I want the Gestapo and Milice to continue spending time and manpower to attempt to capture her. The longer we can make them believe she is still there, the better it will be. I want you to go tomorrow to Bletchley Park and talk to Commander Edward Travis who runs The Park. Explain to him what we would like to do and get his feel for it. It might be as simple as sending some false messages to The White Mouse as if she is still in France and having some of our double agents reply. Anyway, that's just a thought. He might have some other ideas. We want to get this started right away, while the Jerries are still hot to capture Mrs. Fiocca. Don't let on that she is here and a part of SOE–F, the fewer people who know about her whereabouts the better. You may tell Travis that she is no longer in France, but that's all."

Vera Atkins acknowledged her commanding officer and made a note on her pad that she had been carrying.

Buckmaster nodded his head and Vera departed without a word. Buckmaster mused to himself. *I must have the very best job in London, right in the middle of all the action. Today is just another fine example of that belief. I get to interact with all the people who are making a real difference in the war. But it is my agents that I truly care for, each and every one of them. Most are just ordinary people who are being put in extraordinary circumstances. A good number of these brave ones will die and some will vanish without ever being heard from again. My heart goes out each and every time I see an aircraft depart with some of our agents aboard.*

She sat down at her own desk and looked at her messages. She would work late again tonight, the fourth such day in a row. If there was only more time…

Morning reville came early to the new agents at Wanborough Manor. Those fortunate enough to be billeted close to the school had it easier and were able to sleep until 0600. Others were forced to rise earlier in order to make the school's first scheduled classes at 0630. It took a few days, but soon the school's entire class adapted to the new schedule.

For Nancy Fiocca, rising at such an early hour was something of a problem. A self-proclaimed night woman or party-girl, the prospects of early morning running and calisthenics fell just below the tolerance level for the Australian woman. Although she wasn't pleased with the schedule, Nancy kept her mind on her duties and trudged through it all. Class time was another thing altogether. Nancy was absolutely fascinated with the attention to detail the SOE school offered. She was delighted with the fact that many of the intelligence details were updated whenever new information was discovered in France. Also, it soon became apparent to her that the school was being used to flush out those who were incapable of completing SOE-F's primary mission. Any agents who were deemed incapable were sent to a place dubbed 'The Forgetting School' because they often knew too much about SOE-F's activities. These unfortunates were isolated and often sat out the war, or until what they knew was no longer deemed important.

On the third day, Nancy was told to report to the school's motor pool. When she arrived, a non-uniformed female motioned for her to get into a jeep for a ride. The jeep headed in the general direction of London if Nancy recalled her geography and bearings correctly. The uncomfortable ride took almost two hours and little was said during the ride. Nancy wondered where they were heading, but refused to give in to her urge to ask. After all, *I am involved in a spy school. Maybe this is some sort of test for all I know. Better to keep my wits about me and play along with the game. It is sort of a game, isn't it? Our best moves against theirs. Kill or be killed, that's about the gist of it.*

The jeep made its way quickly to the offices of SOE-F. Nancy was shown directly into Colonel Maurice Buckmaster's office where she took a seat on a chaise lounge that sat against a wall. A large map of France hung overhead with a number of colored pins inserted in various places throughout the country. A picture of King George V also hung in a frame on another wall.

Buckmaster took a seat alongside Nancy and extended his hand. "I am Colonel Maurice Buckmaster, head of SOE-F. I am most pleased to welcome you to SOE-F, Mrs. Fiocca. I am sorry that it has taken me this long to do so. My schedule of late hasn't permitted much free time. I hope you understand."

Nancy was charmed by the colonel's words, but asked plaintively, "I don't quite understand Colonel. Do you welcome all new agents like this?"

"Only the one that is called the 'White Mouse', Mrs. Fiocca. I'm sure you know we are fully aware of all your exploits around Marseille."

Nancy was both amused and flattered at the same time.

"I knew we were causing the Huns some troubles in the South, but I wasn't aware of any notoriety until they placed a bounty of 1 million francs on my head. That's when I realized our escape network and activities were really causing them some problems."

"*Five* million francs is the current reward, Mrs. Fiocca. Our lads intercepted a Gestapo bulletin just last week. And the Gestapo has moved you to the top of their most wanted list. You should consider that something of an honor."

"Five million francs, that's a considerable amount," Nancy reacted. "It was good for me to get out of France. Someone would have turned me in for that amount. I am sure it would have happened."

"Quite right. May I call you Nancy? Most of us around here are not so formal."

"Certainly, colonel. I'd be happy if you do."

"Good. Is there anything I can do to help you with the school? Our training is greatly accelerated you know."

"I find everything fascinating, colonel. There is a good deal of information to absorb and I can't wait to experience the remaining weeks of the schedule. There's one thing though, if you don't mind."

"Of course, Nancy. Whatever I can do to help."

"I would prefer that all this White Mouse stuff be kept to as few of us as possible. I want to be just another agent. I think I would be better off that way."

Buckmaster thought a second and shook his head. "I agree, Nancy. Whatever you say. I'll make sure this is carefully handled on our end."

"Bloody marvelous, colonel. I am grateful." She stood up and extended her hand.

"It was a pleasure Nancy. I hope we meet again soon."

"Not *too* soon if you please, Colonel. After all, I have a really busy schedule myself."

Buckmaster laughed and shook her hand. She turned and walked out of the office. After a few moments, Vera Akins appeared and stepped into the office.

"What do you think, colonel? Is she what you expected?'

"What I expected and more, Vera. She is quite a lady and full of spunk. She will be a great asset to us in the future. I wish she had already completed training and was in the field."

"Her training won't last too long, colonel. She will be ready in no time at all."

"Yes, you are right, Vera. I guess I was just hoping. By the way Vera, there's to be no mention of her former exploits to anyone here with the exception of Captain Russell. He might be able to utilize some of her deeds in his classes. "

Vera looked at her superior and smiled. "Righto, colonel," she replied. Vera Atkins then turned and left the office.

For Nancy Wake Fiocca and the other new SOE agents, the four weeks of basic training and indoctrination literally flew by. At the course's conclusion, the remaining group that was slated for work in the field boarded a train. Their destination was Arisaig, a small town in Scotland. Here, the commando training phase of their fledgling careers would take place.

Arisaig was located in the Scottish Highlands and was as remote a location as existed within Scotland. The SOE's main training offices were situated in Arisaig House, but many other local houses and buildings were converted for teaching commando tactics.

The daily schedule for new agents was rough and demanding. Long runs, heavy calisthenics and daily classes in hand-to-hand combat filled the days and nights. Most candidates dropped wearily into their beds at the conclusion of their daily duties.

At 31, Nancy was neither the oldest nor youngest, but the conditioning was quite difficult. She was determined to tough it out even if it took the last breath she could muster.

She took an instant dislike to the Army sergeant who taught the hand to hand combat phase. It was apparent the hardened veteran took exception to the female agents undergoing his tutorage and took great delight in throwing them over his shoulder with ease. He always warned them to be aware of their enemy and delighted when he surprised them with sudden moves and challenges. Most of the female agents had an assortment of scrapes and bruises that they fondly named after the sergeant.

When the final day of training at the desolate confines of Arisaig was completed, Nancy breathed the first sigh of relief since her arrival. The training had been the most difficult experience of her life. She hoped it would prepare her for the job ahead, whatever that might be.

Vera Atkins made sure she was the first meeting on Commander Edward Travis' docket the next morning. She wanted to get in and out of Bletchley Park as quickly as possible since she had other pressing matters to address back at SOE-F.

She had wisely used the term 'priority' and was immediately given the first available appointment.

Commander Travis was seated when she entered his ornate office that had once been one of The Park's libraries. She looked around at the surroundings and caught his eye.

"I didn't want to spoil the ambiance of the room," he remarked. "It seemed almost perfect when I first saw it. The only things I've added are some cabinets over there," he added pointing to his right.

"It's absolutely charming, commander. Folksy, yet efficient. I'd be willing to trade with you any day."

"If you would also trade me the responsibility for this job, you have a deal, Miss Atkins," Travis joked. "Today, if you like."

"I have my own problems, Commander Travis. They might not be as substantial as yours, but they are problems nonetheless."

"Quite. Problems are a most important aspect of war, in my opinion."

"I definitely agree, Miss Atkins. Now, just what is on your mind? How can Bletchley Park help SOE-F?"

"We have a matter that Colonel Buckmaster feels will be up your alley. One of our agents, you can refer to her as the White Mouse, is now part of SOE-F. We want her to become part of your outgoing messages for some time to come. But, you must be careful in referring to her in your messages. You must use the same code names as used before so as not to alert the Gestapo that we have intercepted their messages. We want them to think she is still active in the area even though she has left Marseille and…"

An hour later, Vera Atkins headed back to her desk at SOE-F. She had the complete assurance of Commander Edward Travis that the dissemination of false and misleading information to the German Gestapo in Marseille would soon begin. She was able to garner another brief smile as she stepped into the black British Ford 7Y that would take her back to London.

The job wasn't as tedious as he had expected. In fact, US Army Captain Brian Russell had to admit he was enjoying meeting the new agents and giving them his insights into the inner workings of the German Wehrmacht and Gestapo. His former brush with the Vichy Milice also formed an important part of his lessons.

He met with the agents shortly before their departures, in order that his information could be a fresh as possible. Daily updates from a number of intelligence sources were fed directly to Russell helping him pass on the very latest details to each trainee.

Russell felt a close bond to these people who would soon be risking their lives for their country. He spoke in French with everyone he met and was amazed at the quality of agents that had been recruited.

In the week that he had with each group, Russell attempted to instill a spirit that was both bold and cautious. He warned his trainees that they would face a variety of situations in France or 'the field' as SOE-F preferred to call it. Some of these situations would call for a forceful use of their talents, while others could be met with restraint and patience. Only they could tell which approach would work, and they should follow their intuition in such cases.

"What if we are faced with a problem that seems to have no answer," one new agent asked. "What do we do then?"

Without hesitation, Russell answered. "I have been in such a place and I prayed," he spoke truthfully. "My problem became clearer after that and I made the best of it. You can see that I am here speaking to you, so my praying must have helped, don't you agree?"

The trainee smiled and shook his head. He was joined by the remainder of the class who saw the legitimacy of his words.

Russell grinned at the group and returned to his notes. *I am making a difference for these people; at least it sure seems so. If I help them even a little on their missions, all the better. Too bad there was no one to help me before I set out on my first mission. I might never have been caught by the Milice.*

Another question from the group caught his attention and Captain Brian Russell quickly replied. It was now part of his day's work and he realized he was well-suited for teaching the rudiments of enemy security and its pursuit of individuals. Yet, somewhere deep in his psyche was the desire to return to the field again and take an active part in the fight against oppression. He had no idea when or if that desire would ever be fulfilled.

The next training course for Nancy Wake Fiocca was her most anticipated since she joined the SOE-F. The course was comprised of a number of different aspects, with one in particular holding particular fascination for the newly commissioned ensign. It involved explosives, radios and weapons for the new agent's use in the field. Even since her youth, explosives had fascinated Nancy. It began the first time she witnessed a fireworks celebration in Australia. The awesome power the flamboyant fireworks portended and often displayed held a keen interest for the woman. The prospects of learning to use real explosives in her new career completely riveted the young operative from the day she first learned of the existence of the explosives course.

The remote location was in the Beaulieu Estate, just off the axis between Southampton and Bournemouth on the southern English coast. The old estate consisted of 11 houses of various sizes and names, including The Rings. The Rings was the largest manor house, and contained the headquarters of the training unit as well as the finishing school for all trainees.

The new agents were quartered in different nearby houses. Nancy was delighted when she was told that she would live in a place called The House in the Woods.

"I have always lived in cities" she exclaimed to some of the other agents. "It will be swell to live in the woods for a change. I love the sound of birds and insects, it all seems so peaceful and comforting to me."

The group laughed at Nancy's frankness and went about finding each agent's designated billeting space. Nancy was sent in company with two other female agents who had also been assigned to The House in the Woods.

This should be quite an experience she mused. I am actually looking forward to living in the woods. That's if the place actually lives up to its name. Since the English are sticklers for authenticity and simplicity, there's a pretty good chance it will be quite charming. Anyway, it will certainly be an improvement from the place in Scotland. That was pretty bare to be sure…

The trio entered a dense thicket of trees and followed a narrow path that wound around several larger trees. A tiny sign directed them further into the woods. The sign simply stated

A small directional arrow pointed ahead.

The young woman motioned in the direction of the sign and smiled at her companions. "We must be getting close," she joked as the other two women grinned back.

Another thirty paces and a small clearing developed. Inside the clearing stood a perfectly framed stone cottage that could have easily walked out of a Victorian era novel. The three stopped to admire the place.

It was a single story building with a considerably slanted roof complete with a number of large windows. Underneath the windows, small flower boxes were filled with a myriad of colors of pansies and other similar flowers. Ivy traveled up the sides of the structure and provided an appealing color coat to the entire bucolic scene.

"My God, it's absolutely gorgeous," Nancy piped up. "In fact, I've never seen anything like it in my life. It could easily be an antiquated post card."

Her cohorts agreed and keenly approached the front door. A perfect stone walk accessed the front door of the house.

As Nancy reached for the door handle, someone from within the cottage opened the door and beamed at the trio. Violette Szabo extended her hand and beckoned them inside.

"Welcome to a little bit of paradise," the attractive young woman offered. "The house really is quite a marvelous place. I can't wait to show you around. I got here late last evening and couldn't really tell how charming it was in the dark. When I got up this morning and went outside, I nearly had a fit. A good fit, that is…"

Everyone laughed and introduced themselves to Szabo. It was evident from their unmitigated enthusiasm that the small group would get along well during their stay at the little House in the Woods.

An SS sturmscharfuhrer (sergeant) walked briskly into the office of SS Sturmbannfuhrer Rolf Muhler at the Marseille gestapo headquarters. He clicked his heels stiffly and placed a paper on Muhler's desk.

"We have just intercepted a British communication, Herr Sturmbannfuhrer, I thought you would want to see it immediately."

Muhler looked at the communication and smiled. "Good work sturmscharfuhrer. This is quite interesting. Are you sure it is authentic?"

"Absolutely, Herr Sturmbannfuhrer. I checked it out personally. The message was sent to one of our double agents and he immediately passed it on to us. It used the same code that we attribute to the White Mouse."

"I see. Then she is still active in Resistance actions. I was beginning to wonder. We haven't heard from her in several weeks."

"She was just laying low, Herr Sturmbannfuhrer. She knows her luck can't last forever. She is just playing it safe for now."

"We will see sturmscharfuhrer. We will see."

Muhler picked up a pen and wrote a personal note to SS Oberstumbannfuhrer Ernst Dunker that he attached to the message. He handed them back to the sergeant and waved in the direction of the door.

"Take these upstairs to Herr Dunker's office, but don't wait for an answer."

"Jawohl, Herr Sturmbannfuhrer," the unterofficer barked. He snapped his heels offered a salute to Herr Hitler and briskly departed the room.

Behind his desk, Rolf Muhler considered the message and what it implied. He was still unsure if he would ever get another chance to capture the White Mouse.

Chapter Four

Royal Air Force Warrant Officer Harley Dadswell cut an imposing figure around the Special Operation Executive campus on the Beaulieu Estate. At just over 5 feet 8 inches and 150 pounds, his slender physique hid the fact that Dadswell was all muscle under his uniform. His manner was reflected in his reddish hair and a perfectly groomed handlebar mustache that he waxed daily. The lip decoration was something of an insight into the personality of the almost 25-year veteran airman that had risen through the ranks and been commissioned in 1937. The commissioning ceremony was in fact, the anniversary of his first enlistment date. His prior experience in practically every facet of military duty made him a perfect choice for the SOE Training School when it was first mustered.

His signature prop was a well-made riding crop that he had acquired during his time posted in India, and he was never without the instrument around the Beaulieu Estate. He had, early on, realized its value in making a specific point with the new agents and had used the crop whenever he felt he needed to make a detail clear. This whack caused the chagrin of his students who might have been daydreaming when the whip cracked the relative stillness of their surroundings.

"Point made," Dadswell would announce after the crack, to the now wide-eyed agents in the room. "I am sure you ladies and gents caught my meaning on that..."

If Harley Dadswell had a hindrance, it was the fact that he also possessed a bit of a stutter, a problem only apparent when Dadswell wasn't completely sure of what he was saying. He would first hesitate, and then was only able to issue forth the first syllable. Few realized the warrant officer possessed such a disadvantage, for it was generally conceded that Dadswell was never wrong. Accordingly, the small number of people who realized his minor encumbrance even existed would never think to point it out to anyone else. Harley Dadswell was simply Harley Dadswell and that was that.

He was also a bona fide expert on firearms and explosives, the primary reason the SOE had decided to include him on its training staff. Dadswell's reputation was already established even before the Beaulieu operation was firmly established.

At the SOE's Beaulieu Estate School, U S Army Captain Brian Russell was given the chore of familiarizing the new agents with the workings of the Gestapo and its French equivalent, the Milice. He was constantly updated on intercepted German and French communications that either outlined or changed existing Gestapo and Milice operations. A steady flow of documents and accounts from debriefed Allied escapees was fed to Russell who put them into a working memorandum. From the varied accounts, Russell was able to glean an insight into his formidable foes' various methods of operation and their combined attempts to thwart the work of the French Resistance throughout France.

It was natural that most of the new agents found Russell's classes the best part of their stay at the agents' school. Many of them would owe their very lives to the information that Captain Brian Russell would impart to them before their departure from the school.

Russell was particularly interested in preparing his students for the dire consequences each faced whenever any of the agents happened to be caught by their enemies.

"Always take the initiative," he instructed his wide-eyed learners. "Make your captors believe you are telling the truth. Most of the time they will just be guessing about your involvement, and that's in your favor. If you have a preplanned story that has some actual true facts in it, it will seem all the more convincing. Think about it as soon as you are in the field. The more prepared you are for any eventuality, the better chance you will have."

"Will they really believe us?" an unsure male agent questioned? "Doesn't everyone the enemy questions have a story to tell if captured? What would make our explanation any more real than others?"

"Good point, Agent Blanc", Russell agreed utilizing the man's code name while at the school. "It is up to each of you to develop a tale that actually makes some sort of sense and affords you an alternate explanation for your captors. Use your imagination as I was forced to do once before. It was on my first mission and a member of the French Resistance and I were attempting to escape France through the Pyrénées."

The students propped up attentively in their chairs, not intending to miss one word of Russell's explanation.

"Our cover story was that we were newly married and making a pilgrimage to Lourdes to thank the Blessed Virgin for blessing our marriage. Along the way, I bought a few inexpensive posters of the Virgin Mary to take with us. The idea was that these posters were to be blessed in Lourdes. When we were stopped by the Vichy police and Milice, we stuck to the story and bought ourselves some valuable time while the Milice attempted to check out our story. We were fortunate that the local Maquis were alerted to our problem and were able to rescue us from our imprisonment. We were able to complete the rest of our mission and that is one reason I am here to be able to speak to you. I firmly believe that the posters made our story just plausible enough for the Milice to believe. You must do the same with your cover stories. Attention to detail, even something you might believe to be small and insignificant, might just save your life. After all, I'm living proof that it worked at least once."

The small group laughed and nodded their agreement. Russell's near brush with capture and possible death made their mission seem that much more important. They reflected on Russell's story as he prepared to continue his training.

The report that Colonel Maurice Buckmaster held firmly in his hand had perplexed him for the past forty minutes. The report, filed by Bletchley Park two days earlier, questioned a radio report received from one of SOE-F's operational agents in France. Code name Butcher, the agent was in fact Gilbert Norman, a seasoned veteran operational agent that Buckmaster trusted completely.

A report, supposedly from Norman, had failed to contain the secret security check issued to each agent. Lack of this code was an immediate red flag to Bletchley Park's dedicated coders and the resulting letter cast doubt on the content of the agent's message. Moreover, a check of some 149 prior messages found no such omission, a fact that strengthened the Park's position on the matter.

Buckmaster called Vera Atkins into his office. In such matters, he always considered a second opinion valuable in making a decision.

"Vera, you have seen this report from the Park," he began, handing the papers to his assistant.

"Yes, I have colonel. It upset me when I first saw it."

"Why was that, Vera?"

"Well, we've never had even one problem with Butcher before. His messages are almost pristine with no errors or omissions. I guess I am worried for his safety, Colonel. He and his network are so important to what we are doing. If the Germans…"

"Just a minute now. There's no real indication that the Germans had anything to do with it. He could have simply forgotten. Remember that each of the agents was given two codes to transmit, a buff check and a true check. The buff was a false check. If Butcher was being tortured, he could give the Germans the buff check and not compromise his position."

"I know that colonel, It's just that he's never forgotten before, Colonel. Butcher's not the type to forget."

"Nevertheless, we have no way of knowing what type of pressure he is up against right now. Pressure can make even the most exact of persons a tiny bit forgetful."

"I see your point, colonel," Vera agreed with hesitation. *This is not the time to stand on a soap box. He seems to have made up his mind. I should just agree and go on with my own problems. This will work itself out one way or another.*

"If you don't need me any further, I've my own work to do."

"Righto. Thank you for your input, Vera. It's always good to hear an additional point of view."

Vera departed the room and closed the door behind her. Her thoughts lingered for a few moments on Gilbert Norman and the other agents of the code name Prosper Network. She offered a silent prayer for their continued well-being.

The morning of Warrant Officer Harley Dadswell's first class on explosives was rainy and cold, a fact that some of the agents took as a harbinger of things to come. As the group took their chairs to begin the session, Dadswell offered his perfunctory slap of a nearby table with his riding crop. The sharp noise jolted the agents into strict attention.

"Good mornin' ladies and gents," the diminutive man began. "We are here to delve into the inner secrets of explosives and hopefully not blow each other up in the process." He looked around for a sign that his words were taken wittily, but the array of faces stood transfixed.

Blimey, this group is a bit short on wit. I thought a tad of absurdity might soften them up a smidgen, but I got no reaction. I better find another way to start them off.

Dadswell decided on a softer approach. "Explosives can be your friend," he resumed, "if you treat them with respect they will always perform to your expectations. They can be relied on to do whatever it takes to complete your mission and will undoubtedly save your respective arses on one occasion or another."

The class murmured its agreement and Dadswell almost smiled. The class was his once again to do with what he wished.

"Explosives date back to ancient times," he began his well-rehearsed spiel. "Black powder came from China around the 10th Century and the Chinese eventually used a form of explosive to propel missiles in their fight against their enemies, the Mongols. Modern explosives came into their own last century when an English leather merchant, William Bickford, invented the safety fuse. His invention helped create the type of explosives we use today. As things have evolved, explosives became more powerful as you will soon see.

"In time, I will show you how to build explosives with items that can be bought at any pharmacy in France without question and have powerful aftereffects. That all comes later in the course. Today, we will deal almost exclusively with a simple plastic explosive that the Royal Air Force has named Explosive 808, after the Nobel 808 as it is known worldwide."

Dadswell held up a chunk of green plasticine for everyone to see. "It has the smell of almonds and is the most modern form of explosives that we know of. It only takes small amounts to blow up most of our targets and is absolutely perfect for most sabotage missions that you will undertake. I want everyone to handle this and smell it," he continued. Explosive 808 will become your best friend. If you handle it properly, you will be able to inflict a great deal of damage to our German friends. If you misuse it, you might pay the ultimate price, so be forewarned."

He handed the chunk to the nearest agent and studied the faces of the remainder of the class. Their attention was fixed on the greenish chunk of material as it slowly made it way to each of the new agents. He knew such awareness would remain elevated for the duration of the class.

The general conversation that same evening at the little House in the Woods centered on Warrant Officer Dadswell's class that all four women had attended earlier that day. It was Violette Szabo who expressed the most enthusiasm for the potential of the Explosive 808.

"With enough of that stuff we should be able to kill a lot of Germans in a short time," she offered with a bit of an edge to her voice. "That's what I want to do most, kill as many Germans as I possibly can."

"I'm sure there will be an ample supply," Nancy Fiocca agreed. "When Dadswell said the Germans don't possess anything like Explosive 808, it seemed to me that we have an excellent advantage. I want to be completely sure of how it works. I can see an infinite number of uses for it."

The other women agreed and indicated their eagerness to continue with the training. "Agent Blanc said we would get to handle some of the 808 as early as tomorrow," another agent added. "I can't wait to get my hands on some of it and see just how it works."

"I'm sure we will all have the time to learn," Nancy counseled her younger cohorts. "I'm just sorry I didn't have some of the 808 to work with back in M…" She stopped short of saying the whole word. The other three women looked cautiously at Nancy. They had all been strongly cautioned against sharing any of their prior history with each other should they ever fall into enemy hands. Such information could and would be used to trap them their instructor had warned.

"Sorry, a bit of a slip," Nancy apologized. "I'll try and make sure it doesn't happen again. Good thing there are more than a thousand places in France that begin with an 'm.'"

The four laughed and continued their conversation. So far, their training had been quite stimulating and had held their attention. A bond had formed between the young women and they were quite willing to share their on-campus tales.

After more than an hour of exchanging each other's versions, the quartet agreed it was time to go to sleep. Nancy and Violette headed to their room and washed their faces in the small wash basin that was part of the room.

"These are really good women," Nancy remarked, referring to the other agents. "They will make excellent operatives in France." Violette shook her head in agreement and walked to her bed. She sat on the edge and stared blankly at the nearby wall. Nancy observed her new friend and approached.

"What is it, luv?" she inquired softly. "You look as if you are a million miles away. Is something bothering you? Would you like to talk about it?"

Violette considered the offer and shrugged her head. "Blast the silly rules about our talking to each other." We don't know each other's names, only the code names we have been given. Agent Green, that's who I am and nothing more. Why shouldn't I be able to tell you about what has happened to me? If you are caught all you would know is that my name was Agent Green.

Nancy listened patiently as the young woman released her pent up emotion.

"The first thing is my blasted ankle, the one I hurt while parachute training. The bloody thing gives me fits from time to time and I don't know what's wrong. I took a convalescent leave and it seemed back to normal, but it certainly doesn't feel normal at times."

"Parachute training wasn't good for me either," Nancy admitted. "I didn't fancy being up is the blasted air with everything churning around inside my stomach. I barely made it through the second jump. But your situation is quite different, if you ask me. You should report your ankle to the medical corps and have them take a look at it," Nancy offered. If it's not right, they will fix it."

"I simply can't do that. They might take me out of training again. That would be horrible. The last time I was sent home for months. I couldn't take any more delays in training."

"But, if it hurts you, you should do something…"

"I can hide it for a while longer. You didn't even notice, did you? That is until I just mentioned it …"

"No, I didn't. But, I haven't really been looking. You must admit we are all kept quite busy around here."

"Please don't say anything about it. It will probably get better anyway. Anyway, most of the really physical parts of our training are behind us."

Nancy considered Violette's request and answered. "No I won't mention anything if that's what you want me to do. But, you must promise if it gets really bad you will report it yourself. After all, you can't go into France on a mission with only one good leg."

"I promise," she replied half-heartedly. "If it gets really bad…"

"And, was there something else, luv?" Nancy prodded. "You said first when you began talking."

Violette hesitated a moment, and decided to continue. "It all started a few years ago when I met my husband," Violette started again. "We fell in love from the first time we met on Bastille Day. He was quite dashing in his uniform and it felt like I was in heaven or something like it. We did everything together and finally decided to get married."

Then our precious daughter Tania came along and made our marriage complete. She is a beautiful child and appears to be quite intelligent. She has just turned two. I believe she favors her father, but she is still quite young."

Nancy sat on the bed beside Violette as the story continued.

"My husband was a career officer and when this awful bloody war started, his unit was sent to North Africa. They fought the Germans alongside the British and suddenly his letters became fewer and fewer. One day I received a telegram from the War Office that my husband had been killed in action. He died at some place called El Himeimat, Egypt. I tried to look it up on a map but it was too small to find. I cried every day for several weeks until there were no more tears to offer."

Then I decided to do something about it and eventually found my way into the SOE. My French is nearly perfect so I was sent to SOE-F. My little girl is back in London with my parents so she is safe."

"You mean you left your daughter to join the SOE?" Nancy asked unbelievingly. "Surely there are others who could be doing what you are doing. Your daughter has already lost one parent; you could easily be caught in the same situation."

"I have thought this out very carefully," Violette replied resolutely. "I want to do something to avenge Etienne's death. I want to do to the Germans what they did to me and Tania. It is the only way I can accept Etienne's death."

"Well, if you don't take the cake, luv, I don't know who does," Nancy spoke again. "I don't know if I could have done what you have done. It takes an incredible sort of person to risk everything for what they believe, and that's what you are doing. My hat is off to ya, it really is. I respect your decision and will help you any way I can. You can count on it."

Nancy thought for a moment and continued. "My story is different from yours. When I was a young girl, I came across a book called *Anne of Green Gables*. I think it was written by a Canadian woman and it became my favorite book. Anne was an orphan and managed to get herself in an out of many troubles. I identified with her spirit and read everything I could about her adventures. The thought of her often gives me the will to carry on when difficulties arise."

Before the war, I worked as a journalist and saw some things that really revolted me. Long before the war began, I saw King Aleksander of Yugoslovia assassinated in Marseille right on the Canebière where I was standing. It was a horrible sight and remained in my mind for years. Sometime later, I was in Vienna walking on the Kurfürstendamm when a group of storm troopers began harassing Jewish storekeepers and individual Jews. On another occasion at the city's main square, I saw Jews being tied to large wheels that were then rolled along. A number of fat brown shirts were beating these people as the wheels turned. The whole scene was horrific and I came to understand the Nazis for what they really were…animals out of some dreaded novel or movie. I believe it was then that I decided to do whatever I could to defeat their horrible beliefs and their murderous way of life."

Violette remained silent, absorbing her friend's astonishing account.

"We all feel in different ways. I now understand why you are so driven in the way you approach things. I hate the Germans for what they did to my husband. You despise them for what they are and what they stand for. I'm sure everyone has their own reason for being here and training like we do. In the end, it's all for the same reason---ridding ourselves of the Germans."

"You are right and I appreciate your viewpoint. It really makes sense to me."

"Thank you, I appreciate you also." Violette reached over and gave Nancy a long hug. "We are all in this horrible mess together. It will be over one day and if we all survive our world will be a better place. At least that's my hope."

Nancy did not respond but remained in the embrace. She could not see that Violette's lovely face was suddenly covered with tears.

The hard knocks on his Marseille home's front door awakened Henri Fiocca from a sound sleep. He grabbed his bathrobe from the end of his bed and hurriedly extended his arm for the garment to pass around. He made his way to the front door glancing at the ancient Morbier grandfather clock on his way. The clock's brass movement swung effortlessly within the polished framework. The intricate clock hands showed that the time was just before 3 o'clock.

Merde. Who is banging on my door at this hour? Can it be a problem with one of our ships? They certainly are insistent; they can't even wait for a person to come to the door.

He unlocked the door and opened it to the dark night. Two faces, one tall and the other quite short, each partially covered with a hat pulled down to one side, stood in the light provided from within the house.

"Monsieur Fiocca, I presume," one of the faces said matter of factly.

"Who else would be answering my door at this ungodly hour?" was Fiocca's curt reply.

"We are here for Madame Fiocca. Please get her at once. We are from the Gestapo," the man stated forcefully, producing a silvered identification tag. "I suggest you cooperate and bring her to us at once."

Henri Fiocca suppressed a laugh but instead grinned at the pair.

"I'm afraid Madame Fiocca is not here. In fact, she has left France some time ago to visit a cousin in Australia. I haven't heard from her in some time, but with the occupation ongoing, I guess that's not so unusual."

"Did Madame Fiocca apply for an exit visa when she left? The Vichy government has no record of any such application on file. Without an exit visa, she would not have been able to leave France?"

"My wife did what she wanted," Fiocca said with a shrug. "Those Australian women are very headstrong, if you know what I mean. She simply said she was leaving and the next thing I knew she was gone."

"Did you give her any money for her journey?" the other gestapo agent asked.

"Non-cee always had her own money. Sometimes when I would run out, she would give me some. She was always very handy in that regard."

"So, monsieur, you expect us to believe that your wife just packed up and left on an extended voyage outside an occupied country and you just let her go?"

"Just what was I to do about it? If I told her to stay she would go anyway. I already told you she was a really headstrong woman."

The Gestapo agents looked at each other and leaned over to confer. After several moments the taller agent spoke again.

"My colleague and I want to search the house to see if what you are telling us is true. We have been given information that implicates your wife in some suspected Resistance activities. Once we have completed the search we will take you with us to our headquarters for further questioning."

"If you desire to get dressed while we search, you have permission to do so. Any action of yours that is out of the ordinary will be construed as obstructing our work and will be treated as such. Do you understand?"

"But if this concerns my wife, why am I to be interrogated? I know nothing of her activities. I am busy running my family's businesses and have little time for anything else? Surely you know that much."

"We have already checked on you, Monsieur Fiocca. Of that you can be certain. But, our information on your wife seems to have a ring of truth to it."

"*Merde.* Just who gave you the information in the first place? Are they trustworthy?"

"We are not obliged to give you any information. After all, we are the ones who are asking the questions."

Feigning resignation to the situation, Henri Fiocca shrugged his shoulders and started back inside the house. "I'll go and get dressed. I would hate to visit your headquarters in unsuitable attire."

The two Gestapo agents followed him into the house and turned on lights in the hall that led from the door.

When SOE-F's Prosper Network began to experience troubles, Vera Atkins quickly recalled the episode with Gilbert Norman (code name Butcher) that Colonel Maurice Buckmaster had allowed to slip by. It was quickly becoming apparent that a problem existed within the Prosper Network. Several agents were believed to have been captured and the flow of information from the remaining agents had been suspect at best.

When one of the agency's field operatives, France Antelme, returned to Baker Street and SOE-F's headquarters, he readily confirmed the capture of several Prosper operatives. Visibly shaken, the British Mauritanian had narrowly escaped capture himself the previous day in Paris due to an appointment he had scheduled the same day in Poitiers.

Colonel Maurice Buckmaster was also noticeably stunned by the news since Prosper was one of his main Paris-based networks. He was unused to any of his agents being captured and considered them almost above that sort of thing.

"I must have been wrong about Butcher," he confessed to Vera Atkins when the two were finally alone in his office. "Stupid of me really, not embracing the fact that the true check was the only absolute means we have of authenticating each agent's reports."

"Don't be too hard on yourself, colonel. We are also under a great deal of pressure. We have many people's lives in our hands and we make the best decisions we can about those lives."

"Nevertheless, it was absolutely blind of me to overlook it. I feel I am somewhat responsible for what has happened."

"We will never know the exact circumstances of what took place, not until this bloody war is over. The best thing to do now is to go forward and learn from our mistakes."

"You mean *my* mistakes," Buckmaster said in a low voice.

"I had reservations about Butcher's transmissions, but I never pushed the matter," Vera replied. "I'm also at fault for not pursuing it any further."

Buckmaster considered her statement then shook his head.

"No Vera, you should not feel that way. I am the head of SOE-F and, as such, must be responsible for most of the key decisions that are made here at Baker Street. I am willing to concede that I made a dreadful mistake on this matter. I hope my error in judgment has not caused the deaths of any more of our agents."

"Again, sir, there is no real proof that your actions caused anyone's death."

"That's little consolation Vera. The fact is that one of our top networks has been compromised and possibly some of our other networks also."

"We have nothing to indicate any other networks are having problems, do we?"

"Not as yet, but the possibility exists. We must be extra cautious during the following days to insure all of our agent's safety."

"I will be happy to pass that along, colonel. It will give everyone something extra to think about."

"Very well, Vera. Thank you for listening to me. It means a great deal to me personally."

"Happy to oblige, sir." Vera turned and walked away from Buckmaster's desk. In a few short steps she was back in the hallway headed toward her own office. For some reason, she felt little satisfaction in the fact that she had been right about the Butcher affair. In fact, she felt downright dejected that she had failed to act on the matter.

Chapter Five

The day arrived for the new agents to actually explode some of the Explosive 808 in the presence of Warrant Officer Harley Dadswell. Before the actual exploding began, Dadswell re-emphasized his earlier instructions to the attentive members of his class.

"You will recall my past remarks concerning our little friends here," he began, holding up a brown paper covered piece between his fingers. You will note it states Nobel Explosive No. 808, and carries Mr. Nobel's signature on it. It also says that 'THIS EXPLOSIVE IS ONLY TO BE USED WITH A 1 LB. PRIMER'.

These are the actual explosive devices that each of you will utilize in the field. I have already noted that they are subject to rain and humidity changes, so you must be careful with them anytime you intend to use them. For our purpose here at the school, we will utilize both primal cord and #9 timing pencils to detonate the 808.

Primal cord timing can be designated by length and I suggest a minimum of 10 seconds. That is actually quite a short fuse. You must allow yourself sufficient time to reposition before the detonation actually goes off. The other option is a #9 timing pencil such as the one I have here." He held up the thin object for everyone to see.

"The timing pencil is a small tube contained in a spring loaded detonator which is held back by a thin magnesium wire. At the end of the tube is a glass phial containing acid. When you as an agent want to detonate the 808, you must crimp or crush the glass phial. You ladies should use pliers as the phials are not so easy to crush. Once broken, the acid flows into the rest of the tubs and begins devouring the magnesium wire. Once the acid eats through the wire, the spring releases detonating the attached explosives. Times are rounded to the nearest minute since the acid doesn't always eat through the wire at a constant rate. Timing pencils are available in 10 and 60 minute sizes and also 6 or 12 hour sizes. And, one more thing. Due to the fragility of the acid phial, hard knocks or bumps are capable of arming the detonator prematurely. You all are aware of the consequences of such a mistake."

Royal Air Force WO Dadswell surveyed the class and was delighted to see all heads nodding in agreement. *Good, they understand just how dangerous all this bloody stuff is…too bad a number of them won't be alive at the end of all this to see just how important their work was…*

"Now, can I see a show of hands for the first volunteer?"

Again, Harley Dadswell was pleased that every single hand in the class was raised.

Henri Fiocca had routinely passed by the headquarters of the Gestapo in Marseille at 425 La Rue Paradis without the slightest thought of ever being taken there for questioning. While the upper floors were spacious and attractive, Fiocca soon found the lower part of the building to be quite gruesome. It was now three days since he had been awakened at his residence and the tone of his meetings had suddenly worsened.

The top ranking Gestapo officers in Marseille, SS Oberstumbannfuhrer Ernst Dunker and his subordinate, SS Sturmbannfuhrer Rolf Muhler both stood in front of him with somber faces. Several other SS officers made a small circle around the chair that held Fiocca, his hands bound behind him. Dunker spoke as Fiocca slumped toward the back of the chair.

"We are tired of your excuses, Fiocca. Can't you see your charade is finished? We have exact information as to the fact that your wife was instrumental in setting up an escape route for prisoners of the Vichy Government and the Third Reich. We also know she is hiding somewhere in this area because we have intercepted wireless messages that refer to her current activities. We really don't want you; it's your wife we really want. All you have to do to be set free is tell us where she is or give us information as to how to contact her. Don't be a fool, Fiocca, if the situation was reversed, your wife would turn you in right away."

"You obviously have never met my wife," Henri Fiocca, grinned, "she…"

A blow to the head by one of the SS officers standing behind him cut off Fiocca's reply.

"We have been quite lenient with you so far, you French pig," muttered Sturmbannfuhrer Muhler. "As you will notice, leniency will no longer be the case. Are you prepared for what is to come? I don't think so. In a day or two you will be begging for mercy, and for what? We will eventually find your wife and you will have suffered for nothing. Are you that reckless or just dumb?"

"I have already told you," Fiocca muttered wearily, "I don't know where Noncee is. She just left one day and that was it. I can't tell you what I don't know."

Muhler gestured to one of the SS officers who pulled Fiocca up from the chair. Another officer assisted him as they dragged him out of the room.

Muhler turned to Dunker and spoke assuredly. "Let's see how he is after a day or two in the basement. Our interrogation men have some exacting methods and equipment that have broken better men than he. I'll wager he ultimately gives in."

"I wouldn't be so sure, Muhler. After all, he could be telling the truth. If his wife did leave, she wouldn't want to put him in danger by contacting him. If our informant hadn't told us that both Fiocca and his wife operated the escape network, I'd be inclined to go easier on him. As it is, he deserves whatever he gets."

"I agree Herr Oberstumbannfuhrer. But it will be interesting to see just how much he can endure."

"I think you enjoy torturing prisoners Muhler. It is a sadistic side of your personality."

"We are at war, Herr Oberstumbannfuhrer. I am of the belief that anything is permissible during wartime. The most important thing is that we get the information we need. Don't you agree?"

"The prisoner cannot give us any information if he is dead, Muhler. Just remember that."

"Jawohl, Herr Oberstrumbannfuhrer," Muhler replied with a guileful smirk on his face.

Nancy Wake Fiocca was completely taken by the explosives demonstration and her subsequent incursion into the world of sabotage. When the first of her Explosive 808 detonations actually burst forth, she celebrated with a wave of her fist.

"That's the first of many, lads," she proudly pronounced, "I will see if the Huns can get used to my new calling card."

The feeling of experiencing such an occurrence was almost euphoric to Nancy. Although she had eagerly anticipated the event, the culmination of her first real explosion startled the young woman.

Am I supposed to feel like this or am I somewhat abnormal? she pondered. *The others don't seem all that excited, at least not like me. I can't wait to do it again, and, as soon as possible. And, just wait until I get into the field. I suppose there will be many targets of opportunity to use my 808.*

The rush continued for several hours and lasted until the evening meal. Around a large wooden table that served as their dining table, Nancy talked casually with the other agents.

"We have all been under old Dadswell's whip at one time or another," she confided while referring to Dadswell's riding crop. "He makes such a show of it and sometimes the noise he makes scares me to hell."

"Oh yes," another agent agreed. "He slaps the silly thing for effect. It scares me also."

"I've just thought of something," Nancy continued. "I was going through one of the closets at the Little House and found a box that contained some interesting items."

"Do tell. We're all ears," another of the agents added.

"It's like this. The box must have been left over from some old party or maybe a New Year's celebration. It contained several items and a few of these." She reached into her uniform pocket and produced several small firecrackers."

The other agent's faces suddenly came alive as they realized Nancy's intent. They smiled broadly as the prospects for a simple payback suddenly became clear. Their final class with Warrant Officer Harley Dadswell scheduled for the following day would be one to remember. It would be difficult for the group to wait until the following morning.

St. Pierre Prison was an antiquated, three-story cobblestone series of buildings located at 80 rue Brochier within the City of Marseille's 5e Arrondissement. The prison was but a short 10-minute drive from Gestapo headquarters on the La rue Paradis, but Henri Fiocca was in no condition to even realize that he had been moved from one brutal location to another.

A week had passed since his initial arrest by Gestapo agents and by now Fiocca was a broken man. He thought of Nancy often and regretted not taking her advice to leave with her. He tried to remember her hair, the smell of her favorite perfume, anything that would remind him of her. Only his ongoing pains could cause these thoughts to leave his drained mind.

When the SS's intense torture methods had failed to produce any answers to the incessant questions about his wife Nancy, the German intimidators had finally given up. They all agreed there was little left of the former French businessman, and had ordered him to be sent away to St. Pierre Prison so that his space at Gestapo headquarters could be utilized for other prisoners.

The Franc-Garde soldiers took one look at Fiocca and started betting on just how long he would survive. His bloody clothing hid the fact that Fiocca had sustained broken ribs, a broken arm and severe gastric complications caused by repeated blows to his stomach and back.

Henri Fiocca was thrown into a cell on the bottom floor because no one wanted to carry him up the steps. He lay on a soiled bed and fervently wished that someone would put an end to his suffering and despair. He knew that he would do it himself if only he could summon the energy and means to take his own life.

When the small bowl came that was to be his food, his bloodied eyes looked at the bowl with contempt. And when a dish containing water was offered by the prison's priest, Fiocca could barely gather the strength to sip a few drops.

"I will pray for you my son," the priest offered, "as I pray for everyone here at the prison. It is my hope that you all will be with our Lord as soon as possible."

Henri Fiocca did not hear the last part of the cleric's words. He had thankfully passed out again on his bed.

Two days later, an order came to the commandant of St. Pierre Prison from the Vichy Government. It ordered the immediate execution of Henri Fiocca for his crimes against the nation.

A guard detail was hastily assembled and the almost lifeless body of Henri Fiocca was dragged to an area immediately adjacent to the prison's laundry area.

The Garde corporal drew his SACM *(Societe Alsacianne de Constructions Mecanique)* model 1935A semi-automatic pistol from his holster and pointed it at the back of Fiocca's head. The 7.65mm slug quickly passed through Fiocca's skull and mercifully ended the French patriot's life. It was generally agreed by the guards that Fiocca was not conscious at the time.

The report handed to SS Oberstumbannfuhrer Ernst Dunker the following day outlined the execution of Henri Fiocca in St. Pierre Prison. Dunker immediately ordered his subordinate, SS Sturmbannfuhrer Rolf Muhler, to come to his office.

Moments later, Muhler arrived and gave the Nazi salute to his superior.

Dunker ignored the gesture and threw the papers at the foot of Muhler.

"What is the meaning of this Muhler?" he screamed. "Look what you have done."

Muhler picked up the paper and read its contents. He finished reading and looked up at Dunker's reddened face.

"We could not get any information from him, Herr Oberstrumbannfuhrer. He resisted every possible means we tried. In the end, he was more dead than alive. I believe the execution was a blessing to him in his state."

"Must I remind you that I ordered you to watch out for him?" Dunker returned disgustedly. "Is this what you call looking out for someone?"

Muhler chose not to respond in the presence of his superior's rage.

"You have cost us a valuable prisoner, Muhler, one that cannot be easily replaced. He might have known facts that could have ferreted out other Resistance agents. It might have taken some time, and maybe different tactics would have worked. We'll never know for sure."

Muhler chose to remain silent. The Oberstrumbannfuhrer's temper was well known and it was useless to argue with him. *Besides, the case against Fiocca was all based on the informant's statements. There's no way of telling how accurate the information was... Since we know for sure that the White Mouse is still active in local Resistance efforts, it would seem likely that Fiocca would have given us some information... That is, if Nancy Fiocca really is the White Mouse... Too many questions left unanswered, at least that's how I see it... I'll let the Oberstrumbannfuhrer calm down before I say anything. It's best that way...*

"Your actions will be noted in my report, Muhler. You can be sure of that."

"Jawohl, Herr Oberstrumbannfuhrer. I understand." He extended his right hand and exclaimed, "Heil Hitler."

"Heil Hitler," responded Dunker with little enthusiasm. "You may go now." Muhler clicked his heels, turned and departed the office. For the first time in weeks, Dunker was glad to see him leave.

An air of near playfulness was apparent as WO Harley Dadswell entered his classroom the day after the agents had experienced live explosives. The seated agents were informally talking to each other and only stopped as he appeared to fondle his riding crop.

"Good. I am delighted that I can get your attention so easily. I want to go over what we learned outside yesterday one more time. I feel you can never review the basics of explosives enough. Do you agree?"

The group nodded in agreement and Dadswell continued. "I have always considered explosives my friend," he postulated. "I have always treated them with great respect and they have never let me down. I want to emphasize the respect you must always have for explosives. Due care and consideration for their effects are also most important in their use."

Dadswell droned on for another few minutes, rehashing the prior day's events and adding useful bits of information whenever he saw fit. About eight minutes into his diatribe, he noticed different members of the group taking quick glances at their watches. After another minute, he enquired as to why this was happening.

"Why is everyone checking their watches?" he questioned. "We have quite a bit of time left here before we recess. Is my talk all that boring or do you all have some other place you have to be?"

No one answered, but a few of the agents began to grin.

Not understanding the meaning of the smiles, Dadswell again questioned. "Well, what is it. Is someone going to…?"

Suddenly a loud snapping blast resounded throughout the classroom. Dadswell ducked behind a table while the class burst out laughing.

"W-w-hat the d-d-ii-ckens," Dadswell chortled, attempting to control the situation. "Wh-wh-what was all that about?"

Nancy Fiocca stood as the befuddled instructor scanned the room. "I can explain Warrant Officer Dadswell."

"By all means," he agreed with a scorn. "Please go on."

"Our class decided to test the timing pencil for accuracy one more time in a controlled environment. We set the timer for 10 minutes and attached it to a pair of firecrackers we happened upon. I must report the timing pencil was nearly perfect and went off just a few seconds after 10 minutes."

"You scared the hell out of me," Dadswell retorted, finally regaining his composure. "What was that all about?"

"It's probably closely akin to what happens when you smack that dreadful crop of yours for practically no reason," Nancy replied. "Wouldn't you say?"

From bewilderment, a broad smile broke out over Harley Dadswell's face. He extended his hand to Nancy Fiocca and pronounced loudly, "No harm done 'ere. You're one up on me and I'm much the wiser for it, that's for sure."

The class laughed out loud and approached the warrant officer. They patted him on the back and confirmed he was a really good sport about the whole thing.

"Since our class is something of a shambles," Dadswell proposed, "I think we should end it right now and head over to the mess area for a spot of tea. Everyone agree?"

The consensus of opinion was that it was an extremely good idea and the class departed the room in a matter of seconds.

By the time of the Beaulieu Campus' evening meal, the entire firecracker episode had made the rounds of both the new agent's tables and also those of the faculty. The incident was a welcome relief to the everyday routines and assignments of the SOE School and served to lighten the atmosphere at the place considerably.

For her part, Nancy Fiocca chose to spread the accountability around to her fellow students, informing everyone who asked that it was a mutually agreed upon plan of action and taking no individual credit. Her fellow agents reveled in the attention which made the group even that much closer to each other.

Nancy and Violette Szabo finally went to bed after numerous toasts to SOE-F and each other. A fine light white wine from the Alsace Region of France was found for the occasion. It was the first that any of the new agents had enjoyed in some time.

Violette was the first to speak as she lay down on her bed. "That was quite ingenious of you Agent Jaune. You gave everyone a moment to forget just what we are doing here. I am personally grateful to you."

"No need for that my dear Vert. It was a means of having a bit of fun at poor old Dadswell's expense. He was a good sport about it all. I wasn't all that sure he would react as he did."

"I wasn't sure either. He could have easily been furious and taken it out on us. That wouldn't have been much fun."

"It all worked out for the best. Everyone had a good laugh. I even caught Colonel Buckmaster and Vera laughing when no one was looking at dinner. I didn't expect that at all."

"Well, touch wood or something. I hope our next little antic goes as well."

"You mean you are planning something else along that line?"

"I haven't really considered it, yet. I'm not that keen on getting us all in the pot. After all, we are here to learn to survive, not play around."

"I see what you mean Jaune."

"But that doesn't mean I won't be on the lookout for something to lighten our load, if you get my gist."

"Me, too. I'll also be on the lookout."

"You do that, Vert. It would certainly be helpful. Now, let's hit the pillow. We will be tired tomorrow if we don't."

"Right. See you tomorrow. Good night."

"Good night."

United States Army Captain Brian A. Russell also thought the agents' joke on Dadswell was great fun, and was delighted the students had not chosen their American instructor as the target of their prank. What the new agents might have done to him wafted around his imagination and was quickly dispatched in the good name of reality.

They would really have no reason to try and dupe me, would they? After all, I deal with enemy intelligence and the like, so there's very little they could find that would present an opportunity to clown around. No, I'm safe for now. At least that's how it seems to me.

Russell returned to his daily dispatches. A particular paper, lifted by the good people at Bletchley Park from a coded Gestapo message, caught his attention. It was a message sent from Gestapo Headquarters in Marseilles to the main Gestapo Headquarters on avenue Foch in Paris. It detailed prisoner movements in the Marseille area and included a name that caught Russell's attention.

It read: **FIOCCA, H. TRANSFERE A ST. PIERRE PRISON.**

Fiocca, that rings a bell for me. Where do I know that name? He thought a minute and his mind finally clicked. *Nancy Wake Fiocca, our Agent Jaune. Her last name is Fiocca. I had better let Colonel Buckmaster know about this. It will be his decision as to what we do about it. I certainly can't let Agent Jaune know without his permission.*

Russell picked up the telephone and dialed Buckmaster's office. Vera Atkins answered and informed Russell that Buckmaster was out on the Beaulieu campus but should return in a short time.

"I need to see him as soon as possible when he returns," Russell said politely.

"Certainly, Brian. I'm sure he'll see you as soon as he returns. As a matter of fact, why don't you head over here now? I know he will be back in a matter of minutes."

"I'm on my way," the American officer replied. "See you in a sec."

Vera Atkins smiled at the American's abridging of the English language.

The radio operations section at SOE's Beaulieu Estate belonged to Agent Denis Rake from the first day he set foot on the Hampshire campus. Thoroughly trained and battle tested, Rake was a perfect fit for the tight knitted teaching community. His bouts with depression behind him, Denden, as he had become affectionately known, attacked the job of teaching new agents the wireless with the same abandon that had made him a performer on the British theatrical circuit. His homosexuality, a fact that he made no attempt to hide, bothered no one at Beaulieu. There was simply too much important work to be done by all concerned to be troubled by such an asymmetry.

Rake was also a master radio operator who was able to provide interesting anecdotes of his own adventures in occupied France to his eager students. He tried to instill in each agent a specific cadence and style that would serve as a specific signature for each operator. A trained operator in England could easily distinguish a specific hand on the other end of the wireless. If a security question was raised about a field agent's transmission, the agent's signature could be used for absolute verification.

Denis Rake spent countless hours with his students and became very valued to most. Female agents were particularly drawn to Rake whose easy charm and demeanor made their difficult job of learning Morse code and the rudiments of radio transmission that much easier.

The instructor spent enough time with each new agent to be able to identify each one's transmissions personally, storing such information in his gifted memory.

61

He also lobbied Colonel Buckmaster for improvements to the existing radios and equipment.

"Too heavy, these are colonel," he repeatedly professed. "And they draw too much power. Why, the Jerries in Paris were takin to cutting off power to certain sections of the city where they suspected transmissions were oraginatin'. And it worked, too. A couple of agents were arrested while they were transmittin'; at least that was the word in Paris."

Buckmaster took Denis Rake's comments quite seriously. He was aware that testing was already underway on the new MkIII sets, which weighed only 9 pounds with batteries and accessories. With any luck, these sets would be ready shortly and distributed to the departing agents. Buckmaster chose not to disclose the development of the MkIII to Rake until he received the first sets. Had Rake known, the former entertainer's exuberant personality simply could not have waited to utilize the first sets, and Buckmaster considered that something of a problem. He felt it was better to wait until delivery to inform his instructor of their existence.

Rake also became a close confidant of US Army Captain Brian Russell. Russell was the chap on campus who always learned of new techniques the Germans had employed to locate the wireless and its transmitters through his steady stream of intelligence data. When the enemy began employing direction finding teams to locate SOE operatives, Russell found the information from intercepted German communications that alerted the SOE to the Germans' improved techniques. Along with Rake, the two quickly devised a shorter transmission format that lessened the opportunity for the enemy direction finders to locate the source of the SOE agents' transmissions.

The two also became close friends outside the confines of the SOE grounds. Russell regarded Denis Rake as a real individual. They shared a love of France and the fact that both had formerly been operatives within occupied France. A small inn in Beaulieu Village was the only watering hole available for enjoyment for the SOE staff, but was too small to hold more than a few of the instructors.

Russell and Rake preferred to make the short trip to nearby Southampton, a much larger city on the River Test. They located a small hotel there, the Grand by name, but, in reality, a smallish, somewhat antiquated building. The Grand came equipped with an intimate café and bar that catered to the seamen who frequented Southampton's busy harbor. The two SOE instructors were made at home and soon became regulars at the establishment. Rake even entertained the crowd with a selection from his theatrical repertoire when in a particularly festive mood.

On this particular evening, Rake confided to Russell that his present class of agents was far ahead of most classes. "Two of the female agents, Vert and Jaune, show exceptional abilities with the radios. They picked up Morse right away and could easily be radio operators if they chose. I've taught them everything I know and my class isn't even finished."

"I have only had them for a day or two," Russell responded. "Agent Jaune seemed sharp as a tack and Vert was so beautiful it was hard to take my eyes off her."

"I wouldn't know about that," Rake countered naughtily. "I'm only interested in their abilities as future agents." He smiled to himself as he finished his Campari.

"I get that group next week," said Russell. "I will be on the lookout for both of them. From what you said, they should be able to pick up my stuff quite easily."

"Agent Jaune might be able to *teach* your material, Brian. You had better watch out or you might just be out of a job."

"And, Denden (Rake's nickname around the campus), would they send me back to France in that case? That's what I have been hoping for the past year or so."

"You know my feelings on that," replied Denis Rake. "I wouldn't mind givin' the Jerries one more shot at my sweet little arse."

"You break me up, Denden. After all the close calls you've had, you are willing to tempt Fate again. Sheer bravado it what it is, old man. Sheer bravado."

"For some reason I just don't think the Germans will ever get the better of me, and that's the truth. Nothin' specific, mind you, just the wee feelin' that my demise won't be at the hands of a kraut-eatin' devil from the North."

The two friends ordered another round as the small bar began emptying for the night.

Colonel Maurice Buckmaster returned to his office less than ten minutes after Russell had arrived. He quickly strode around his desk and offered Russell a seat.

"Just what's on your mind, Captain Russell? From the look on your face it must be something important."

"I believe so, sir. I found it in some French dispatches that came through my desk." He produced a single page of paper and handed it to Buckmaster.

Buckmaster read the contents and peered at Russell. "Are we sure this is her husband?" he asked plaintively.

"It would seem so, colonel. After all, the prison is in Marseille and the name Fiocca isn't all that common in France. Nancy's husband's first name was Henri and I believe that would cement the fact."

Buckmaster pondered the situation and finally spoke. "I will make some inquires just to be sure. I wouldn't want to break her heart if I wasn't completely certain about it. Please hold off on saying anything to her until we are positive."

"As you wish, colonel."

Russell rose and departed the office. He was relieved that the burden of confronting Nancy Fiocca with such horrible news was removed from his shoulders.

Chapter Six

The Auvergne Region of France is located in the south central part of the country that is sparsely populated. Its northern section is quite hilly while the southern part is mountainous and dotted with colorful pastures that make the area almost pastoral. The Auvergne is France's only volcanic region, having formed about 70,000 years ago. While no eruptions have been recorded for the past 6,000 years, the area remains volcanic in nature with numerous protrusions remaining to remind of its lava-related past.

Two main rivers, the majestic Loire and its left tributary, the Allier, dominate the area from their source in France's great Massif Central. The area derives its name from the Auverni, a fierce Gallic tribe that fought in vain against Julius Caesar's formidable and dominant Roman Legions.

The Auvergne is also the location of Vichy, the elegant spa town that is headquarters to the capitulated government of France under the Great War hero Marshall Pétain. As such, the very word Vichy has become despised by most French citizens and in particular by the SOE-F who constantly seeks to disrupt the Vichy Government's attempt at collaborating with its German occupiers.

The head of the local French Resistance was Colonel Émile Coulaudon, a 37-year old with firm Socialist beliefs. Born in Clermont-Ferrand, he was taken prisoner at Gerardmer in late June of 1940 and escaped less than three weeks later. His first involvement with the French Resistance was the establishment, in Clermont-Ferrand and more southerly Brioude, of an actual fighting unit to harass the Germans. Coulaudon's Resistance handle was Gaspard and he was quickly respected by his peers and members of his unit.

Included among his subordinates was Captain Henri Tardivat. Prior to the war, Tardivat served as a teacher of mathematics and enjoyed success as a rugby player in his hometown of Montluçon, almost due north of Clermont-Ferrand. At the outbreak of hostilities, Tardivat immediately initiated his anti-German activities. He eventually became the leader of the local Montluçon Maquis segment that was ultimately overseen by Emile Coulaudon.

One of Coulaudon's other top associates was a woman, Christine Allard, a beautiful brunette who had been a part of the French Resistance since its early inception. In the beginning, she was part of the Resistance network with Pierre Bond (code name Victor) around the town of le Puy-en-Velay in the Haut Loire. Christine was quite successful in her Resistance efforts until a most unfortunate occurrence changed her luck.

Originally from the town of St. Flour, Christine broke down when confronted by her father about her ongoing Resistance activities. She tearfully admitted her work with the secret organization and fully expected her conservative father's stern disapproval. To her surprise, the town's watchmaker took great pride in his daughter's accomplishments and even voiced his approval on a subsequent social meeting with some of his friends at his favorite bistro. One of those friends was a Vichy sympathizer who afterwards reported the conversation to the local Milice office. Luckily, a French Resistance member worked in the Milice office as a double agent and was able to warn Christine of the Vichy Police's impending attempt to capture her.

She quickly left her parent's home and headed north to Clermont-Ferrand where Pierre Bond knew she could contact other Resistance operatives. Christine came to the attention of Emile Coulaudon who immediately enlisted her in his operation. New identity papers were forged utilizing the name of a local young woman who had fled the area prior to the Nazi occupation.

By accomplishing a number of hard projects for Coulaudon, Christine Allard soon became a top operative and Coulaudon's trusted aide. The Resistance leader rewarded her courage and expertise with additional responsibility. He was keenly aware that no job or assignment was too difficult for the striking woman. Her code name was also changed from Jeanne to Sofian to insure she remained clear of any possible Milice or Gestapo traps.

Vera Atkins' work load had increased significantly during the past few weeks. A briefing took place with a top ranking officer of the Allied Expeditionary Forces from Camp Griffiss, Bushy Park, Teddington, just southwest of London. The officer, an American full colonel, had called on Colonel Buckmaster with little advance notice. Buckmaster had insisted that Vera sit in on the meeting, a fact that pleased Vera immensely. The full Colonel came complete with a decided drawl to his speech, but spoke with complete authority as to his mission.

"Colonel Buckmaster," he began earnestly, "everything I say from this point must be considered completely top secret. The contents of our discussion will not be reviewed with any other members of your staff unless absolutely necessary. Is that clear?"

"Certainly, my dear man. After all, we are in the business of keeping secrets aren't we?" Buckmaster declared back to the American officer.

The colonel eyed his fellow officer and continued. "The day we have been waiting for is finally developing and that's why I am here. The information I am about to give you is too sensitive to put into any sort of communication. Plans for the invasion of France are already underway and I must tell you the operation is going to be the largest ever attempted.

Due consideration has been given to a number of possible landing sites along the French coast including the Pas de Calais and Cherbourg. Cherbourg seems too heavily defended to attack and the Pas de Calais has been chosen as the sight of a feigned attack, one that will make the Germans think that it is the actual point of attack."

Buckmaster and Vera listened attentively; captivated by the idea that such an event was finally becoming a reality.

The American officer continued. "Our timetable calls for an invasion of Normandy sometime during the month of May, with weather and a vast array of other dynamics permitting. We know some of the physical problems associated with Normandy, but it has been chosen because it offers the best possible chance of success with the fewest losses of life.

It will be an allied operation under the title name of Operation Overlord. You must commit the name to memory, please don't jot it down anywhere."

Buckmaster looked over at Vera with an engrossed look on his face. Vera was also totally immersed with the officer's words, but managed to shake her head in agreement.

"As you can well imagine, your SOE-F will play a large role in this operation. It is vital that the French Resistance render as much of the Jerries equipment and troops inoperable as possible. If our enemy's communications are cut, it will be a tremendous asset to the operation. Anything we can come up with to harass the Germans' response once the attack has begun will mean a great deal to our success. Our Commander, General Eisenhower, has directed that all our resources be made available to you as soon as you deem necessary. Equipment, airplanes, boats, whatever it is you need. He also wants you to get as many of your operatives into the southwest section of France as you deem necessary. That also involves your decreasing your training times if necessary. Am I clear on that?"

"If you mean I am to send unprepared agents into a battle area, that's simply not possible, colonel. Am I perfectly clear on that, sir?" Buckmaster retorted edgily.

"Yes, most certainly Buckmaster. Untrained agents won't do us much good, will they? I simply meant that it will be up to you to have as many personnel in place to help the overall effort. And that includes your training staff. If any of them can be spared and you feel they can be of help, I ask that you find an assignment for them in France. I'm sure you understand the importance."

"You have made that perfectly clear, Colonel. I will sit down with Miss Adkins here and see where we can tighten up a bit. I will make this a priority as of now."

"Thank you so much, colonel. I knew we count on your cooperation. I'll mention it to Ike when I get back to headquarters. He will be pleased. Thanks again. I hope I haven't inconvenienced you too much."

"Not a jot, colonel. You will find the SOE quite responsive to such requests."

"It has been quite easy to work with all of you. I hope I didn't seem too pushy when I started. I can get carried away about all this. It's such a large operation that it is all mind-boggling."

"Quite, my dear chap. If I understood as much as you do, I'm sure I'd be feeling quite the same."

"I have some papers to leave with you. They are all Extremely Top Secret and apply to the upcoming mission. I'm sure you will want to get into them right away."

"I will start on them immediately, to be sure. I must tell you that I can hardly wait to see what we have in store for Jerry."

"We are going to kick some serious German butt, Colonel. I can promise you that."

"By all means, colonel. I must thank you for taking time to share this with us."

"It's my job, Colonel Buckmaster. And, I take it very seriously."

"To be sure, colonel. We all do."

"Well, thanks again. I guess I'll get on the road. I have other stops you know."

Buckmaster extended his hand and shook vigorously. It wasn't every day that someone brought such exhilarating news to Baker Street. As soon as his visitor departed, he opened the first of the envelopes and began reading avidly. Vera Atkins returned to her desk, her head swimming with the potentialities of the information she had just learned. She knew she now faced even more extensive work days ahead.

Émile Coulaudon, code name Gaspard, signaled his meeting of the Auvergne Maquis leaders to order with a nod of his head. The meeting place was an old barn located on the southeastern outskirts of Clermont-Ferrand. Set back from the road, the site commanded a full view of movement from either direction. A lookout was stationed out of sight in the barn's upper level.

"We have just received word of a major airdrop mission that will provide us with the means of giving our German friends even more problems," he began earnestly. "This is the drop we have been expecting for the last month. If everything goes correctly, our British allies will provide us with some rocket- propelled and anti-tank weapons. You all know how much we can use them."

The Maquis nodded in agreement as Gaspard continued. "There must be something big happening in the near future; we have never received these heavier weapons before. We must be extremely careful that nothing happens to even one of these precious pieces. They will be taken to the caves just north of Clermont-Ferrand and carefully hidden. No traces of our presence should be left, so we must take special care. I am leaving it up to you to insure this all happens. Use only your best men and tell no one else about your actions. The Nazis are still looking for us and I don't want anything to happen to these weapons."

The assembled leaders again shook their heads in accord.

"The drop is scheduled for tomorrow night around 2200. We will use the drop zone that is far enough from the city as to not attract any attention. Your fires should be lit 10 minutes before the scheduled drop time. There are two small trucks available to carry the weapons. Time will be of the essence and I want enough Maquis assigned to this to insure the weapons are protected. There are also two Citroëns that will precede the trucks. If we are unlucky enough to encounter any German patrols or roadblocks, the cars will be able to alert the trucks. Maintain a sufficient distance between the cars and trucks so there will be enough time to alert the trucks if we have any problems. Each car and truck team will use a different route to the caves so that one should certainly get through."

Gaspard looked into the faces of his battle-hardened partisans. Everyone knew their job and what was expected during this important mission.

"If there is nothing more to discuss, I suggest you all return to your homes or wherever you are staying. Tomorrow night will come soon enough."

The small group stood and filed out of the old barn. Hardly a word had been spoken since the group arrived.

Gaspard beckoned to the lone woman in the group to stay.

"Sofian," he said softly, utilizing her code name. "You stay a minute. I want to discuss something with you."

Christine Allard stopped and adjusted her beret. The chilly spring weather was still active and sent cold quivers down her back. She shuddered and waited for Gaspard to begin.

"This is what we all have been waiting for Sofian. I really believe this is the beginning of the big push to rid us of the Germans for good."

"What makes you say that Gaspard? Have you received any other messages to confirm your beliefs?" she answered.

"Nothing that I can put my finger on at this time. It's more of a feeling. We are getting better cooperation from London and more agents are being dropped in than ever before. It seems to me that the elements of a major operation are underway. There is nothing specific, but it all adds up."

"You always have a good sense about such things, Gaspard. It's part of what makes you a great leader."

"Thank you, Sofian. I am glad you think so."

"We all believe in you, Gaspard. Every one of us."

"We have all fought this cause together. The Maquis and the Resistance are one in our effort. It is a great statement for our beloved country that has seen so much pain and suffering."

"We have been very fortunate here in the l'Auvergne. We have caused the Bosch many setbacks and much distress. Their time here has not been very pleasant."

"I think it is the same everywhere in France," Christine asserted. "There are so many who are a part of our fight. It's the only way we can beat the bastards."

"Very true, Sofian. It takes a great deal of effort. Now, I have something special I want you to do before the drop tomorrow night…"

When United States Army Captain Brian A. Russell was briefed by Colonel Maurice Buckmaster on the Allied Expeditionary Forces plan called Operation Overlord, he asked the first question that came to his mind.

"Why are you telling me all this, Colonel Buckmaster? I'm not really sure what it has to do with me and what I do here. I think it's incredibly daring and undoubtedly important, but I just don't see how I fit into it."

"Righto, Captain Russell. I half expected you to ask something like that." He paused, searching for the correct course for his response. At length, be began to explain. "I have given this matter a great deal of thought and what is expected of SOE-F for the immediate future. As of now, you are the only other faculty member here at Beaulieu who is aware of this plan. As of now, I am unsure of whom else I will bring into the loop.

"When this invasion actually happens, the Germans will undoubtedly react to it with all of their possible resources. They will put priorities on the railways to get their heavier equipment and troops moving toward Southwestern France. The two main railway systems they can be expected to utilize are from the south and through the Auvergne. Needless to say, it is imperative that we make every effort to stop these movements. If Jerry can't reinforce his troops quickly, then we will have a huge advantage."

Russell studied the large map directly behind Buckmaster's desk.

"I see that, Colonel. The Auvergne route is actually a day or two shorter if I am correct in my thinking. I would think they would put more emphasis on that way. At least, that's what I would do."

"Undoubtedly, my boy. And that's where you fit in."

"I'm not sure…"

"Let me explain. The Resistance forces in the Auvergne have been really successful of late and we had already made plans for reinforcing them with some of our agents. There is a sizeable Maquis force in the area and we believe we can make their numbers work in our favor. If the Germans have things to worry about in their back yards, they won't be so quick to commit troops to stop the allied invasion. We intend to do the same in other sections of France, wherever we have a real Maquis presence."

"I'm still not sure where I…"

"I'm not quite finished, Captain Russell. "In order to do the best possible job, I need an experienced agent to go in ahead of our other agents and literally scout the entire area. I need someone with actual experience and the ability to estimate what the enemy might be able to do if we planned a definite attack. At the same time, I would want the entire railway section of the Auvergne studied as to how we can best stop troop and equipment movement. We would have to know which areas are heavily defended and which are not. We can't rely on the Resistance for these pieces of information due to the fact that the Gestapo has some agents working within the Resistance. We can't alert the pricks to our intentions or interest in the railroads. It won't be an easy task, and it must be done rather quickly. We don't really have that much time to work on it."

Brian Russell again moved closer to the map on the wall. He studied some of the points on the map and then turned to Buckmaster. "In order to do what you want I would have to have complete access to the railway system. I don't think that something like that is at all possible."

"You might be surprised, my boy," Buckmaster answered back. I've just had a chat with some of the boys at BCRAL *(Bureau Central de Renseignements et d'Action Londres)* and they gave me an idea to consider. They have an agent in the City of Vichy itself who is an inspector for SCNF, the French national railroad system. He is a part of another Resistance group, *Resistance-Fer,* a group that is made up mostly of railroad workers and railroad executives. I wasn't even aware of the unit's existence until I enquired at the BCRAL.

Anyway, it seems you are about the same age and height as this inspector who lives in Vichy. I thought we might make use of that and have some credentials made up for you. If we can switch the two of you for a few days, there's no telling what you might be able to find out. The inspector can lose himself in the mountains for a short time. We can have you parachuted in to take his place. His daily duties include frequent trips on the trains so your moving around won't be suspicious."

Buckmaster paused, allowing Russell to absorb the details of his proposal.

"It might just work, colonel, provided I don't run into too many people who know the real inspector. That wouldn't be so keen."

The BCRAL thought of that also, Russell. There is a minor flu outbreak in Vichy at this time so many of the residents are wearing flu masks around the area. You would fit in nicely with one of your own."

"It seems as if everything is covered, colonel. Do you have any idea when I depart?"

"Your credentials are being finalized at this very moment and should be delivered sometime tomorrow. If the weather cooperates, you will be in France tomorrow evening."

"And who will look after my duties here at Beaulieu, if I may ask?"

"I've already asked Vera to spell you. That gives you today and whatever time is available tomorrow to bring her up to snuff."

US Army Captain Brian Russell smiled politely at his British superior. Once again, it seemed to the young American officer that little had been left to chance by the SOE.

Gaspard's instructions to Christine were very specific and required a degree of planning. She was instructed to set up a vantage point about one-half mile from the projected drop zone where she could observe any ground movement toward the drop area. She was given one of the hand held SCR-536 handie-talkie two-way radios that had been recently airdropped from England. It would be Christine's job to spot any possible interference from German ground units that might conceivably compromise the mission. Another Maquis fighter would tend the other radio and would remain in close proximity to Colonel Gaspard in case of a problem.

The following morning, Christine took a ride on her bicycle to the vicinity of the drop area to scout a beneficial position. The daylight was a boon to her efforts as she navigated the rough, uneven terrain. She eventually estimated her distance from the drop zone and began to look for a clear vantage point.

A high ridge arose to her left and Christine climbed up to take a look. The verdant landscape unfurled below her, ostensibly pristine in its early spring splendor. She took a moment to enjoy the beauty, a sensation she had not experienced in quite some time.

It is really quite beautiful around here. The mountains and valleys seem perfectly suited to each other. The sounds of birds and insects blend into the surroundings in one musical accord. This is a place that should remain unspoiled by war. Too bad that's not the case...

She turned toward the upcoming drop spot and was able to distinguish the trees and fields that occupied the site. Convinced she had found a reasonable vantage point, she began the climb down.

She remounted her bike and began pedaling back in the direction of Clermont-Ferrand. Minutes later, her keen sense of hearing alerted her to the fact that a motor was coming from the direction of the city. Christine quickly dismounted and hurriedly pushed her bicycle behind some nearby brush. She crouched down and peered around her cover.

A German armored car came into view traveling at a low rate of speed. It featured an angled armored body and turret, with a large bed frame antennae on the top. The turret was open and a German soldier with goggles stood erect inside the turret, peering around.

Christine looked closely at the car. Its design was something she had never seen before. She took care to note as many details as possible and committed these features to her sharp memory. As the car rounded a bend in the road and disappeared, Christine stood and retrieved her bicycle. She would hurry and get the news of the vehicle to Gaspard.

That was a bit too close for me. Another few seconds and the Germans would have seen me. I wonder what they were doing around here. This isn't a heavily traveled road, in fact, it is somewhat remote. Well, Gaspard will know...

·

The small group of new agents realized their training time at the Beaulieu Estate was drawing to an end. Classes were concluded and the small aspects of their covert activities occupied their days and evenings. Attention to detail was now paramount in the SOE-F's attempt to safeguard their lives while in occupied France.

Some of the SOE's special needs were met by people who never expected to be part of the spy business. Claudia Pulver was, by trade, a fashion designer and expert seamstress prior to the outbreak of war. It was her job to make agents sent into France look as if they belonged there. Pulver was assigned the job of matching an agent's clothes to the area in which the agent would operate. Since people from different sections of France wore different clothes, it was up to Pulver's department to see that correct regional dress was afforded each new agent sent into France. These clothes were accurate down to the labels of actual stores located within the region. Female agents were measured and fitted as if they truly lived in the cities to which they were being sent. The shoes were always French and were deemed as comfortable as possible given the actual circumstances.

The final touches were provided by someone like Bert Adlington. Adlington was a plaster sculptor who initially helped the SOE design exploding devices for agents to use in the field. He then became the SOE's premier ager, the person charged with making new items appear to be old. New clothes, suitcases and the like would quickly raise German suspicions so Adlington, and others like him, would treat the items and make them appear used and old. This process was invaluable to the agents whose very lives depended on their ability to blend into their new environment.

It was Nancy Fiocca and Violette Szabo who appeared together at Adlington's door to pick up their new wardrobes. They were ushered in and handed two bags each of clothes, shoes, and personal items. They were instructed to lay the clothes out and try on the dresses to insure they fit. Adlington left the room as the two agents eyed their new clothes.

Violette pulled out a dress and held it up. "We won't be very fashionable in these," she offered as she removed her blouse. "In fact, I think this one is downright ugly if you ask me."

"Don't be so quick to judge, Jaune. The idea is that we do not attract any unnecessary attention. Fashionable clothes would be a quick giveaway, and we would be the ones that would be dead," she said lightly.

"Oh, I know all that," Violette answered back. "I was just feeling a bit sorry for myself, that's all. I wasn't really disappointed in the clothes. They have even provided me with two bras. I hope they got my size right."

Nancy smiled back at her younger friend. She fingered her assortment of clothes and was happy to see some pants and walking shoes in the collection.

"Someone has been quite thorough in thinking out all this crap," she uttered. "It looks as if I am going to be out in the country if I read all these clothes correctly. There is only one dress and it's a bit floppy for my taste."

Violette regarded the dress as Nancy held it up and smiled broadly. "That might impress a German, but never a Frenchman. I agree with you, it's almost hideous."

The two friends bantered back and forth as they tried on all the clothes that were contained in the bags. As they finished, Bert Adlington reappeared at the door.

"I thought you two might be finishing by now. Is everything up to your impeccable standards, ladies?"

Nancy began to laugh and Violette quickly joined in. "As good as possible Mr. Adlington," Nancy beamed. "And, they appear well used. You have done a marvelous job."

"Just part of our service here, ladies. I am happy you are pleased with our efforts."

Nancy and Violette looked at each other as they repacked the bags. Adlington stepped to another part of the room and returned momentarily. He handed each a small, well-used brown suitcase and motioned for them to place the bags inside.

"Now you are both all set," Adlington finished. "I wish you good luck on your missions."

Both women offered a sincere "thank you," as they departed the room carrying their suitcases. They knew they were finally ready for their next assignments.

Chapter Seven

The olive drab Austin 10 Royal Air Force staff car hurried toward RAF Tangmere in West Sussex. The base, near the English coastline, offered US Army Captain Brian Russell a brief respite from the non-stop activity he had recently experienced at the SOE's Baker Street complex. For the past 30 hours, the young American officer had seen a whirlwind of faces that were all concerned with preparing him for his upcoming mission into South Central France.

He had been photographed for his new identity card, measured for his uniform as an inspector for the SCNF French Railway System, provided with a thorough collection of updated maps of the railway system, and another half-dozen activities that soon became a blur to the American.

The fact that he was carrying a new lightweight wireless MkIII radio set that was carefully hidden under a fake compartment in his lone suitcase was of little consequence to Captain Russell. He sincerely hoped his off-time Morse transmissions lessons with his pal Denis Rake at Beaulieu could now be put to good use. He tried to recall the alphabet from his memory but was simply too exhausted to remember the full table. He closed his eyes and attempted a few moments of sleep.

Nearly an hour later, the Austin rolled to an abrupt stop at a cottage directly across from the entrance to RAF Tangmere. The WAAC (Women's Auxiliary Army Corps) corporal who had driven Russell from Beaulieu Estate stepped to the side of the car and opened the door.

"We're here, sir," she piped out loudly, breaking Russell's slumber.

Russell looked around, barely cognizant of his surroundings. He managed a weak, "Yes, thank you," and stepped from the automobile. Placing his hat at a crooked angle on his head, he looked wearily at the cottage and then across the road at the entrance to RAF Tangmere.

"You are to report to the cottage, sir. I'm sure you remember..."

"Oh yes, now I do," Russell mastered his response.

The corporal closed the door and returned to the driver's seat. "Good luck, sir, and I truly mean that," she said as she started the car and lurched forward.

I must really be a mess, Russell thought. *What with no sleep and all the grilling I've been through, it's no wonder I'm fit to be tied. I must gather myself right away. After all, I'm only hours away from departure time.*

He approached the cottage and rang a small doorbell. A face appeared from within, a small man wearing rimmed glasses, who closely regarded the figure in the doorway.

"You must be Captain Russell, my dear fellow. We have been expecting you. Please come right in."

"Might I be able to take a quick nap somewhere?" Russell suddenly found himself saying. "I'm really beat and I'd be in much better shape if I had a few minutes to catch some shuteye."

"That could easily be arranged, Captain Russell. You won't be departing for several hours and there's a cozy corner with a cot that just might fit you."

The words were like music to Russell's tired mind. He smiled and followed the SOE official into the cottage.

It took the SOE-F several weeks to select the first mission into France for Violette Szabo. The time delay also worked in Violette's favor as she was able to spend some time with her daughter Tania who was now nearing her second birthday. Along with visits to family, friends and an occasional trip to the nearby cinema, Violette was careful to get some important business completed during the break in her schedule. Knowing her incursion into France was wrought with danger, she decided to provide for her daughter's future.

She stopped at a neighborhood stationary store and purchased a standard form that could serve as her last will and testament. She took a pen and carefully noted the following:

This is the last Will and Testament of me Violette Reine Elizabeth Szabo of 36 Pembridge Villas Notting Hill W11 in-The county of London made this Twenty-fourth day of January in the year of our Lord one thousand nine hundred and Forty-Four.

I HEREBY revoke all Wills made by me at any time heretofore. I Appoint Reine Blanche Bushell of 18 Burnley Road Stockwell SW9 to be my executor, and direct that all my Debts and Funeral Expenses shall be paid as soon as conveniently may be after my decease. I GIVE AND BEQUEATH unto My daughter Tania Demaris Desiree Szabo, 59 Fernside Avenue Mill Hill Edgware N7 All of which I die possessed.

V. Szabo

Violette asked Vera Atkins and another SOE-F Officer, Major R. A. Bourne Paterson, to witness the will and left the document in Vera's care.

Shortly thereafter, word reached Violette that the date for her first mission had finally been arranged.

She reported to SOE-F headquarters and found that a number of personal items awaited her arrival. Her clothes were ready along with a French handbag and French shoes. Once dressed, the clothes were again checked for any possible items that could mark her as British. Her new papers identified her as Corinne Reine Leroy, a commercial secretary whose address was 64 rue Thiers in Le Havre. Her birth date was her own, but her place of birth was switched from Levallois-Perret to Bailleul, a fact that allowed her to travel to coastal and port sectors.

The mission itself was both simple and complicated at the same time. One of SOE-F's agent circuits, Salesman by name, was thought to have been penetrated. Most agents were located in and around the Rouen area and also operated in the vicinity of Le Havre. Another SOE agent, Philippe Liewer, one of the original organizers of the Salesman network, was to accompany Violette and attempt to ascertain what had happened to the members of the setup.

Vera Atkins drove with Violette to the premises of Gibraltar Farm, the stopping off place for Royal Air Force Station Tempsford and pick up location for the B-24 Liberator Bombers of the United States Army Air Force's Eight Air Force Special Operations Group. The bombers were part of the so-called Carpetbaggers Squadrons, four American squadrons whose duty was providing resistance assistance for France, Holland, Belgium and Norway.

As the car wound its way past the de Havilland Aircraft Company in Hatfield, Vera Atkins looked at the excited young woman seated next to her. For some reason, she had taken special notice of Violette and had silently noted the striking young woman's progress through SOE-F. Some of these thoughts raced through her mind as the car's engine continually ground through the early evening air.

I hope this all turns out well for her. I have always had some misgivings about this one. For one thing, she speaks French with an English accent and that will be curtains if she is ever closely interrogated. She is also injury prone and I'm not completely sure her ankle has completely healed. She makes up for all this with her enthusiasm and her hatred for the Germans. She even puts the revenge she seeks ahead of her little girl, a decision I'm not sure I could make myself. If we weren't so damn short of agents, I'd probably try and find an excuse to keep her here in England and not expose her to any possibility of being captured.

Oh well, I guess I'm getting a bit soft on things. It all comes with the job. Even so, I'll be quite happy when I see her back here in a couple of weeks. I'll come out to meet her when she returns. You can count on that.

Philippe Liewer was already waiting when the car carrying the two women drove up. He shook hands with Vera and renewed his liaison with Violette. The two were given parachutes and were thoroughly checked by the crew of the Liberator that was waiting nearby.

They boarded the huge B-24 and were shown the "Joe Hole" opening that would serve as their departure point. Violette became more nervous as the four engines eventually roared to life.

"Want a fag?" Liewer offered Violette a Player's Navy Cut cigarette. "It will help your nerves. This is my first real jump; I'm a bit anxious too."

Violette shook her head and declined.

If I took a puff of one of those, I think I'd throw up all over the place. I can't believe I'm so nervous. I have thought of nothing but this for the past year. Maybe if I have a sip of water. She fingered a small canteen and unscrewed the cap. She lifted the metal container and took a small sip, then a larger one. The water was cold and felt good in her throat. She took a deep breath and forced herself to relax.

Violette settled back in the uncomfortable canvass seat as the bomber roared down the runway. The big bird slowly gained altitude as it headed toward the French coastline. She recalled her last kiss with Tania and the tears that followed.

His nap stretched out to more than five hours and helped reinvigorate Brian Russell immensely. He awakened with renewed energy and made good use of some cold water in a nearby sink to thoroughly rinse his face.

It was already dark outside and Russell was motioned to a side door and then into a waiting jeep. The jeep turned and entered the main gate at RAF Tangmere and was waived through by the heavily armed RAF guard on duty.

"No credentials check?" Russell asked the driver, a young RAF leading airman.

"No, sir. The guards know whatever papers you show them are fakes anyway so they just waive us through. They saw that you came out of the cottage like everyone else. That's what's convenient about bein' so close to the main gate."

Russell mulled over the airman's words. *So everyone knows I'm a spy as are all the others like me. It kind of makes sense in an offhanded manner. Why check papers that are all forged? As long as I came out of the SOE's cottage, that's good enough for them. Well, it seems to be working...*

The jeep turned toward the active taxiways and stopped not far from a row of Westland Lysander MkIIIA's that were parked in a ready area.

"This is your drop off, sir," the airman announced cheerily. "I wish you good luck on your mission."

"Thanks, young man. I'll probably need all the luck I can get."

The airman nodded and put the jeep into gear. In another few seconds, he was headed away from the Lysanders.

Russell looked around in time to see a short, bald man in his mid-fifties approaching. He looked at Russell and asked, "Inspector Patout, I would presume."

"Yes," Russell answered, nodding. "Are we ready to go?"

"To be sure. As soon as your parachute and pilot arrives, you'll be right off."

Russell looked around the Lysander, a rather snub-nosed single engine aircraft that had become the workhorse of SOE's operations. The short man approached when he saw Russell eyeing the Lysander.

"Great lil' aircraft 'ere if you ask me. Can take off and land on a dime and flies too low for anyone to see 'er. You would have to fly directly over someone for them to see you and she doesn't really make that much noise. Come and gone 'fore anyone can do anythin' about it."

Russell nodded his agreement and patted the black fuselage. He conceded in his mind that the small craft would be no more than a spec in the night sky.

Another person approached, carrying a parachute in his arms.

"Flight Lieutenant Bob Whitaker," he introduced himself to Russell. "I'll be your chauffer tonight. Here's a parachute for you to put on, but I doubt you will need to use it. Our landings of late have been fairly steady, and I have another agent to pick up for the return flight. You'll only have to jump if the conditions warrant it."

"Good, I'd prefer that," Russell answered with a grin.

"I've already pre-checked our bird, and she's ready to go. You climb into the back seat and strap yourself in. We have provided a handrail to make it easier to get in," he advised, pointing at a short rod attached to the side of the aircraft. "We can talk once we are airborne, on the intercom. I'm sure you know how that works."

Russell nodded and started up the Lysander. He adroitly stepped toward the rear and climbed into the back seat without using the handrail, a fact that was not lost on Flight Lt. Whitaker.

Once aboard, the experienced flier quickly started the motor and began rolling toward takeoff. There was little activity at RAF Tangmere at that hour so he immediately moved to the takeoff holding position. RAF Tangmere tower gave immediate permission to begin takeoff and the Lysander swiftly moved forward.

Russell was amazed at how little runway the small plane covered before it gently lifted off the ground. The black Lysander climbed to 500 feet and Flt. Lt Whitaker adjusted the throttle and turned toward France.

A moment later, he called back to Russell on the intercom. "Neat little bird, isn't she?" he asked possessively.

"Neat," replied Russell. "Hardly any effort to take off and she used very little runway if I am correct."

"Quite, old boy. She can get up even faster, but there was no reason…"

"Absolutely. Save the short ones for when you really need them."

"So, you've had some prior experience with aircraft?"

"Not really," Russell replied honestly. "A little here and there. Mostly, I pay attention to things. You know what I mean."

"Precisely. You never can tell."

"And you will get me close to Vichy tonight? That would seem to be quite a feat, considering that Vichy is the seat of French government at this time."

"It's not all that difficult. After all, it's a relatively small city and it's in the mountains. Mountains tend to hide the sounds of an airplane engine if the aircraft is low enough."

"Low enough?" Russell questioned.

"R-r-ight," Whitaker affirmed. "But, no fear. The most difficult problem tonight is picking out the correct set of mountain tops so we can approach the landing field from the proper direction. I've studied the charts and I think we will be all right."

He thinks we will be all right. He damned better be right. It would be a shame to wrap my pretty new uniform around a blasted mountain top for nothing.

Russell settled back and studied the passing terrain. The French coastline came and slowly disappeared behind the Lysander's tail. Few lights were able to be seen, a direct result of the German blackout of occupied France. A series of rivers and lakes passed below, hopefully a trail of landmarks for the veteran RAF pilot in the front seat.

It won't be long now, bud. This is what you dreamed about, being back in the action of things. I wonder what's on tap for me for the next few days. Whatever it is, I know I am ready. I wonder ... his thoughts suddenly drifted back to Christine Allard and their parting at the Pont d'Espagne more than three years ago. *Has it been that long? Three years...it can't be that long. I wonder what has happened to her...is she still alive?*

A sharp break in the steady drone of the Lysander's engine suddenly cut into Russell's thoughts as Flight Lt. Whitaker banked the small plane in preparation for landing. His time for action with the French Resistance was once again about to begin.

Émile Coulaudon, known as Gaspard to all his Resistance and Maquis supporters, fingered the manual that he had just retrieved from its hiding place in the old barn that was his headquarters. He started paging through the book as Christine peered over his shoulder. He finally stopped and turned to Christine.

"Is this the vehicle you saw on the road?"

Christine looked intently at the photograph in the manual and declared firmly, "Yes, that's it. I'm sure of it. I was just like the picture."

"So our enemy has finally figured out how to monitor us..."

Christine was puzzled and asked, "I'm not sure..."

"According to the manual, it's a direction finding vehicle. It uses triangulation to find the exact spot of a radio transmission. It takes our own signal and uses it to help find where we are transmitting from. It requires additional vehicles so there are probably more of these around."

"You mean we can no longer transmit our signals?"

"Not exactly, Sofian. It just means we have to make our transmissions shorter and move our positions around. It will take them time to figure out just where we are and if we are quick about it, we should always be a step or two ahead."

Christine was unconvinced and stared dubiously at the manual.

Gaspard took note and tried to reassure her. "I might just have another idea for our new friend," he spoke. "We might take two of those big anti-tank guns with us tomorrow evening. If one of these fellows happens along, we could give it a nasty reception."

Christine's eyes widened at the thought of such an idea.

I would love to take out this monster with one of the big guns. One well aimed shot would be all you would need. That would teach the Bosch to leave us alone.

She handed the manual back to Gaspard and smiled confidently. Gaspard saw her look and correctly figured out what she was thinking. He would give his top assistant the honor of drilling the German direction finding vehicle if the occasion arose. She had earned that honor many times in past missions against their enemies.

The totally blackened Westland Lysander circled the landing field in search of a correct code from below. A series of flashes from the ground told the pilot that all was in order for his landing. The craft swooped in low and touched down almost immediately on the grass of a long field about seven miles from the City of Vichy.

Several partisans with berets approached the aircraft with their guns drawn and mounted a guard around the airplane. Russell stepped down and waved up to Flight Lt. Whitaker with thumbs up.

The pilot returned the salute with a broad smile.

A female figure approached the Lysander and nodded to Russell to take off his parachute. She took the chute and expertly placed it around her shoulders. She turned away from Russell and pondered the best way of boarding the plane. Russell saw her predicament, stepped forward and offered his hand to help her reach the boarding rail. She pulled herself up and jumped into the back seat. She looked down at Russell and mouthed a 'thank you' to the American officer. She put on the headphones and was soon adjusting her seat belt. In a few moments, the Lysander's engine began purring as the craft began its taxi. Fifteen seconds later, it was airborne and headed back toward England.

Russell was impressed with the operation's preciseness and professionalism.

I don't think the Lysander was on the ground more than five minutes total. It really makes sense, there's no point in giving the enemy a chance to capture either the agent or the Lysander. These chaps know their business and that's in our favor. I hope it works as well with me when I try and leave next week.

One of the Resistance members approached Russell and spoke. "We have been expecting you Inspector Patout. If you will please follow us…"

The small group left the meadow and walked about a half-mile to a spot where an old Citroën T23 was parked. Its canvas top was speckled with numerous tears and an Imbert Generator was attached to the vehicle's rear section. The Imbert generator converted firewood into a combustible gas under the influence of heat and fed it into the Citroën's engine that had been simply adapted. The wood started burning and the truck's driver started the engine. A brief chug later and the Citroën truck started forward. Russell looked at the generator and marveled at its utter ingenuousness.

You must hand it to these people. No gasoline available so they find a way to use wood that is in great supply. This is just another reason why we will ultimately win this war. It is a simple case of too many people finding ways to overcome their problems.

Russell sat back as the truck lumbered its way back toward Vichy. He adjusted his inspector's cap and looked around at the other Maquis seated in the back of the old truck. Two smoked and the other two closed their eyes in a state of semi slumber. One of the smokers nodded to Russell who returned the gesture.

These sure are remarkable people. They are up all night and go about their jobs the next day as if nothing has happened. It must be hard to be a Maquis fighter. They never know when or where their next meal will come from. These guys don't seem all that emaciated. They must be getting some decent food on a regular basis. That's what it takes. Feed an army and it will fight all day and night. Starve an army and they will barely fight.

The truck bounced as it neared the outskirts of Vichy and its cobblestone streets. A few minutes later the truck came to a halt. One of the Maquis motioned for Russell to alight. He did so and was immediately greeted by another partisan who stepped out of the shadows.

"Inspector Patout, nice to see you again," he greeted Russell and extended his hand. He was wearing a white face mask and offered another mask to Russell. Russell produced his own mask as the man looked down at it.

"Better you have one like the others at the hospital," he advised. "Yours is a bit different and might just give you away. I'll dispose of yours if you put this on."

"Russell obliged the Frenchman who gestured for Russell to follow. The two marched two blocks to an address at 129 rue Voltaire. The Frenchman knocked twice and the door opened. He stepped inside and motioned for Russell to follow.

Inside, a large woman of about fifty surveyed the new arrivals. Not unattractive in a country sort of way, she looked Russell over and nodded approvingly.

"He favors the real Inspector Patout, all right. Unless it was in the bright sunlight, I could never tell them apart."

The Frenchman nodded his agreement and walked to a nearby cabinet. He extracted a corked bottle of wine. He poured each a small glass and raised his hand. "To a Free France and God bless all those who fight in her name."

The three clinked their glasses lightly and began talking. "Early tomorrow morning I will take you to a place where the real Inspector Patout will be waiting. He will explain in person what your normal duties involve. He will also tell you who might be dangerous for you and your mission. I'm called Herve. At least that is my code name. He pointed to the woman. "Her code name is Odette and she will prepare a small breakfast for us before we leave. Now I suggest we get some sleep, the dawn will come early for all of us."

Russell was shown to a small room where a neat bed was already turned down. He felt secure in the fact that the French Resistance was totally prepared for him and would meet any needs that surfaced. He was still tired from his recent efforts and welcomed the chance to get another small measure of sleep. He rested his head and was asleep within thirty seconds of hitting the pillow.

Violette Szabo went about her assigned task of finding out the fate of the compromised Salesman network. She walked about the narrow streets of Rouen and attempted to contact other members of the network. The news she was able to unearth was gloomy at best.

First of all, she saw wanted posters of Liewer and Bob Maloubier, resisters of the Salesman circuit. Not considering the possible consequences, at one point she tore down one of the posters and put it in her purse to show to her superiors in London. The thought of being caught with the poster never entered her mind.

She managed to find out that the Francheter family was still free and living at their apartment at 7 Place des Emmurés. They had provided Liewer a home while he set up the original Salesman network. Practically everyone on Violette's list that she had committed to memory was either dead or arrested.

Violette then moved over to Le Havre, but her efforts there met with similar results. There was no trace of any other agents, a fact that affected Violette greatly. She considered her mission almost a failure and with a heavy heart boarded a train for Paris where she would again meet with Liewer.

Liewer was terribly upset with her findings since he knew most of the missing and dead agents on a personal basis. He was determined to inflict whatever possible damage on the Germans who had killed his friends and fellow agents.

He told Violette that a Lysander pickup had been arranged for them two days hence and that she was free to see Paris with the spare time they had been afforded.

As a child, Violette had lived in a Paris that seemed a far cry from the near empty streets of the German occupation. The taxis that she remembered so fondly were now replaced with vélo-taxis, a cousin to the oriental rickshaw. These odd contraptions were pedal powered by former cyclists from the famous Tour de France.

She also found it hard to get used to the sound of wooden clogs that were worn by many Parisians due to the shortage of leather.

Violette was, however, eager to do some shopping while in the grand city. She was still carrying the French Francs given to her by the SOE-F prior to her departure from England. This amounted to a formidable bankroll and Violette determined to bring back gifts for her mother and baby daughter Tania.

She also visited the imposing, multi-columned Eglise de la Madeleine on rue Royale. This was the church of the beautiful painted domes and colored marble that Violette and her late husband Etienne had pledged to visit after the war. Now she prayed for the soul of her dead husband.

Exiting the church, she walked down rue Royale toward the Place de la Concorde. The couturier Molynex's shop caught her attention and she entered. There she purchased a number of dresses as well as a yellow jumper that she would pick up the following day due to a few minor alterations. The following morning she appeared at the shop to pick up her purchases.

Violette then met Liewer and the two rode out to the scheduled pick up that night in a small field southwest of Châteauroux, some 100 plus miles from Paris. The car passed through Versailles and then Orleans on its southerly course. At the landing site, designated as Hercule, two Lysanders of the 161 Squadron arrived within minutes of each other around 2300 hours. Recognition codes were given and the two aircraft landed successfully. Violette and Liewer each quickly climbed aboard one of the waiting aircraft.

The Lysander pilot with Violette aboard took a homeward course that brought him perilously close to the German-controlled airport at Châteaudun. Suddenly, a number of searchlights lit up the sky and shooting erupted from the airfield. The pilot, Flight Lt. Bob Large took evasive measures to get the relatively slow Lysander out of trouble and inadvertently switched off Violette's microphone. The series of maneuvers had a negative effect on Violette who was thrown around the back cockpit and became quite hysterical in the pitch black night. She screamed into her microphone but received no reply. She finally gave up hollering as the plane levelled out and continued on its way.

Large managed to get the plane back to RAF Tempsford but the landing proved to be tricky. One of the German shells had found the undercarriage of the Lysander and shredded one of the tires. The Lysander bumped down and ground-looped, once again flinging Violette about in her seat.

Flight Lt. Large jumped out of the plane in an attempt to rescue his passenger. Violette was not able to see him jump out of the plane and thought they had landed in enemy territory. Large was young, tall and blonde as were many German soldiers.

She yelled a series of French expletives at him. Large took the abuse, unaware of Violette's ability to speak English. Moments later, a car arrived and things began to get sorted out. When she realized what had happened, Violette smiled broadly and uttered a plaintive, "*Vous êtes pilote!*" and kissed him squarely on the lips. It was an altogether fitting ending to her first mission for SOE-F.

Chapter Eight

Nancy Wake Fiocca had completed her training and was adamant about being sent back into France at the first possible chance. Since it had been more than a month since she had completed the regimen she was naturally eager to begin her duties as an agent with SOE-F. She decided to take matters into her own hands and approached Vera Atkins about the subject on a particularly windy day on Baker Street.

Vera was pleasant to the younger woman, but offered little help. Her time would come just as it had for all the new agents before her. Nancy would just have to wait.

"That's a bunch of crap," Nancy replied, seemingly agitated. "I spend all this time getting ready and then all I do is sit around and twiddle…"

"Everyone is treated the same, Mrs. Fiocca," Vera replied formally. "Certain agents fit certain situations. Not everyone has the same set of skills."

"I'll see Colonel Buckmaster if you please."

"The colonel is quite busy at this moment. I'm afraid you must wait until he is ready to see you. I'm sure you understand."

Nancy did not understand one bit and shot back. "He'll see me or I'll walk my arse out of this building. You'd better believe I will."

Vera picked up the phone on top of her desk and began speaking into the instrument in a low tone. After a minute, she looked up at Nancy and spoke. "Colonel Buckmaster said to tell you that your leaving here is your choice. He will, however, make time for you after 1600 hours if you care to wait. He is in an important meeting and doesn't wish to leave at this time."

Nancy looked at her watch. *1600 is four more hours. I really don't want to sit here with my thumbs up my bum. I have put my foot in it this time; I certainly don't want to leave for good. I know what I'll do...*

Nancy stepped back and summoned up her resolve. "I'll return at 1600, Vera. Please thank the colonel for taking time to see me." She turned and left the office.

Vera smiled to herself and returned to her paperwork. *These agents are really something else. They are brave and loyal, but they live in a world that is not altogether real. They act as if every day is their last and I can't really blame them for that. If I were going into what they are, I'd probably be a little high strung myself. And, Nancy Fiocca might be the best agent we've ever had here, all her instructors agree. I actually enjoy her personality, even if it is a little brash at times.*

◆ ◆ ◆

Nancy arrived back at Vera's office at exactly one minute before 1600.

Vera motioned her into Colonel Buckmaster's office, which was through a connecting door. Nancy acknowledged Vera with a head gesture and opened the door.

Colonel Maurice Buckmaster was sitting at his desk and looked up when Nancy entered.

"Please have a seat, Nancy," he motioned to a chair positioned next to his desk. I'm sorry to have kept you waiting so long. These days are so full that I'm not always in control of my schedule. What may I do for you?"

"Colonel, I want to see some action," she said directly. "My courses were finished more than a month ago. Right now I'm just sitting around accomplishing nothing. I know you will understand. I just want to get moving with my life."

Buckmaster studied the young woman. *God, what I would give for more like her. Always wanting to take the bull by the horns, no matter what the dangers involved.*

He chose his words carefully and answered in a level voice. "I most certainly understand, I would feel the same if I were in your shoes."

Buckmaster stood up and walked to the wall map behind his desk. He motioned for Nancy to join him.

Should I tell her what is about to happen? In a way, it will involve her and all the rest of our agents. Hell, why not? She is a seasoned operative that knows how to keep really important matters to herself. He pointed to France and began his elucidation ...

The first day of US Army Captain Brian Russell's masquerade as Inspector Patout of the SNCF French railway system started off quietly enough. He was taken to his offices in Vichy by the same Resistance partisan whose code name was Herve. The offices were adjacent to the main railway station at the intersection of the Rue de Paris and la Place de la Gare. On the way downtown, Russell had passed the Centre Hospitalier de Vichy, a large structure that seemed quite busy.

Herve motioned to a door that had PATOUT, A. painted in large block letters. He motioned for Russell to go inside and tipped his beret as a token of good bye and good luck. Russell acknowledged the gesture and took the key he had been given and unlocked the door. The lock moved easily and Russell stepped inside the small office. Inspector Alex Patout rose to greet Russell. "I'm to tell you about your duties as best I can. It shouldn't take too long. I don't want to be around here any longer than I have to. Well, you must first…"

After the real railroad official departed, Russell observed that Inspector Patout was a very neat person whose desk was almost immaculate. He committed to memory where everything was placed with the intention of leaving it the way he found it. A schedule of train movements was lying face up and Russell opened the pages to today's date. He noted an eastbound train was due in about five minutes.

I want to be sure and catch that one, no sense hanging around here any more than necessary. Northbound trains are the most important to my mission, so this will be a good start.

He placed the timetable inside his uniform jacket and adjusted his face mask. *Damn thing is a bit scratchy, but I think it will do the trick. It is natural to give someone wearing a face mask a wide berth, and that will also help.*

He picked up a clipboard and attached a number of pages to the board. Satisfied he was prepared for his role, Russell opened the door as another uniformed French SNCF officer passed by. *"Bonjour,"* the officer offered. Russell answered, *"Bonjour"* in a scratchy voice as the other man walked away. When the other Frenchman had passed, he made his way to the train platform and waited for the oncoming train. A minute later, the local passenger train pulled into the station and stopped. Russell boarded a coach and waived to the conductor who tipped his hat at the inspector.

Russell was pleased at his reception. *Maybe I can get away with this after all. If it all goes this smoothly, I shouldn't have a great deal of trouble,* he posed. *After all, I am doing the same job that the real inspector would do. My being here is not out of the ordinary in the least.*

The train's current destination was the City of Moulins, with a number of local stops. Russell was sure to position himself at a window view to see what preparations the German army had made to defend the different areas. He also took notes as to possible sites along the route that might provide sufficient cover to Resistance and Maquis members' intent on derailing the train. The steam powered locomotive pulled into the small town of St. Pourcain. A sign noted the Sioule River as the train crossed a narrow bridge. Russell observed that no military installations were apparent anywhere in view. The bridge itself seemed a plausible target with its foundations resting in the riverbed. He jotted a quick note to himself and returned to his gazing.

After several hours and two delays, the outskirts of Moulins rolled into view. Here, German Wehrmacht military vehicles and even some machine gun emplacements were visible from the train. Russell made some additional notes and determined to stay on the train as it headed further north.

So far, so good. I have seen several spots along the tracks that would make great places for knocking out a train, but the local Resistance people probably have those figured out also. I think I'll stay tonight here in Moulins and scout around the place. This a marshaling spot and most German trains should pass through here at one time or another. It won't hurt for me to have a closer look see and find out if there is any apparent weakness.

Russell waited until the train had stopped and then alighted. He waived to the conductor who waived back. He walked north by northwest toward the center of the city and came upon an unusually large church that totally dominated the skyline of Moulins.

This is probably the famous Cathédrale de Moulins if I am correct. I believe it dates back to the 14th or 15th Century. If I have time, I'd like to visit it. From what I have heard, it's one of the most beautiful in France if not the entire world.

Further down the street, Russell came to a multi-storied building with a sign proclaiming *Hotel de Paris Depuis 1834.* A small second sign hung below that said simply, *Spa.*

This is for me, Russell quickly reasoned. *A good massage will just do the trick. These sort of places usually have good food, so I will win on both fronts. And, the SOE-*

F was kind enough to give me plenty of cash in case I needed it, so I will put a little of it to good use. This might be the start of a most enjoyable mission.

He entered the hotel and was amazed at the place's interior. A large painting dominated the entrance hall and high quality antique chairs dotted the entire first floor. Russell stepped up to the desk and inquired about a room.

"Certainly, Monsieur Inspector. We have many rooms to select from," a genial clerk offered. "Since the war started, we have rarely been full. And since you are with the SNCF, we have a special rate for you."

"Excellent," Russell answered. And, can I impose upon you to have a masseuse sent up as soon as possible? I am in need of a good hard rubbing."

"Of course, inspector. The massages we offer are a specialty of the hotel. I know you will be completely satisfied."

"Just call my room and let me know the details. I think I'll go and lay down for a few minutes."

"As you wish, inspector."

Russell took the key and headed for the nearby lift. His room was on the second floor, number 212. He entered a found a pleasant room with ample furnishings. A magnificent serpentine chest with six drawers, two sitting chairs and a larger than usual bed filled the room nicely.

A large wash washbowl rested on top of the serpentine chest and Russell poured some cold water into the vessel. He cleansed his head thoroughly and unpacked the small valise he had brought with him. He placed the objects on the chest and rolled back the covers on the bed. He lay down softly but found the bed somewhat harder than he expected. He adjusted his position and was soon asleep.

The first thing Violette Szabo did after returning to England was to visit her parents at their Burnley Road home. She assured them she was safe and that her mission had been quite ordinary. She did not feel that she was in danger at any time. Violette next went to see her daughter.

Tania was living under the care of Vera Maidment, a close friend of Violette's, at her home at 59 Fernside Avenue in suburban Mill Hill, about eight miles north of downtown London. Violette had hoped to have her daughter live with her at her Pembridge Villas flat but realized her missions would disrupt her daughter's life. Besides, Mill Hill was sufficiently clear of the dangers from possible bombings that Londoners had learned to tolerate on an irregular basis after the London Blitz of 1940.

She presented her daughter with the new dress bought in Paris and found it too large for the little girl.

"You will grow into it in a short while, my darling," Violette reassured her daughter. "And then Mummy will be able to show you off to the entire world."

Violette returned to her flat to await SOE-F's next mission. She saw several members of the agency and even went out some evenings for drinks and dinner. It was generally conceded that long intervals existed between missions, a fact that made none of the agents happy.

Shortly after her return, SOE-F rewarded Violette's initial Rouen efforts. The SOE applied to First Aid Nursing Yeomanry, Violette's actual home organization, for a commission for Violette. Two weeks later word was received that Violette Szabo was commissioned an ensign in the organization.

While Violette was pleased with the commission, she yearned to return to France and her private war with Germany. She visited SOE-F several times but was told to be patient and that her chance would come in due time.

Waiting was not easy for Violette Szabo, and the time passed slowly. She missed her husband a great deal and was more determined than ever to avenge his death at the hands of the Huns. With events in Europe about to come to a head, Violette would not have long to wait.

Christine Allard (Sofian) had been assigned a particularly difficult mission by Émile Coulaudon (Gaspard). She was to lead a group of ten Maquis fighters to reconnoiter the huge Michelin tire factory in Clermont-Ferrand for a possible attack or some sort of sabotage.

The French Resistance had tried to penetrate this complex the year before but failed. Subsequently, the RAF had bombed the plant that was Germany's chief producer of tires for its Wehrmacht and Luftwaffe. While the bombing was considered successful, the plant was again operational and considered a prime target for the Allies.

Christine chose her Maquis fighters well. All were former residents of Clermont-Ferrand and well versed in getting about the city without arousing suspicion. They were also properly dressed as opposed to many of their country cousins who fought as partisans.

The mission was simple, but wrought with danger. Anyone getting close to the Michelin plant was checked thoroughly by the Milice or even Gestapo agents that routinely roamed the exterior streets around the plant.

Christine selected a particular guise that had worked well for her in prior missions within Clermont-Ferrand. A cousin of one of her Maquis was a dispatcher for the city's sewer system. When asked, he would provide uniforms and even trucks that would serve as the Maquis' transportation. He would also secure work orders that would allow the Maquis close proximity to the plant itself. Since the trucks and uniforms were generally foul and smelly, they were always given a wide berth by most passers-by. That group included Milice and Gestapo officers who found the workers repugnant.

The group suited up and drove the two Citroën trucks that had been provided to two different spots that Christine had selected. Both provided excellent vantage points to entrances to the one-story sprawling complex that was highlighted by distinctive angled rooftops. Each unit was to spend one-half hour at each location. Next, they would move to two additional locations that were not near entranceways but seemed to afford possible sites for sabotage.

The uniform that Christine wore was ill fitting and smelled. She managed to keep her hair under a work cap that was a least two sizes too large.

The men exited the first truck and quickly set up work barriers around the vehicle. They extracted some gear and removed the manhole that was closest to their truck. One Maquis descended into the hole while another handed equipment to him.

A lone figure approached. He regarded the men and truck and stated bluntly, "Milice. What are you doing here?"

"The worksheet is in the truck if you need it," a gruff speaking Maquis answered. It's on the seat, behind the wheel."

The Milice officer moved away from the group and approached the truck. As he neared the vehicle, he suddenly stepped back. "Why, it is nasty inside there. It smells as if it *is* the sewer."

"What do you expect?" the Maquis responded. "We get dirty when we work down there. If we were all clean you might suspect we weren't working too hard."

The Milice officer shrugged and began to walk away. He turned around and spoke again. Get your work order out now," he ordered. "No more fooling around."

"Yes, officer," the Maquis replied hesitantly. He reached into the truck and fumbled with some papers.

Christine moved forward sensing some sort of problem. She fingered the weapon she had hidden under her work clothes. She thought of pulling the gun out but stopped as the other Maquis finally emerged from the cab of the truck.

"Here it is," the Maquis exclaimed. It was under some other papers." He handed the smudged work order to the Milice officer.

"Even your papers smell," the officer said despairingly. "It's a disgrace."

"You want to change jobs?" the Maquis returned. "It's okay with me if we do."

"Get on with it you filthy piece of shit. And be quick about it. Any loitering and I'll be right back."

"Whatever you say, officer," the Maquis replied, smiling to the other workers. He looked at Christine who nodded back in return. She was already well into making note of their surroundings.

The same basic scene unfurled around the second truck. The Maquis went about their business and scouted the area for any possible weak spots. Twenty-five minutes later, they moved to their second location that was near the rear of the factory. There was little activity to note, just a seemingly endless line of windows with heavy metal grillwork surrounding the buildings. If one wasn't aware it was a tire factory in the middle of the town, the buildings could easily be misidentified as something else.

Their job completed, both trucks were returned along with the pile of smelly uniforms.

"I want to take a bath before I do anything else," Christine commented. I smell like a toilet or something."

"We all feel like that Sofian," another Maquis responded. "I'm going right to a place I can bathe myself."

"You will all be contacted when we need you," Christine promised. "You all did a good job. Stay low and stay safe."

With that she walked briskly toward the flat she shared on rue Terrasse, not far from the splendid *Cathedrale Notre-Dame de l'Assomption*. She sincerely hoped she would not encounter anyone she knew on her walk home.

The days passed swiftly for the fake Inspector Patout of the SNCF. He went about his job unobtrusively, and encountered few minor problems. He visited a large portion of the Auvergne and made stops in Montluçon, Nevers and Bourges for the night.

On his final day's trip back toward Vichy, Russell was finally confronted by someone he supposedly knew.

Another Frenchman with a similar inspector's uniform took a seat next to him as the train headed steadily southward.

"Alex, my friend, it's nice to see you again. It certainly has been awhile."

Russell looked up to see the smiling face, portly and about thirty years of age. He desperately hoped he could pull off his charade.

"I've been sick, my friend," he said hoarsely, as if he could barely speak. "You know the flu has been quite serious in Vichy. Everyone is sick, and some have even died."

"Yes, I heard about it. But you are the first person I know that has seen it in person."

So far so good, I don't believe he knows the real Inspector Patout all that well.

"I've missed work for a week but now I have been ordered back to work, sick or not. You know how that is…"

The other inspector nodded in agreement. "Yes, the SNCF doesn't appreciate anyone missing work. They are tough on everyone."

"Yes and the fact that the flu is highly contagious make little difference to them. They give us these face masks and expect the best."

"Alex, you sound a little funny to me. Are you sure you are all right?"

Russell coughed and wheezed for effect and replied. "I guess I'll be all right. Most of the others with the flu are already improving. I guess I'm the one where the infection lingers."

"Your accent seems a bit strange. I don't remember you even having an accent."

"You are mistaken," Russell replied weakly yet forcibly. I'm the same as always, can't you tell?"

"I guess so. You just seem different to me."

"Let me catch some sleep while I can. This train is drafty as hell."

"If you wish, Alex. I will see you again." The man looked as Russell and departed.

Damn it all, just when things were going so well. I had better take care of this guy and get the hell off the train as soon as possible. He wasn't at all convinced I was the real Inspector Patout. We have an hour before reaching Vichy. The next stop is in Saint-Germain-des-Fossés. I'll get off and make a call to Vichy.

◆ ◆ ◆

Russell was off the train before it came to a complete stop. He quickly entered the SNCF office and picked up a phone.

I just hope that other inspector doesn't follow me in here and check on me. I'd have to make a run for it and that would be bad.

The person on the other end answered and Russell explained what he wanted to do. He asked that someone come and pick him up along with a change of clothes. Satisfied he had taken the correct course of action, the American officer stepped to the rear of the station and left by a back door. He resigned himself to the fact that he now had to wait for the Resistance to come and fetch him.

An hour later, the real Inspector Patout, complete with face mask, jumped on the approaching train just before the Vichy station platform. He took a seat in the same car that Russell had traveled in and waited for the train to come to a complete stop.

He waited as the passengers cleared the doorway and stepped down on the train platform. A thin, beak-nosed man wearing a trench coat and fedora approached and produced a silver medallion from his coat. He pushed the medallion toward the inspector.

"Gestapo! Produce your identity card and remove your mask at once," he ordered.

The other SNCF inspector from the train wandered over and peered at the two men. Inspector Patout removed his mask and addressed the other inspector. "Cecil my friend, I guess this is all your doing."

"Er, Alex. I just sensed something was wrong. Your voice was different and you seemed to speak with something of an accent. I thought it would be wise to make sure."

"Everything seems in order," the Gestapo officer announced. Turning to the other inspector he said bluntly, "You have wasted my time. This man is who his papers say he is."

"Oh, yes," Cecil answered contritely while he sweated profusely. "I have made a terrible mistake. I hope he will forgive me."

"It's all right, Cecil. Even the best of us makes a mistake now and then."

The Gestapo agent departed and the two men walked toward the SNCF office.

Back in Saint-Germain-des-Fossés, US Army Captain Brian Russell had taken a seat in an old Citroën C4G that had just arrived to take him to the departure point for his return flight to England. He was unaware that his ruse had worked to perfection and that the genuine Inspector Patout was safe and back at work in Vichy.

Gaspard and his band of Auvergne Maquis had been active for the past two weeks. And, they had been quite lucky. A member of their band had received information about intended troop movements in the region. Gaspard had acted quickly and dispatched several groups of Maquis to deal with the Germans. The reports proved to be correct and the Maquis made the most of their opportunities.

A pair of bridges was blown up and a pitched battle in an extremely tight and mountainous road proved costly to the Germans. In the end, the Maquis had managed to completely disrupt the operations and inflict heavy damage to the German equipment as well as inflict numerous casualties to the Wehrmacht soldiers that were part of the operation. Only one Maquis fighter had been wounded in the action, an amazing feat in itself.

Next, the Maquis commander received several additional reports that immediately perked his interest. Another Maquis sympathizer had spotted a pair of strange looking armored vehicles with large antennae protruding from their tops. The pair was parked next to each other behind the local Wehrmacht headquarters in Clermont-Ferrand. The place was guarded, but, according to the informant, not overly so. The vehicles had been spotted around 1000 hours and Gaspard sensed they might be there around the same time each day. He decided to attempt to add these armored vehicles to the Maquis list of unusable weapons.

He recalled Christine's wish to be involved in any operation regarding the direction-finding vehicles and set up a meeting with her. He told her of the sighting and ordered her to take another Maquis with her along with one of the anti-tank guns they had received from the RAF airdrop. She was to scout the area around the headquarters and, if she thought it possible, attempt to destroy the two vehicles.

Christine was delighted with the chance Gaspard had given her. She chose a strong young Maquis fighter named Paschal to accompany her. Pascal would carry a loaded anti-tank gun and she would tote an additional round for the gun. Even though a second shot might be impossible, Christine knew that such situations could never be expected to go as planned.

That evening, the pair was dropped a few blocks from Wehrmacht headquarters located just off the Boulevard Lafayette, not far from the Musée Henri Lecoq. Christine moved slowly and silently until they came to a semi-wooded area that was perpendicular to the headquarters buildings. She took care to put the gun, which had been covered with a rug, in a hiding spot behind a small shed. She located the two direction finding vehicles that were parked immediately behind the headquarters building behind a low fence. A solitary Wehrmacht guard with a shoulder rifle patrolled the area.

"We have an almost clear shot," Christine exclaimed to her cohort. "I can't believe the Bosch are so stupid as to leave the machines unprotected. It's almost as if they want us to blow them up."

"Maybe they think that no one knows what use they are," Paschal offered. "I wouldn't have known what they are if you hadn't told me. I would have just thought they were strange looking tanks of some sort."

"You must go and retrieve the PIAT (Projector, Infantry, Anti-Tank). That place just behind the trees," she pointed to a nearby setting, "seems a really good spot to shoot from. I will stay out of sight until you return."

Christine thought to herself. *It is about 150 yards to the vehicles. That is well within the range of the gun. If I can just be lucky enough to hit something vital...*

Paschal left and returned a few minutes later, puffing with his heavy load. "This is heavier than it looks," he said, removing the rug.

"I could not have carried it," Christine replied. "But you are young and strong."

Paschal smiled and nodded. He turned to Christine and asked." I might have an idea about the guard. My gun here has a silencer," he continued. "If I can get off a good shot and wound or kill him, he won't be able to shoot back at us."

Christine considered the youth's request. "You are an excellent shot, Paschal. Go ahead and see if you can get close enough. I'll be ready and if I see the guard go down, I'll fire at once."

"Good. I'll come back as soon as I fire so we can get away."

"If we are separated, go to the house I told you about on rue Vermanouze. There are friends waiting there for us."

"I remember, Sofian. I know the house."

"Now, be off with you. Take careful aim, your shot is important."

"You also, Sofian. You are the reason we are here anyway."

Paschal departed and was soon obscured by the bushes and trees.

103

Christine loaded the anti-tank gun and rested it on a small branch of a tree. She adjusted the sight and waited.

Too bad there is that little fence to cope with. I could actually aim for a tread or something specific. The round will go right through the fence; I don't think that is a problem...

A few minutes later, the Wehrmacht soldier who was walking guard suddenly stopped and fell over. Christine waited to see if he moved but it was apparent that the soldier was either dead or severely wounded. Christine expected some commotion to follow, maybe even a few soldiers running out to see what happened.

Nothing. The entire scene was eerily still until Paschal appeared in front of her.

"You should be taking your shot," the young Maquis implored. That was the plan."

"You are right, Paschal. Let me make it all right."

She lined up the site again, adjusted the pillow to her shoulder to lessen the recoil shock and tried to cock the PIAT. Nothing happened! She attempted to cock the weapon again but it wouldn't budge.

"*Merde!*" she almost shouted. "Come help me get this thing cocked."

Paschal attempted to cock the PIAT and finally managed to work the stubborn mechanism. He looked at an exasperated Christine.

"Good thing no one has been alerted. This fool thing is hard to operate."

She again felt the trigger and sighted the weapon. She adjusted the pillow and the finally squeezed the elongated trigger. A definitive whoosh originated from the gun as the 2.5 projectile sped toward its target. Seconds later, a loud explosion and fire erupted from the parking area of Wehrmacht headquarters.

"I hit something," Christine exclaimed. "I want to see the smoke clear and see if we can take another shot."

"Must we wait, Sofian? I'm not sure that's a good idea."

"No one has even come out to see. We can wait a moment."

104

The smoke cleared and Christine was delighted to see one of the direction finders on its side, smoking heavily. The second vehicle was facing in a different direction, seemingly intact. The fence around the area was almost completely destroyed.

Christine saw her chance and decided to take it. Some heavily armed German soldiers were now apparent in the area, looking around to see what had happened.

She quickly reloaded the PIAT and attempted to cock the gun. To Christine's joy, this time the mechanism worked perfectly.

She sighted again and squeezed the trigger. Another round left the barrel and headed toward the German vehicle. It exploded with a loud bang and everyone around it ducked for cover.

"Let's go," Christine literally pulled Paschal along. "It will be quite busy around here for a while."

Paschal needed no urging as the two slipped out of their hiding place with the PIAT in tow. Paschal quickly wrapped the gun as they ran. A few short blocks and the safety of a friendly Maquis family awaited their arrival. Christine was full of adrenaline, and tried to calm herself. The feeling of firing such a weapon and having sent two German vehicles to the scrapyards was a joy unto itself.

Chapter Nine

The mood surrounding Nancy Fiocca for the last month was nothing short of miserable as her friends and fellow agents were acutely aware. It was evident that the fiery woman was tired of waiting for SOE-F to assign her a mission and she was vocally outspoken about the matter on several occasions.

"I wish the bleepin' powers that be would make up their mind about me," she fired off after several glasses of champagne on one outing. The setting was the famed Astor Club in Piccadilly and her companions were other SOE agents and instructors.

"Your time will come, Nancy. We all must be patient."

If I have heard that once, I've heard it twenty times she thought. The band blared up In the Mood and Nancy Wake Fiocca took another sip from her fluted champagne glass. *My, this tastes good. Wonder what it is.* She picked up a bottle and read from the label. *Veuve Clicquot Ponsardin, Maison fondée en 1772, 1937.*

This is really good stuff. If I remember correctly, 1937 was a banner year for champagne, or that's what my dear Henri once told me. Henri...I wonder just how he is doing...He is such a dear, the love of my life. Maybe a bit too practical at times, but definitely good for the likes of me. I still think it was an unwise idea for him to stay in Marseille...I know he's in great danger there, even if he wouldn't admit it to me...I hope I can one day get word to him that I am okay...I don't want him to worry needlessly...

The band broke into a faster song and blare of the trumpets caused Nancy to break her train of thought. She returned to the present and swore loudly, "Piss on our wonderful leaders. Let's have fun in spite of them. She ordered another bottle of champagne and accepted a dance invitation from one of her friends, a handsome young officer named René Dussaq.

We'll make this a great night, even if it's one of our last. If I am to go down, I intend for it to be fighting. My pals here are all in the same boat, so each of us should drink and have fun as if it is our last time to do so. Even if this party lasts all night, we'll make the most of it.

Around 0400, the remaining survivors finally made it to the street and headed toward Piccadilly and Nancy's flat. About every thirty yards, a member of the group would do a parachute roll they'd just been taught---arms forward and bent to minimize the fall. Of course, their legs were joined together.

They voiced a song at the highest level their voices could attain:

> *'Gory, gory what a helluva way to die.*
> *Gory, gory what a helluva way to die,*
> *and we ain't gonna jump no more...'*

Even at such an ungodly hour, the group attracted more than their fair share of attention from anyone they passed along the way. No one in the group was even aware of the stares.

There was little fanfare attached to U S Army Captain Brian Russell's return to Great Britain. After landing at RAF Tempsford, he was quickly taken to SOE-F's headquarters at Baker Street. It was only 0700 in the morning, but he was immediately shown into the presence of the section's leading French railroad analyst who spoke dryly to the American officer.

"Okay, Captain Russell. Let's have it."

Russell complied and handed over his notebook from the mission.

The balding man of about fifty looked over his rimmed glasses and perused the small book.

"Excellent, Captain Russell. "You have followed the code exactly. I expect we will find a great deal of top notch information inside."

Russell chose not to comment, and waited for the man to speak again.

"This will take some time to break down. If you have something else to do, I would suggest you go about it. You must stick around so we can question you fully, but I see no reason for you standing here until then."

Russell smiled at the British manner of stating the obvious and turned back into the hallway.

I might as well get it over with now. With any luck, I might even get in to see him now. It is quite early, but I would think he will already be in his office.

Russell made his way toward the upper floors of the building where the section's brass made their offices. He came upon Vera Atkins' door and knocked softly. A resolute "Come in" immediately followed. He opened the door and met Vera's suddenly smiling face sitting behind her desk.

"Nice smile for this early in the morning, Vera," Russell spoke.

"I always smile when one of our agents comes back safely Brian. May I offer you a cup of tea?"

"Coffee would be better, but I'll happily take tea," he answered politely.

She rose and walked to a small table where a tea pot rested on a brass tray. She poured a cup of tea and asked, "You Americans prefer sugar in your tea, don't you?"

"This American surely does, Vera. I consider it the civilized thing to do."

She looked closely at Brian Russell and decided he was teasing her back. *If I didn't know better, I'd think he was flirting with me.*

"So what brings you here so early?"

"I was told to hang around the campus for a while. I need to see Colonel Buckmaster if he is available. That's about it."

Vera Atkins picked up the phone on her desk and softly spoke into the mouthpiece.

"You are in luck. He says he can see you right away. You may go right in and you can take your tea with you. The colonel is already working on his second cup."

"Thanks, I will. Good seeing you again Vera." He winked at her and started toward Buckmaster's door.

Vera blushed and turned her head.

Dammit. He does that to me all the time. He's not really flirting, but just being himself. But he is so very good looking. I wonder what his tussled hair would look like on my pillow. If only he would be flirting...

Russell came to the door and entered Buckmaster's office. The senior officer rose and extended his hand.

"Good to have you back Russell. I hope your mission proved to be productive."

"I would think so, colonel. I was able to move about the Auvergne quite freely and was able to take an enormous amount of notes on my travels. I believe the information will be most useful."

"And you encountered no problems."

"Only one, on my last day. I was able to phone ahead and the real Inspector Patout was able to meet the train. I have no way of knowing, but I trust he was able to protect his identity. Another SNCF inspector became suspicious of me and I think was about to report me. I hope it all worked out for everyone."

"I will make some inquiries into the matter. If I hear back, I'll be happy to let you know."

"Thank you, colonel. I also have something important to discuss with you."

"By all means, young man. Please go ahead."

"On the flight back here I made a decision, colonel. I really enjoyed being back in the thick of things, if you know what I mean."

Buckmaster nodded, and Russell continued.

"I would like to be assigned to another undercover mission in France as soon as possible, sir. I know the job we are doing here is most necessary, but I feel I am more valuable as an agent. I hope you understand."

Buckmaster paused, choosing his words carefully.

"Your request makes sense, captain. If I could get out of here I'd certainly like to do some field work myself. The feeling of being on the edge of things is what makes a really good agent."

"Precisely, sir. I hoped you would understand."

"But, Russell, you must consider what you do for us here at Baker Street Irregulars is also vitally important. I simply must take that into consideration."

Brian Russell's heart began to sink at Buckmaster's choice of words. He was sure of what was coming next.

"So, I must tell you that you have to wait until I can find an adequate replacement for you. I have no idea how long that might take. Until then, you just have to wait and make the best of things."

"I can handle that, colonel. As long as I know there is an end in sight."

"You have my assurance, Captain Russell. I will let you know as soon as possible."

"Thank you, colonel."

Russell rose and departed the room. Along the way out he again winked at Vera Atkins who blushed appropriately. It had been a great homecoming and an even better reception of his request. First, he would finish with the railroad analyst and then get some sleep. Then, he would call his old pal Denis Rake and get together for some heavy drinking. There was ample reason to celebrate and he was not one to miss such an occasion.

Two days after her all night bash, Nancy Fiocca was awakened from a deep sleep by a knock on the door of her flat just off Piccadilly. A courier brought a note from Baker Street that she was to report as soon as possible.

Nancy quickly dressed and applied her makeup. Satisfied she was presentable she quickly made her way to Baker Street. Upon arrival, she was directed to Vera Atkins who was waiting in her office.

"Good morning Mrs. Fiocca," Vera offered cheerily. "It seems the day you have been waiting for has finally arrived."

"You mean you have finally gotten off your arses and assigned me a mission?" Nancy answered equally cheerfully. "It's about time if you ask me."

111

Vera ignored the barb and continued. "This will be a most important mission for SOE-F. We thought long and hard about this and feel you're the right person to send on this."

Nancy listened attentively, but said nothing.

"The situation in the Auvergne has heated up rapidly and it is time for us to act. The Maquis there are becoming stronger every day and we have finally begun to supply them properly. There is adequate leadership in place, but there are several factions to deal with. What we need is a unified force that can deal the Huns a real blow. You will be going in as part of a team to help organize the Maquis and bring it up to real fighting standards, whatever that might be.

The area is also a vital railway access for the Germans and we suspect they will be using these routes quite a bit in the near future. There are some big plans afoot on our side, but for your own good, you need not know any of the details. I'm sure you will hear about them sooner or later, and then you will understand.

In some ways, the Auvergne is the key to our success in Central France so we must send in our best people for the job. Now you might understand why we have taken so long to assign you a mission. We were saving you for the big job, and we trust you are up to it."

"Thank you, Vera for your confidence."

"Don't thank me. Thank Colonel Buckmaster. He is the one who selected you. To be honest, I had some reservations about the type of job you would be facing, but the colonel felt otherwise. I respect his judgment and, after all, he is the boss here."

Nancy let her answer slide, the news was simply too good to believe.

"You will start your preparations as soon as we have finished our little talk," Vera renewed her dialogue. "As you are aware, we take great pride in setting up our agents so that they blend in perfectly. These preparations should not take more than a day or two, but strict silence about your destination and mission are in effect from this moment on. Please make sure there is no idle chatter, we can never tell when such prattle can wind up doing someone harm."

"I understand perfectly, Vera. You can be assured I won't say a word."

Vera looked at Nancy and raised an eyebrow. "I certainly hope not, Mrs. Fiocca. Any breech of secrecy and you could be pulled off the mission."

Nancy fought the urge to say something discourteous in return but refrained.

"You should report to the outfitting section and get your clothes. They have been informed of your destination and are busy making sure our clothes match the area. Do you have any questions?"

"You have been quite thorough, Vera. I expected as much."

"Right. Then along with you. If everything goes well and the weather remains favorable, your flight should depart tomorrow night." She extended her hand to Nancy. Good luck, Mrs. Fiocca."

"I do wish you'd call me Nancy," was the reply. "It seems a bit less formal."

"I'll give it a try, Nancy. Now, get going."

"I'm off like a jackrabbit in heat," Nancy cracked as she turned and left.

Vera Atkins half smiled as the agent left her office. *I know I am rough on her but she is the toughest of our agents and I think she enjoys the banter. She is headed into a most dangerous situation, one that will test her abilities to their limits. But, if anyone can succeed in such a mission, it will be she.*

Baker Street was unused to children, so when Violette Szabo brought her daughter Tania with her to inquire about a possible upcoming mission, the staff was predictably amazed. Several staff members questioned Violette's sanity at wanting to fight Germans with such a darling little girl in tow.

Violette heard some of the whisperings, but chose to ignore them. *After all, it's my life to live, isn't it? I'm an adult and I am free to make my own decisions. I did well on my first mission into France, everyone said so. I've even been promoted so I must be doing something right.*

She wondered into the assignments office but was told there was nothing new for her.

"You must be patient, my dear," one of the clerks spoke. "Your time will come again soon. There are others waiting that have been in line longer than you."

Violette left with little hope for an immediate assignment. She took Tania on a long walk and wound up at the London Zoo in Regent's Park. The zoo was almost closed for the war, but a portion of it was being used as an air raid shelter.

The walk was saved when Violette spotted some of the beauties of Queen Mary' Gardens that was nearby. Planted in 1934, the gardens were a sheer delight to the eyes. Roses were in particular abundance as were a number of flowers that Violette correctly identified to her daughter as begonias.

There were also the purple, lavender and white stilettos of the delphiniums that added grace and color to the surroundings. Tania found the surroundings irresistible and couldn't decide on which varietal she liked most. An older gardener was working nearby and offered to cut the little girl some flowers to take home. Tania agreed and wound up with a handful of assorted flowers wrapped inside a piece of newspaper. She carried the flowers like a torch and proudly showed them to anyone who crossed their paths.

Violette was both disappointed and nearly exhausted when they finally finished their outing. She put Tania to bed and lay down on her roll arm sofa that was upholstered with a red antique country print. She began to cry softly and thought of her husband Etienne who could never enjoy the delight of being around their child.

The tears lasted but a few minutes and were replaced with an even firmer resolve to avenge her husband's death. *My time will come again and I will make the most of it. No tears for me, I must be strong about all this.*

A few minutes later Violette was fast asleep and dreaming of killing Germans. In the dream, she was trapped with a number of Resistance partisans in a cave that was their base of operations. The Germans had discovered their cavern and had attacked during the night. Violette had grabbed her weapon and taken a position at the entrance to the cave. She was returning fire when a German hand grenade was lobbed into the cave. She saw the grenade and was attempting to cover the explosive but she was a bit too late. The grenade exploded just as Violette woke up from the dream. It was a recurring nightmare that had visited her sleep several times in the last few months.

Denis Rake, or Denden as he was widely known to everyone, had also been summoned to the SOE-F's Baker Street headquarters. He arrived at the appointed hour and was shown into Colonel Maurice Buckmaster's office.

"Rake here, sir, reporting as ordered."

"Sit down, Denis. No need for such formalities here."

"Yes, sir," Rake returned, moving a chair closer to Buckmaster's desk.

"I sent for you for a specific reason, Denis. You must have realized that by now."

"I did, colonel. But I still have no idea why."

"You are friends with a certain US Army Captain named Russell if I am not mistaken. He speaks very highly of you."

"I know and respect Captain Russell, colonel. We are sometimes known to bend an elbow if you catch my meaning."

"He told me as much," Buckmaster replied. "He also told me you might be eager to return to France one day."

"He is right, colonel. Even though I had a few close scrapes with the Jerries, I don't think they will ever get me. For some reason, I am always able to escape their nasty clutches."

"I have your record, Denis. I know you have been quite slippery."

"So what do you have in mind for me?" Rake asked bluntly.

Buckmaster paused a second, and answered the question. "Some things are about to light up that I am not at liberty to disclose. Here at SOE-F, we have been tasked with a number of operations that will deter our enemy from responding to these events. One of the most important areas of concentration will be the Auvergne and we will need our top people..."

The sight that greeted the B-24 Liberator crew that was to take Nancy Fiocca and Major John Farmer (code name Hubert) on their trip over France was almost hilarious to the airmen.

Nancy was dressed for any occasion. She looked positively lumpy to the men, with good reason. For her airborne departure out of the Liberator, she wore a favorite camelhair coat on top of her regulation army overalls. Her legs were covered with silk stockings and very stylish shoes, but her ankles were heavily taped to attempt to cushion her bones from the shock of the landing. On her head was a tin hat, ordered by the powers that be. She also had a pair of revolvers that were hidden somewhere within the pockets of her clothes. Nancy carried a small backpack that contained several changes of clothes, a pair of nightdresses that were hand-embroidered that she had insisted on bringing with her. She also included her favorite red satin cushion.

Nancy Fiocca's handbag had been carefully stuffed with over a million French francs to aid the Maquis she would meet. She also included articles of feminine hygiene as well as her favorite red Chanel lipstick. A final inclusion in her second button on the cuff of her left sleeve was the cyanide pill that was issued to every departing agent. It assured the user of instant death if the user decided to make use of the pill.

Someone had also provided spam sandwiches for the departing and Nancy had hesitantly started eating one once the Liberator was airborne. In a few minutes, the awful tasting sandwich had turned her stomach into a tumbling frenzy and driven Nancy to a state of near vomit. She tightened her stomach and struggled to remain composed. To take her mind off her present intestinal problems, she returned to thoughts of her childhood heroine. *I hope that Anne of Green Gables is with me tonight. She would get herself through all this. I wonder if her stomach ever reacted like mine has. I simply must control myself. Puking over this bomber would ruin everything.*

Nancy was still fighting to control her intestinal distress as the intercom on the B-24 suddenly announced 'dropping zone up ahead'. The signal was given for her to move toward the Joe–hole on the aircraft. Nancy made it upright and checked her parachute for the fiftieth time. She was sure the chute would open correctly, but checked again to insure her safety.

Standing there she gazed into the pitched blackness beneath the Liberator. *There, I see some bonfires and a light blinking off to the side. We actually found the correct place. God bless the navigator. And the pilot,* she added hastily.

The B-24 circled the landing field several times in order to pick the correct line for the drop. Finally it was time to jump and Major Farmer went first. His static line went taut and automatically released the chute.

Nancy watched him disappear into the darkness and grasped she was next. She hesitated a moment and next received a big push from the aircraft dispatcher that she had arranged with before the jump. A rush of cold air slapped her face and engulfed her, rendering her helpless in the strong arms of the wind. She waited for the sudden upward surge that would accompany the flaring of her parachute. It came abruptly and she slowly began the drift toward the earth below.

Observing that the wind was carrying her away from the field and the welcoming bonfires, she pulled hard on the parachute risers in an attempt to steer the parachute back on course. Nothing helped in the strong wind and she drifted awkwardly into a massive tree that was part of an adjoining field. The entire area was pitch black and she was unable to see the bonfires located in the next field.

Then a distant voice called out in French. *"Aah, voilà un parachute là-bas!"*

The fact that the words were in French did not mean that Nancy was safe. She drew her revolver as the voices approached her tree.

A kindly French voice spoke from directly beneath her. *"Aah, que l'Angleterre doit nous envoyer une si belle fleur."*

Nancy was frustrated by her awkward position in the tree and shot back. "Cut out that French bullshit and get me out of this tree."

Her extraction was completed in minutes and she finally stood next to her French contact. Henri Tardivat was leader of the Maquis at Montluçon. Nancy surveyed the handsome man and found his presence reassuring.

Nancy attempted to destroy her parachute as she had been directed back in England, but Tardivat stopped her. "We can use this fine fabric in a number of ways," he reasoned. "Fabric like this is rare in wartime France and I simply won't see it buried."

"We have our orders," Nancy barked back. "And you will not stand in our way of doing what we were told."

Major John Farmer looked on with an amused grin on his face. He knew Nancy only slightly before the mission's start, but he had heard about her stubborn reputation.

Finally, Henri Tardivat had had enough of the brash woman and said to her. "It's time to leave. We have a car for you both."

"A car?

Her SOE training had advised that cars were only used for and by Germans and should be avoided at any costs.

"Actually, it's a *gazogène*. Come, I will take you to your friends," Tardivat offered.

Nancy and Major Farmer boarded the car that took them to the home of a sympathetic Maquis couple in Cosne-d'Allier who immediately offered them a good meal accompanied by a number of drinks. Glasses were raised to the success of their mission. The entire repast was crowned by a marvelous *pousse-café*, the wonderful combination of coffee and brandy. When it finally came time to sleep, the agents were shown into a room that contained one double bed.

Nancy regarded the bed and then John Farmer. Farmer regarded the bed and then the surprised French couple. The couple regarded their guests with a sense of bewilderment. *What could possibly be wrong with one bed!*

Arrangements were finalized since there was little choice. Nancy finally slept beneath the bedclothes while Farmer (Hubert) slept on top with several layers of coats over him.

The SOE plan for the agents was for them to wait until another SOE agent, Maurice Southgate, came to pick them up. In fact, three days later, one of Southgate's men, Hector, did arrive at the Maquis safe house. Hector promised that Southgate, or another of his men, would return shortly for them.

A long week passed for the two agents, with no word from Southgate or any of his men. Something had gone wrong, and Nancy was becoming edgier by the day. Their mission was to eventually reach Gaspard, but that was becoming more difficult with each passing day.

Finally, Nancy had enough of waiting. After getting Farmer (Hubert) to agree, she confided in her host, Jean, as to their wish to contact Gaspard. Jean knew nothing of Gaspard, but was aware of the possible location of one of his chief lieutenants, code name Laurent.

The next morning, the ancient *gazogène* was fired up and the journey began.

The trip took most of the day and encountered frequent stops as Jean attempted to locate Laurent's whereabouts. As night approached, they finally reached Laurent's camp in a deserted chateau some ten to fifteen miles outside Montluçon.

Nancy closely regarded the Maquis who gathered around the old car. The men were ragged, thin and definitely unwashed owing to their general body odors. Laurent himself was a middle aged Frenchman with a jovial nature. He promised to get them in touch with Gaspard as soon as possible. He explained that the Gestapo was actively looking for both him and Gaspard at that very moment.

Nancy took the news in stride even though it meant spending some time in the less than regal surroundings of Laurent's mountainous camp. She passed out a good amount of the money she was carrying to insure the Maquis could buy some much needed food and provisions. She carefully explained that the Maquis should buy the goods in different places so as not to arouse suspicion. The Maquis were surprised that this woman was so well-informed and conscious of their everyday activities. They readily accepted her into their band of Maquisards.

The desire to return to France on an active mission was a daily nuisance for US Army Captain Brian Adams Russell. He found his daily job at SOE-F more routine each day and noticed himself daydreaming at certain times during the day. These sessions would not last long and did not affect his work, but the thought of returning to France occupied his thoughts a great deal of the time.

He observed some of the other SOE-F staff around him for a possible replacement, but realized that each one was close to being expert in their particular field. Plus, the workload at SOE-F had been recently increased, a fact that meant all personnel were working longer days and nights.

When Denis Rake stopped by his desk late one afternoon, he found Russell with a blank look on his face.

"Troubles, mate?" Rake questioned. "Want to talk about it?"

"Not really, Denden. "But I am in the mood for a pint or two. Want to water down with me?"

"You're on, my bucko," Rake replied. "No time like the present."

A nearby pub, The Boar's Breath, was only half full when they entered. Rake selected a booth near the door and ordered two pints on tap.

Rake looked Russell in the eye and said gently to his friend," Now, what's all this about? I've rarely seen you down in the dumps. It's not very becoming."

Russell thought for a second and replied to his friend. "I've just been worrying about ever getting back to France. I went to see Buckmaster but he said I won't be going until he finds a replacement for me here. That could take some time if you catch my drift."

"Rather so, my good captain. I will think about it. I might just know someone who would fit the bill as your replacement."

"Really? That would be just swell. Who is it?"

"I'd rather not say and build up you hopes. I'll check it out shortly and let you know. It all has to be on the hush-hush, you know."

"Everything we do is on the hush-hush, Denis. I am well aware…"

"How about making this a truly wet outing to celebrate my new status?" Rake added.

"New status? I haven't heard."

"It looks as if I am going back to the bushes, the French bushes if I am correct."

"They're sending you back to France on a mission?" Russell questioned almost incredulously. "Of all the lucky bastards. And, you didn't even ask to go, did you?"

"Not really. I heard a good friend of mine sort of suggested I would be available, a good friend from an affiliated Army."

Russell's face sank visibly when he realized his friend was poking him.

"I only mentioned to Buckmaster that you were the best possible radio operator we had and that I thought you might be open to another assignment. I hope I didn't go too far…"

"Not at all, chum. I actually welcome the chance to give our little German friends another dose of my wit and charm. Seems they didn't get enough last time and still have me on their wanted lists," he announced playfully.

"Do you know when you are going? Have they told you anything about what you will be doing?"

"Nothing at all, but that's not unusual. They wouldn't take to me blabbing about it all over Piccadilly. Not that I actually *blabber* anyway..."

The friends laughed heartily and downed their pints. Russell immediately raised his hand and another round quickly followed. "A few dozen more toasts to your new good fortune are just what the doctor ordered," Russell saluted.

"Correct, *Doctor* Russell" Rake quickly returned. "You take the lead and I will surely follow."

When the two finally walked out into the late spring air it was already dark. A few birds stilled chirped and double decker busses slowly chugged along with their bellies full of human cargoes. Both Russell and Rake agreed that their late afternoon was well spent would be one to remember for quite a long time.

Maurice Southgate was a thirty-one year old former Royal Air Force officer that had been educated as a youth in Paris. He looked more like a Frenchman than many true French and survived the British Expeditionary Force's ill-conceived invasion of France in 1940. He joined the Special Operations Executive two years later. His French fluency targeted him for the SOE-F Section where Colonel Maurice Buckmaster quickly found his other skills to be of great use for his agency.

Early on, Southgate was given the responsibility for setting up an agent network that was located in the French Region of Limousin. The main city in the region was Limoges, home of the world famous porcelain that bears its name.

The agent network was called Stationer and was one of the most successful operated by the SOE-F. Southgate had grown it to around 2,500 members. Its efforts in sabotage and disruption had made it a constant thorn in the side of the occupying Germans.

He had been called back to London when the word of the planned Allied invasion of France was developed, and was quickly returned to Limousin to help plan Stationer's efforts to support the invasion.

Southgate parachuted in safely near Toulouse and began the enormous job of coordinating the efforts of his now large group. His success had made him a top target for the Gestapo bound to protect the area.

On the same day he was supposed to meet with Nancy Fiocca and Major John

Farmer, a trap was set for him as he was attempting to visit his new wireless operator, René Mathieu, in Montluçon. Weary from his enormous workload, the thin, mustachioed officer failed to note the secret signal that marked the house as unsafe.

He was arrested and subjected to a great deal of punishment and subsequently sent to 84 Avenue Foch in Paris, the Gestapo's counter-espionage home. He was later sent to Fresnes Prison with other captured agents.

A total of thirty-six captured agents were next send to Buchenwald concentration camp where they awaited their eventual fate. Word of a pending execution reached some of the prisoners and in particular, Alfred Balachowsky, an esteemed entomologist that had been born in Russia and a former SOE sub agent for the ill-fated Prosper network in Paris.

Balachowsky had formed a friendship with Southgate, and sought out his friend.

"Because of my work here, I am fortunate to get certain information from the Office of the Commandant. You are on a list of particularly undesirable prisoners of the SS. A directive is about to be issued and you will most surely be included. You must fake a stomach ache and get admitted to the hospital at once," Balachowsky suggested. "They will not mark you if you are in the hospital. Put on a good show when you go there and you should be safe."

"Thank you my friend," Southgate replied. He immediately went to the hospital and was admitted and assigned a bed. The following morning, word was received inside the camp that sixteen prisoners were marched to the Buchenwald's main gate and hanged.

While in the hospital, Southgate actually developed real stomach problems and remained in the hospital for several weeks. Upon his release, he was assigned to the camp's tailor's shop where he sewed pajamas for present and future prisoners.

Knowing that the SS was particularly interested in him, Southgate kept an almost invisible profile and even spent time in the area known as the Little Camp.

His Stationer network was divided into two parts and continued harassing the enemy as D-Day approached. It was a tribute to Maurice Southgate's exceptional organizational abilities that the units continued their heroic work without his presence.

122

Chapter Ten

It was almost a week since Nancy Fiocca and John Farmer had arrived in France and their time to meet with Émile Coulaudon (Gaspard) had reached fruition.

A wild ride that crisscrossed a great many back roads finally took the couple to a site located deep within the forests near the walled commune of Saint Flour. They had finally reached the sylvan citadel from which Gaspard operated.

Shown into the presence of the notable man, Nancy observed their host. Gaspard was tall, not unhandsome, with a tendency toward a receding forehead. He looked at his visitors with a certain amount of disdain.

"I do not know you nor have I been informed of your visit," he began sourly. "I am not really prepared to receive you."

Slightly taken aback, Nancy tried to explain their presence. "We come to you to offer our services and to bring you some financial aid to help your Maquisards to eat and clothe themselves in a proper manner. We appreciate the fact that you have not been warned of our coming, but these are truly difficult times. Our agent who was to have met us did not arrive and we fear the worst for him. We took the chance of finding Laurent so that we could eventually locate you. Laurent was happy to see us as were his men. We were able to give them some money that changed their ability to fight with full stomachs."

Gaspard listened, seemingly unimpressed. "I am expecting help from de Gaulle's Free French forces in North Africa that should arrive any day," he responded. "So I do not really need your money. You also seem to be without a radio operator that would be very useful to us right now. Am I correct in my assumption?"

"He will be along shortly," Farmer answered. "You can be sure of that."

Gaspard was still unimpressed. He summoned a few of his top men and began talking. Nancy and Farmer stepped around a corner and also began talking. Fortunately, their new position was next to a window that afforded Nancy a chance to hear Gaspard's men's discussion that was loud and animated.

Somehow, Gaspard's men believed the pair was carrying a great deal of money. This money, they all agreed, would be quite useful to their efforts. Eventually, one of the men volunteered to seduce Nancy, relieve her of all of her money and then kill her.

Nancy was incredulous! Of all the nerve of this character. I'll break his fucking neck. Who do they think they are dealing with? She recalled her SOE training that made her tap the lower sides of her hand on wooden tables to harden them, thereby turning her hands into lethal weapons.

Later that afternoon after lunch, the Maquis man Nancy had heard made his first move by asking if she would like to accompany him on a little walk.

The feisty woman fired back at point blank range.

"Je suppose que tu veux coucher avec moi?"

He answered meekly, unsure of the direction of the conversation.

"Je, Je serais très honoré" he responded. She stepped forward and grabbed his arm, twisting it behind his back. Her move took him completely by surprise.

"And then kill me and take the money…is that the plan?" Nancy spoke with complete confidence.

"Non, non, non?" He winced in pain as Nancy twisted his arm even harder.

It was immediately clear that Nancy was far stronger and much smarter than the stunned Maquis fighter had first thought. The tall female visitor was definitely more than he had bargained for and his head dropped in frustration. She released his arm and shook her head at the now pitiable Maquis.

It was a standoff---of sorts.

Several hours later, Nancy heard about a raid that had been planned that very evening on the sports store of a known *collaborateur* in Saint Flour. The idea was to drive into the town under the very noses of the German garrison and smash the store's front windows. The Maquis would then help themselves to whatever they could find, boots, tents and every other type of camping equipment. Nancy Fiocca fancied the idea and insisted on joining the raid.

An unknown woman, even one with Nancy's particular skills, participating in such a dangerous raid was unthinkable to the strapping Maquis named Judex, who was organizing the raid. Nancy pleaded with him to go, using many of the graphic French phrases she had learned through the years. She continued her tirade and Judex finally gave in. To stop her ranting, he agreed that she would accompany the raid that evening.

Around 2300 hours, an old covered gray Mercedes L2500 truck rumbled through the business section of St. Fleur. Its seven inhabitants disembarked and methodically broke all the windows of the store and silently carried off all they could handle. Each made several trips and by the time they were finished there was little of value left on the shelves. In their minds, the *collaborateur* had been repaid for his disloyal viewpoint.

The raid had taken all of five minutes and not one German soldier had responded to the noise created by breaking glass.

Nancy thought the whole scene was eerily quiet as the truck made its way back into the countryside. *It actually feels good to have taken part in all this. I like the sensation it gives me. This is the first time since this bloody war started that I feel I am giving rather than receiving. I want to take this fight to all our enemies.*

The truck rumbled effortlessly through the winding roads and eventually brought its passengers back to Gaspard's hideout. The raid had been an outstanding success and everyone reveled in its accomplishment. Nancy felt particularly good about the outcome. In one fell swoop she had become one of the everyday Maquis. She could now use this trust to help the partisans in many different ways. Elated with the future prospects of her mission, she was unable to get to sleep when she attempted to do so about an hour later.

Christine Allard made her way back from her dangerous mission unscathed. The explosions she caused by blowing up the two German direction-finding vehicles tended to make most residents in the area close their doors and windows. She made sure that she was away from the danger area as soon as she fired the second projectile.

She was elated with her success and was impatient to tell Gaspard of her accomplishment. Destroying both of the German vehicles was even more than she could have expected. When she arrived at the Maquis safe house that had been designated for her after the mission, she was visibly disappointed to find her leader absent.

"He is late, that's all," another bearded Maquis told her. "Don't worry. It's not at all unusual. With the Gestapo trying to catch him more and more each day, he must be sure of where he is going. The goons set traps everywhere and there are just enough Vichy pigs around to help them."

"I know he is all right," Christine replied, somewhat mollified. "I had just hoped he would be here when I arrived."

"You might as well have something to eat," the Maquis added. "I just bought a fresh *saucisson* that is absolutely delicious. There's some bread and a piece of *bleu d'Auvergne* that will fill you up. Help yourself to the wine, it too is local but isn't all that bad."

"Thanks, I will. All the excitement has left me with quite an appetite."

Christine cut a piece of the sweet sausage and placed it between two pieces of bread that she had cut from the *baguette*. She next placed some of the aromatic blue cheese on top of the *saucisson*. A nearby apple was then cut into pieces and placed on top of the cheese. Satisfied she had completed her creation, she poured a small amount of red wine from the container on the table. She smelled the liquid that was both floral and fruity. She tasted a small bit and was pleased.

Not at all bad. The Maquis was right. Not a great wine but certainly a pleasant one. Should go nicely with my little culinary masterpiece.

Christine took a large bite and smiled to herself. The various flavors merged together and presented her palate with an almost sensuous feeling.

Am I just that hungry or is this really that good? It tastes like something a fancy restaurant would make.

The beautiful young Resistance fighter finally decided the food was a mixture of both flavor and appetite and settled down to enjoy the remainder of her meal. Even if Gaspard wasn't able to share her recent achievement with her, she realized her efforts were incredibly important to the French Resistance's overall struggle. She relaxed and let her thoughts wander for the first time in weeks. She recalled her earlier duties with the Maquis and even her first real assignment for the Resistance.

She thought tenderly of her American Army captain, Brian, and how much she really loved him. *I wonder what he is doing now, or even where he is. Is he still alive? Does he still love me? I guess I am just being a silly woman, letting my imagination and heart get the best of me. I know he still loves me, and I still love him the same as when we parted.*

Christine regenerated the thoughts from long ago and felt a warm sensation sweep her body. *Will I ever see him again? Will Fate ever intervene?*

She finished her meal and prepared to leave. She would see Gaspard as soon as the next opportunity presented itself.

As **Nancy Fiocca** and Major John Farmer waited impatiently for the arrival of their radio operator, Gaspard softened his attitude toward the pair a bit and assigned them to one of his lesser leaders, Henri Fournier (Laurent).

Fournier's Maquis group was located in the idyllic village of Chaudes-Aigues, in the neighboring *département* of the Cantal. True to its name, the village was the site of a number of soothing hot springs.

It was actually the intent of the dubious Gaspard to shovel them off to Fournier since he had no real interest in them and fully expected money and arms from the Free French. The resilient Resistance leader had no way of knowing that he was doing the SOE-F agents a major favor in the process.

Fournier was a former hotelier, and after a short time, proved to be a very upright man. He had used a good deal of his own money to finance his band of Maquisards who held him in extraordinary esteem. He soon agreed that Gaspard could be quite a handful, a fact that pleased Nancy Fiocca to no end. After a few days, Laurent decided it would be in the pair's interest to move to a smaller village even higher in the mountains called Lieutadès until their radio operator finally arrived. Nancy and Hubert (Major Farmer) questioned the possibility that the radio operator had been captured or killed.

"This is maddening, not to have a radio man," Nancy complained acrimoniously as the two were seated inside their safe house. "Here we are, fully trained, with all the money in the world to work with, and no connection to London. It's hopeless, that's what it is. Hopeless!"

"We simply have to wait Madame Andrée," he replied. Madame Andrée was the name Farmer always used whenever talking to Nancy. "I'm as frustrated as you, but there's simply nothing we can do about it."

"If I ever get back to London I'll damn well do something about it," Nancy barked back. "I'll make sure someone's head rolls."

"And, if he has been killed or captured? What will you do then?"

"I don't bloody well know, Hubert. I don't know."

Denis Rake had found a new lover and was completely taken by the latest man in his life. The day after his meeting with Buckmaster, he practically disappeared from the face of the earth until the frantic efforts of the SOE-F finally located him in his new lover's flat.

Once contacted, Rake frantically rushed to Baker Street where an exasperated Vera Atkins informed him that his aircraft was leaving in about six hours and that he had better be there for its flight. He was told to immediately report to the departure area where he would receive his credentials, new clothing and accessories. When Denis awkwardly asked if he had time to make a call to his new friend, Vera became visibly upset and called an armed guard into her office.

"Don't let this person out of your sight," she instructed." If he tries to leave or make a phone call, shoot him. Wound him if you can but kill him if you have to."

Denis Rake couldn't believe what he heard. As a valued and veteran member of the SOE, he was insulted to be treated in such a manner. He huffed his way out of Vera's office and angrily protested when the armed guard gently pushed him from behind.

Part of his departure duties was to meet with a briefing officer who explained where he was going and with whom he was to work. When Nancy's Fiocca's name came up, Denis Rake's disposition was suddenly improved.

At least I'll be with someone who really has balls, he surmised. *Nancy's a regular whirlwind. She has a keen head on her and always seems a step ahead of everyone else. I will enjoy this in spite of old Aunt Vera and her verbal tirade! Now, if I can only figure out how to call my new friend without getting shot, everything will be just peachy...*

Vera Atkins thought it best to let Colonel Maurice Buckmaster, head of SOE-F know about Denis Rake's less than serious attitude toward his position in the section. The fact that she had been unable to contact the radio wizard for nearly two weeks was a personal effrontery to the dedicated woman and shook her confidence in Rake's commitment to the SOE cause. Once he heard the facts from his assistant, Buckmaster was in no mood to grant Rake any quarter.

"I knew you were having some trouble locating him," Buckmaster offered, "but I had no idea it took that long."

"I also had to have several others helping me find him. If I hadn't thought of heading down to that faggie pub where they all hang out, I might never have located him," the exasperated Atkins replied. "Our agents in France have been waiting for him for more than a week. No tellin' what sort of uses they have had for him."

"Quite, Vera. I think it's time to reign in our little dandy a bit. Too bad he's already departed or I'd pull him off the bloody mission."

"And just who would you send? That's the reason he's going in the first place. This is a critical mission and we wanted someone with real experience. We are quite limited these days, and we have more requests for people than we have actual people."

"You are quite right, Vera. He had to go. No question about it. But he needs some handling; I believe we both agree on that."

"Certainly, colonel. Whatever you say."

"Please call Captain Russell in, will you. I want to have a chat with him. He and Rake have become quite close lately."

"Quite close? colonel," Vera asked with disbelief.

"Not in that sense Vera. They are just drinking buddies if I am correct."

"I see," Vera sighed, visibly relieved. "I will see to it that he is here as soon as possible."

"That will be all. I have a number of papers to check and I am way behind on several important plans."

"Yes, colonel." Vera left Buckmaster's office and began walking toward another part of the Baker Street campus. She knew just where to find Captain Brian Russell. A wide grin covered her face as she turned the last corner.

It was a bright, sunny morning in mid-May and Nancy Wake Fiocca had walked to a small graveyard in Lieutadès just down the road from their hotel. She hopped up on a small rock wall that surrounded the cemetery along the road and took in the beautiful scenery.

Here I am again sitting in this beautiful place with nothing to do. I would love to come back here after the war and simply relax and enjoy nature. She started to think about Henri and how the war had affected her beloved husband. She promised to make it all up to him once the war ended.

Her ambiance was broken by the sound of an approaching automobile. The small black Citroën 11CV pulled to a stop where Nancy was sitting. A familiar face jumped out and quickly asked, "Have you picked out a suitable plot for yourself?"

"Denden, you darling man," Nancy shot back excitedly, "Exactly where in the hell have you been?"

"Don't ask," was Rake's curt reply. Nancy wisely decided not to pursue the matter any further. His very presence meant their mission could actually become a reality.

The two returned to the house where Hubert was waiting. Rake was not pleased with Major Farmer from his earlier encounters during training and greeted him casually.

"Where have you been?" Farmer demanded brusquely. "We have been waiting more than a week for you."

Denis Rake was about to explode when Nancy stepped in. "Denis was detained back in England, Hubert. Let's leave it at that if you will."

The British officer looked at Rake and decided to hold his tongue.

Nancy spoke again. "We need to get some information back to London as soon as possible. We need their instructions as to just how to proceed here."

"I will be set up in about five minutes," Rake promised. "It will not take me any time to send your message. Is it written or just in your minds?"

"I never write anything down in case we are captured," Nancy countered. "You know that Denden. I am ready whenever you are."

The pair watched as Rake set up his radio to transmit. Two minutes later, the initial part of the message was already being received in Kent for forwarding to London. Rake's finger was a veritable whirlwind as he effortlessly tapped the WT No 2 8AMP key to his machine.

United States Army Captain Brian Russell was both excited and thrilled to hear the news about his upcoming mission to France's Auvergne Region. The fact that the mission involved his friend and drinking buddy Denis Rake didn't come as a surprise to the young American officer.

Trouble seems to follow Denis for some reason. He's an okay fellow, but he tends to rub people the wrong way. His sexuality has never bothered me, but I'm sure it affects some people differently. I can't believe he was AWOL for almost two weeks, but I guess it's true. I'll wait to hear his side of the story before making judgment, but I guess facts are facts. It will be good to see him again and also Nancy Fiocca. They should make one helluva team. I would hate to be the Vichy police or the Germans.

This time a B-24 Liberator jump would send Russell into the mountainous area of the Auvergne where he would find the other SOE-F agents. A landing spot in the nearby commune of Lagarde that was flatter than any around Lieutadès was selected for the drop. A message was sent to Laurent's band that an additional SOE agent would be joining them shortly with the exact date and drop point carefully coded.

Russell found he was actually looking forward to the parachute jump and made quick plans to brush up on the mechanics of the vault. He carefully reminded himself of the initial fall, and most importantly, the exact procedure for hitting the earth at relatively high speed.

Satisfied he remembered the drill, Russell sat back and puffed on a cigar as he waited to board the B-24. He had started smoking the delicious weed some months ago and had even learned that his favorite cigar was a Cuban panatela, a long, thin and elegant cigar that had a great draw. He had nearly finished the cigar when he was summoned to board the aircraft. He took one long puff and dipped the lighted end in a nearby puddle.

The trip east was short and sweet. When the loudspeaker finally announced their approach to the drop zone, Russell stood and attached his static line. He proceeded to the Joe-hole and waited for the signal to prepare to exit. When the thumbs up finally came, he pushed himself into the hole and out into the cold night wind. His fall went as scheduled and his parachute opened gently above his head.

A pair of lights below waved to him as he descended toward the earth. He saw the outlines of trees and even some water off to the side. His course remained constant as he came closer and closer to the lights shining below. All at once Russell saw he was there. He executed the parachute landing fall that he had been taught by the Royal Air Force Parachute School and rolled safely on his side.

A pair of hands extended to help him up. "Welcome to France, Monsieur," a friendly voice said from nearby. "That was a nice landing. We will take you to your friends."

"As soon as I bury my chute," Russell replied.

"That will not be necessary, Monsieur. We will take it for you. Please follow us."

Russell saw no reason to argue and handed over the parachute. He followed the men to a nearby road where they walked briskly to the safe house where Laurent, Nancy Fiocca, Major John Farmer and other Maquis were waiting.

Christine Allard was finally able to see Gaspard when the Maquis leader finally returned to his secluded hideout two days after her most recent mission. He sat with her in private and listened to the details of her operation.

When she had concluded, he spoke to her in an almost fatherly tone.

"Sofian, while you accomplished what you set out to do, I feel you took some unnecessary chances," he began. "Staying around for the second shot put you and Paschal in even more danger. You might have been captured or killed."

"But there was no one coming out of the German headquarters, Gaspard," she answered defensively. "I saw another chance to destroy the other vehicle and took it."

Gaspard looked over at his assistant and thought, *If only all my Maquis were as good as this one. She thinks like a man and certainly fights like one. To be that brave and beautiful at the same time is almost incomprehensible. Too bad she has never shown any interest in me, this is the type of woman that would always make one's life interesting.*

He spoke again. "Yes, you are right, and you were successful in destroying another German vehicle. But what I want you to consider is what would have happened if you weren't so accurate with your shot and the enemy was coming from somewhere you couldn't see them. What would have happened then?"

Christine considered Gaspard's words and hesitantly agreed. "I guess you have a point. It might have all ended differently."

"I'm glad you see that much, Sofian. It means you are still able to consider all aspects of our mission. I would hate to have to replace either one of you."

Christine nodded her agreement with a slight bob of her head, but was still not convinced that her leader was completely right. *What he says is true, but I still feel I did the right thing. The fact that we escaped unhurt speaks for itself. The next time I am in a similar situation, I will try and make myself consider all the consequences. That's what a good leader would do.*

Nancy Wake Fiocca was already starting to doze off when the two Maquisards entered the dwelling in Lieutadès that served as the Maquis' headquarters.

Damn, this mountain air makes me drowsy at all hours of the day and night. All I want to do is nap.

She shook off the momentary lethargy and rose to greet the newcomer. Seeing it was US Army Captain Brian Russell, she extended her hand in his direction.

"I never expected to see you here..."

"Thierry," Russell responded quickly. "It's nice to see you again Madame Andrèe. I hoped I might surprise you."

"You certainly did," Nancy replied, realizing there was more to Russell's appearance than it seemed.

"You old cow," Denis Rake chimed in. "You didn't tell me you were scheduled for the Auvergne."

"Didn't know until the very last," Russell responded. "But I'm glad to be here in one piece."

Nancy again spoke. "Thierry, this is Laurent, the leader of this fine band of Maquis. I have already sent word back to London of Laurent's accomplishments."

"Good. Madame Andrèe, may I have a private word with you?"

"Of course. Let's step into the next room."

Russell followed Nancy into the next room, a small sitting room with a medium sized sofa and armchair. Russell gestured toward the sofa and took a seat next to the female agent.

"I know you are wondering why I am here, Nancy. For the record, so am I. It seems that Buckmaster took Denis' AWOL quite seriously. You are aware of what happened to our Denden aren't you?"

"Not really," Nancy replied. "When I questioned him about his tardiness, he simply answered, 'Don't ask.'"

"It figures. I'm sure he's not proud of what happened."

"So, exactly what did happen?"

Russell proceeded to tell Nancy the entire story of Denis Rake's amorous fling and its resultant delay. He also mentioned that Buckmaster wanted to insure that Denis towed the line while in the Auvergne and it was his job to see that the high-spirited man do just that.

Nancy smiled and sighed. "Our Denden is one of a kind all right. I love and hate him at the same time. But, he is the best radio person I know about, so I will have to make do with him."

"I don't want him to know why I am here. I'm afraid his ego wouldn't take it well and it would make my job even harder."

"Most certainly, my dear captain, er, Thierry."

"I have some additional things to do, including a meeting with Gaspard as soon as possible."

"Good luck with that one. He hasn't been happy with us here since we arrived. Seems he's expecting some money and help from the FFF or something. He's been an absolute shithead to us. That's why we are up here with Laurent. Gaspard wanted nothing to do with us even after I told him about the money."

"I have a feeling he is about to change his mind when he hears what I have to tell him," Russell related. "He's certainly not going to like the message I bring."

"Be careful, Captain Russell. He even approved of one of his men seducing me and killing me for the money."

"He actually thought he could do that to *you*?" Russell poked. "He didn't know you very well did he Nancy?"

"He didn't know me at all. It's his loss as far as I am concerned. I don't give a shit if he ever gets any of our money or help."

"Unfortunately, his Maquis control the entire Auvergne at this time. We must deal with him, or else. We have little choice. Let's see if he changes his attitude after our meeting."

"I will wait and see," Nancy ended. "Let's get back to the others. We even have a bottle of wine saved for your arrival."

"Sounds good to me. I could use a bite to eat if possible. I forgot to eat something in all the rush to get over here."

"Leave it to me. I'll rustle up something from the kitchen. Our money has made most of the basic food stuffs available again."

The pair walked out of the sitting room and rejoined the group. In seconds, the conversation was once again highly animated.

Chapter Eleven

Back in Marseille, it was apparent to both Gestapo officers that their efforts to capture The White Mouse were failing miserably.

"Nothing has worked in this matter," SS Oberstumbannfuhrer Ernst Dunker spoke despondently to his subordinate, SS Sturmbannfuhrer Rolf Muhler. "Even the five million franc reward hasn't proved effective. It's also possible that we have been receiving some false information from the enemy about her operations."

"We have followed up on every lead. Nothing has been overlooked," Muhler replied. "Whenever we set a trap, she fails to show up. She is either the luckiest person in the world or she doesn't actually exist."

Dunker thought for a moment. "What if she somehow escaped and made it back to Great Britain? The authorities there could have made use of her information and transmitted misleading information about her."

"I seriously doubt she could have escaped, Herr Oberstumbannfuhrer. We have closed most of the escape routes the French Resistance have been using. It is quite difficult to get into Spain at this time."

"*Most* of the escape routes? Why haven't they *all* been closed?" Dunker demanded.

"There is simply too much ground to cover, Herr Oberstumbannfuhrer. "And, we are forced to use the Milice and the Franc-Garde. Some of their troops are absolutely worthless. Some are even Resistance members. When we unearth them we immediately execute the bastards, but they continue to torment our efforts."

Dunker did not respond. He was thinking as Muhler's words finally died out.

"What if we try something ingenious ourselves, Muhler? What if we announce that the White Mouse has been captured and the reward taken? Won't the British react in some way to such news?"

"I'm not sure what you mean? Won't they know it's a trick if they have her in England?"

"If all communications pertaining to her ceases after the news of her capture, we will know she's been there all the time. We can stop trying to arrest her and concentrate on other matters important to the Third Reich."

"Jawohl, Herr Oberstumbannfuhrer. I see what you mean."

"Good. Then see to it at once. Follow the usual channels so it won't seem suspicious. It will be interesting to see how our enemy reacts."

"I will get on this immediately, Herr Oberstumbannfuhrer. I will report back to you after its completion."

Muhler left the Gestapo colonel's office and walked directly to the communications room. The notice outlining The White Mouse's capture would be broadcast in a short time.

When Dennis Rake's initial radio reports from the Auvergne about Gaspard's reluctance to cooperate were received in London, SOE-F had reacted swiftly. They contacted BCRAL *(Bureau Central de Renseignements et d'Action Londres)*, the agency that was the direct link to De Gaulle's Free French Forces. The short meeting determined that, while sending money to Maquisards in the Auvergne and elsewhere was an important aspect of their operation, it was severely limited by lack of funds at the present time. Money would be sent back to France at a time when and if such finds became available. The BCRAL official also stated that he felt such a time was not in the immediate future.

The meeting was also a deciding factor in Colonel Maurice Buckmaster's mind that sent US Army Captain Brian Russell to France. Russell's first important job was to inform Gaspard of the realities of the situation.

As he made his way to an agreed upon meeting place with the French Resistance leader, Russell hashed over the problems he now faced.

If Nancy and Farmer are correct, this guy is a pain to deal with. He is a bit out of touch if he thinks the Free French are his hope for survival. How should I play this? If I come down too hard, he might react badly. That would do no good at all.

If I seem too soft, that would not help either. I need to find a tightrope that I can walk that is neither too hard nor too soft. I think it might be best to give him some room to choose for himself...

The place for the meeting was a three-room wooden schoolhouse located in a grove of trees in the town of Messeix, south southwest of Clermont-Ferrand. Russell and his Maquis guide arrived at the designated spot and found it deserted.

It's around 1000 hours and this is the middle of the week and there are no children at the school Russell theorized. *This just doesn't feel right to me. If something doesn't materialize in the near future, maybe I should get my American butt outa here and live to fight another day.*

He turned to his Maquis guide and explained his concern. The Maquis shrugged his shoulders casually as if he had no opinion whatsoever on the subject. Russell looked around again and was preparing to leave when a single figure appeared from a clearing at the edge of the grove.

The man carried no apparent weapon and walked straight toward Russell.

"You wanted to meet with me?" the Frenchman asked abruptly.

"If you are Gaspard, then, yes I do," Russell replied. "I have traveled a long way to see you."

"You wouldn't mind giving me the current code word, would you?"

"Basset," Russell replied quickly, studying his challenger.

"So you know the password. It seems a number of people do..."

"So you are Gaspard. I've heard a lot about you."

"Your French is absolutely perfect," Gaspard offered. Are you from Paris?"

"Paris courtesy of the Sorbonne," Russell replied.

"Ah, the Sorbonne," Gaspard sighed. "Before the war I wanted to be a teacher myself. I always wanted to go to the Sorbonne but was never able. My family business prevented it. I was always expected to follow in my father's footsteps."

He isn't all that bad, after all. I sort of feel sorry for him.

"I was fortunate to attend. I made some great friends there."

"But, you speak perfect French, and yet, somehow, I don't feel you are French, monsieur."

"Please call me Thierry, Gaspard. It's the name I have been given."

"Are you really French, Thierry?" Gaspard repeated.

Should I tell him the truth? Maybe in this case, honesty will have a good effect on him.

"I am an American," Russell replied. I studied in Paris for several years."

"And learned to speak French like a Parisian. My compliments, Thierry. Most people would never question your speaking. I study accents, sometimes it comes in handy in our work."

"I understand. One can never be too careful in these times."

"Precisely. I have many Gestapo looking for me right now. Sometimes, they seem a little too close."

"Can we get down to business?" Russell asked. "I don't want to take up too much of your time."

"Of course," Gaspard answered. "Let us go inside the schoolhouse. There should be at least three chairs inside that will fit us."

"And where are the children?" Russell questioned."

"They received a holiday today, much to their delight. I didn't think it wise having a meeting with children about. One of them might just see something and tell their parents. Not everyone around here supports our cause."

The three stepped inside and brought three chairs together. Russell spoke first.

"London has asked me to convey some information to you, Gaspard. I'm afraid it's not really good news. When you have heard what I have to say, I would invite you to check on its authenticity with your Free French forces. I presume you still have radio communications with North Africa, right?"

Gaspard nodded affirmatively, as Russell continued. "London has confirmed that there are no funds at present for the Free French to send to the Maquisards anywhere in France. This includes your operation here in the Auvergne. If and when the situation changes, I'm sure you will get funds, but right now there is little chance. We have made an arrangement with BCRAL to supply you and others like you with the resources you need to make your daily lives easier. We want you to have food to eat and clothes to wear. We intend to begin supplying you with better weapons and as much ammunition as you need to accomplish your mission. That was the point of sending Madame Andrée here in the first place. She has already provided Laurent and his band with ample moneys to make them a better fighting force."

"She told me as much," Gaspard replied. "At the time I was expecting money from our own source. If what you say is true, I have probably made a mistake in not accepting her help."

He seems to be speaking straightforwardly. He doesn't appear to be all that irresponsible, maybe just a bit stubborn. I will let Nancy know that so that she will be able to work with him in the future.

"But," Gaspard added, "I will first check out what you have told me. Until then, I want nothing from you. I hope you understand."

"Of course. That would be the smart thing to do. How long will you take to find out?"

"Two, three days at the most. I will send word to Laurent. Until then, you must wait with him."

"I can wait three days."

"Good. Our meeting is ended. Your guide will take you back to Laurent's camp. Maybe we will meet again."

"I certainly hope so, for your good and that of your men."

"*Merci*, Thierry."

The Maquisard leader walked out of the schoolhouse and headed back toward the clearing. He did not look back at the two men still standing in the door of the schoolhouse.

As the senior Gestapo officer in Marseille, SS Oberstrumbannfuhrer Ernst Dunker was privy to the latest detailed information gathered by Germany's intelligence agencies. His own agency operated under Heinrich Himmler's personal supervision and as such was immune to most of the bureaucratic infighting that took place in the country's intelligence community. Dunker knew Himmler only slightly, but that association was enough to insure his own stability within the Gestapo.

Dunker was absorbed in a communication he had just received from the Gestapo's headquarters on Prinz Albrecht Street in Berlin. The multi-page document covered a variety of subjects and served as the Gestapo's update for their activities throughout Europe.

A particular aspect of the report had caught Dunker's attention. It stated that a number of French Resistance members had been caught and interrogated in recent weeks. Detailed information from these prisoners had been gleaned through the use of scopolamine and other methods of interrogation and was thought to be genuine. The report stated that an unusually large number of agents had been infiltrated into France and the Gestapo held the belief that these infiltrations were the precursor to some big buildup or operation, possibly the invasion of France by the allies.

All ranking Gestapo officers were directed to put added emphasis on deriving any additional information from any Resistance members that were captured. The officers were authorized to use any means possible to extract additional information.

Do the wizards back in Berlin think we are just sitting around waiting for information to fall into our laps? We are doing everything possible to provide information that will help the Third Reich. Ever since the Schutzhaft (use of protective custody) was instituted, we've been able to do as we please with these bastards. But, Berlin just might be on to something with their notion of a big buildup of new agents in France. We have been expecting something like this for several months, so this time they might just be correct in their thinking. I will send a notice out to my interrogators to ask some pertinent questions of anyone who we catch. We might just be able to add to Berlin's intelligence cache.

He took a pen from a drawer on his desk and wrote a detailed note for distribution to all officers in his area. He outlined several courses of action for questioning of suspected French Resistance prisoners. He called for his sergeant, who appeared almost immediately. He handed the paper to the non-commissioned officer and instructed him to see that the note was sent out as soon as possible.

The Maquisard messenger from Gaspard's band arrived at the hotel in Lieutadés early in the morning two days after Russell's meeting with the Resistance leader. He found Russell, Nancy Fiocca, Denis Rake and John Farmer sitting together over a petit déjeuner of cheese and bread along with cups of warm coffee.

He addressed Russell, while gazing benignly at the steaming coffee.

"Colonel Gaspard sends you word that Madame Andrée will be most welcome in his camp. He also extends his apologies for any inconveniences he has caused."

Russell broke into a grin and gestured toward the coffee pot on a nearby table. The man smiled appreciatively and headed toward the coffee.

"He probably hasn't had any coffee since the war broke out," Major John Farmer remarked in English. "None of Laurent's men had either, that's until we came and handed out some money. Amazing what the black market can provide, even here in Lieutadés."

"I hope he goes back and tells all of Gaspard's men about it," Nancy added. "It would do wonders for their morale."

"Quite a switch on Gaspard's part," Russell said. "I guess he was able to confirm that there was no money coming from the Free French forces. I imagine he will turn out to be our best friend from this point on."

"He will still be stubborn," Nancy chimed in. "The only reason he's being nice to us at all is that he has no other choice. If he wants arms and money to feed his men, he has to come to us for it."

"Well, that's why you are here, for better or worse. I expect your job will be a great deal easier from this point on. I'm sure he will do whatever you want of him. It would make sense," Russell opined.

"I sure hope so. We've already wasted a good deal of time just sitting around." Nancy looked over at Denis Rake who chose to ignore the reference.

Russell again addressed the Maquis messenger. "Can you take Madame Andrée back to Gaspard's hideout?"

The messenger nodded his agreement and Russell spoke again.

"I think it is best you go and see him now. Take Denden with you and get some word back to London as soon as you have met with Gaspard. They will probably set up a schedule for some airdrops as soon as possible. I am going to make a scouting expedition to see if I can find some targets. London made me commit a list of places and things to destroy to memory before I left. I hope I can remember it all."

"I have a good map that Laurent gave me when we arrived. All the German checkpoints are marked, at least the ones he knows about. It should help you get around."

"Is there a bicycle I can borrow?" Russell asked. "I don't want to have to walk my way through the Auvergne if I can help it."

"I think that can be arranged," Major Farmer spoke up. "Laurent's Maquis has a number of them at their disposal. Bicycles are the one commodity of which we seem to have an ample supply."

"Good. I want to be off as soon as possible. Please let Gaspard know what I am attempting to do. I don't want to hurt his feelings or make him believe we aren't working closely with him."

Nancy shook her head. "We'll let him know all right, he'll think he's the King of Sheba or something."

"I believe it was the Queen of Sheba," Farmer injected.

"King, queen…who gives a shit," Nancy retaliated. "You got my message."

Major John Farmer chose not to answer the spirited woman. Russell regarded the entire scene and thought to himself. *She really is a strong-willed woman. This area will be in good hands. I just hope she leaves Farmer's head on in the process.*

The gathering broke up and departed in different directions. In a few short hours, the plans that SOE-F in London had carefully prepared would be put into operation. The planned strategy had taken a good deal of time to reach fruition.

Christine Allard, or Sofian to her French Resistance cohorts, had been given a mission to gather information on a German supply depot that was supposedly located near the town of Brioude. She had commandeered a bicycle for her mission and was pedaling steadily as she crossed a bridge of the Allier River.

She spotted a German checkpoint directly in front of her and prepared to stop and present her papers. As she approached the checkpoint, another bicyclist was just leaving the German position, a man with a black beret whose head was turned away from her. Something about the man seemed familiar to Christine, but the German soldier facing her had already raised his hand for her to stop.

Christine glanced back at the diminishing bicycle and turned to the young soldier. Two members of the Franc-Garde stood in the background with rifles slung around their shoulders. She addressed the Bosch soldier with an almost genuine smile.

"Here they are," she spoke softly as she handed the papers to the man. He regarded the attractive woman and read from the book."

"So you are from Ambert on the other side of the mountains?" he questioned.

Christine replied softly, "Yes. I am also a seamstress as my papers indicate. I am delivering some finished dresses to a customer in Brioude. You can examine them if you wish." She handed him a small package that was tied together with string. The young soldier untied the string and assessed the contents."

Satisfied the package contained dresses, he handed it back to Christine.

"Aren't you going to re-tie it?" she asked pleasantly. "After all, you just undid it."

"German soldiers don't tie string around packages. Tie it yourself if you want it tied," he replied in broken French. "And, be quick about it."

Christine carefully retied the packages, looked the soldier in the eye and remounted her bicycle. She began pedaling toward Brioude when she suddenly recalled the bicyclist she had passed nearing the checkpoint.

No, it couldn't be she mulled over to herself. *It just looked a little like my Brian, that's all. It's been so long since I have seen him. He couldn't be back here in France, right in the middle of the Auvergne. It must have been someone who looked like him. I guess I'll never know...*

145

The follow-up meeting with Gaspard went even better than Nancy Fiocca could have imagined. The change in the Maquisard leader was apparent from the beginning and that fact made Nancy a bit uneasy.

If someone can change his disposition on the flip of a coin, then he can change right back just as easily. I will have to handle this one with kid gloves, no doubt about it. London wants things to run smoothly here, and I'm given that responsibility. Let's just see how far I can take it...

Two important aspects of their mission were agreed upon by Nancy Fiocca and John Farmer during their meeting with Gaspard. Nancy would be responsible for assessing the Maquisards needs and then organizing the airdrops that would supply the fighters. Farmer would serve as a military advisor on tactics and mission strategies and Gaspard would take his suggestions to heart. All their activities would need to be reported to London. Denis Rake would remain with Gaspard's troops to make these reports.

Nancy decided to spend her time between Gaspard and Laurent's camps, depending on the proximity of each mission. She wished to remain on top of everything that was being planned and she felt her time was best suited to such activities by spending spells in both camps.

An airdrop was scheduled immediately after Rake contacted the English receiving station in rural Kent where all transmissions were monitored by a 500-person staff. Provisions were made for an arms drop later that night on a plateau in close proximity to Chaudes-Aigues. Bonfires were lit at the prescribed hour. Nancy and a group of about forty Maquis patiently waited for the sound of an approaching airplane engine.

Several hours later, doubts had begun to creep into the minds of the Maquis. No plane had arrived and the bonfires had been doused. Shortly before midnight, a sound from the northwest sprung everyone into action. The bonfires were relit and all eyes lifted skyward. Minutes later a large number of arms cases began floating gently toward earth in their parachutes. The excited Maquis leapt forward and started opening the cases. Satisfied with the contents, they began placing the cartons on several horse drawn carts that had accompanied them to the drop spot.

Nancy was as excited as any of the Maquis. In her mind, the drop proved to her partisans that she meant business, even if the drop was a few hours overdue. She accompanied the carts back to the camps (one went to Gaspard and the other to Laurent) and stood proudly with arms folded as the cartons were opened. Gaspard was duly impressed.

"I should never have doubted you Madame Andrée," he said wistfully. "But I had no way of knowing. War makes for dubious choices, don't you agree?"

"If you say so, colonel. I have such an honest face that I would have immediately agreed to everything if I had been in your position."

Gaspard looked at the woman and smiled. "You certainly do, Madame Andrée. I agree that it would have been the correct thing to do."

"Let's get all this counted so I can send the message back to London. I'm sure you will want to disperse a number of these guns to your other groups."

"It's already being taken care of. There are trucks on the way to get them to our other units. They will all be thankful."

"We must all work together, colonel. With our resources and your brave men, we will persevere."

Gaspard nodded and continued supervising his men. It was already one great night for the fighters of the Auvergne, a night than none of his men would soon forget.

The day after the Allied invasion of France in Normandy, word quickly swept through the British capital of London. With the sheer numbers of personnel involved in the invasion suddenly absent, the streets of the great city seemed practically deserted. As boats and ships from the great armada that had been assembled returned to their ports, rumors suddenly turned to fact as the naval participants hit their favorite pubs and hangouts. While no reports of any successes or failures surfaced, it was entirely evident that a great military operation was underway that would eventually restore the democratic way of life to most of Europe.

At SOE-F's Baker Street offices, plans were now put into effect to continue clandestine support of the amphibious and air attacks along the French coastline.

One of those plans involved Violette Szabo who had anxiously awaited her next call to duty. She was ordered to report the following day to Baker Street for briefing and assignment.

Good, she thought. *I will just have enough time to get down there and see Tania before I have to report. She has been such a lovely child through all this. Never really complaining and only a tear or two when I had to say good bye. I will do something wonderful for her when this is all over. Maybe we can both go on a trip or something. I will never be apart from her again after the war, I swear to that.*

Violette dressed herself in one of the dresses she had purchased in Paris and hurried toward the railroad station. She had memorized the train schedule to Hampshire and Havant in particular. It was there that the Yew Tree Lodge was located, the nursery that cared for Tania when she was not with Violette.

She reached the train platform at Waterloo Station with about five minutes to spare. A hanging sign confirmed she was on the correct platform for the train to Hampshire and points southwest. Violette caught her breath and adjusted the small hat she had chosen for the occasion.

At least I will look nice when I see my daughter. She is always so excited when I show up unannounced. I'm not sure Mrs. Edwardes approves of my just appearing out of the blue, but I know she understands.

The train rolled to a stop almost in front of her and Violette boarded one of the rear coaches. In about an hour, she would see her daughter again.

SS Sturmbannfuhrer Rolf Muhler finally collected all his notes and made his way to the office of his superior, Obersturmbannfuhrer Ernst Dunker. He disliked being the bearer of bad news, particularly when it concerned the status of the Gestapo's ongoing investigation into the whereabouts of The White Mouse.

"I'm afraid there is no change in the British radio signals to The White Mouse Herr Obersturmbannfuhrer," he began in a muted tone. They are still directing her to operations around Marseille."

Dunker thought for a moment and replied, "I still think those are false signals that are intended to dupe us. I want all our activities around her halted."

"Jawohl, Herr Oberstrumbannfuhrer. I will see to it at once."

"And Muhler, have we had any success in obtaining any further information about a possible invasion from any of our prisoners? It would be helpful to be able to report to Berlin that we have some intelligence that might help determine what is happening."

"No, there is nothing to report. If any of the people we have arrested know any-thing about such a thing, they certainly aren't willing to admit it. We tortued a pair of Resistance people for hours this very morning, but nothing new was learned. I was informed that one of the prisoners died just after the interrogation."

Dunker remained silent as he considered his subordinates words. Damn stub-born people, these partisans. *They would rather die than disclose even the smallest bit of information. I must admit they are a formidable adversary.*

"I have an important meeting in the city, so I must leave you Muhler. When I return we can discuss this further. My car is waiting on the street."

Muhler hand saluted his superior who waved casually back.

Dunker walked briskly down the stairs and approached the front door. A non-uniformed Gestapo agent stationed at the door opened it and allowed the SS officer to pass through. Dunker was pleased to see his Mercedes Kubelwagen Type 170VK ready with its motor running and its top and side windows down.

It's a nice day out and I can enjoy the fresh air, he decided. He signaled to his driver and the car started moving. A passing truck slowed and a bag was tossed out of the passenger window. The bag landed on the hood of the Mercedes as both Dunker and the driver watched. The driver applied the brakes to the car but it was a moment too late. A loud flash and explosion erupted that spun the car around in circles. Dunker was thrown out of the back of the vehicle and landed against a nearby tree. Smoke engulfed the entire area and a number of people inside the Gestapo headquarters poured out into the street, several with their Lugers drawn.

Dunker was still alive when the first Germans reached his side. He was bleed-ing profusely from wounds to both his scalp and face. His right arm was also punc-tured and was hemorrhaging badly. He was immediately rushed back inside the building where a doctor had been summoned to tend to his wounds.

Chapter Twelve

One of the ideas that had been postulated to US Army Captain Brian Russell, prior to his departure from SOE-F in London, was the possibility of an actual large scale armed attack by the combined forces of the Maquisards in the Auvergne. To that end, Russell was directed to search out potential targets of opportunity within the region and also assess the plausibility of the success of such a plan.

Since large scale attacks were not the primary function of the Maquis to this point in their existence, such a daring change in strategy would require a great deal of intelligence and pre-planning on the part of the partisans. SOE-F would be required to supply the type of weapons necessary for such an encounter along with sufficient expertise to assure the plan had a high degree of success.

In his mind, Russell wasn't sure of exactly what he was searching for, even though the concept had been thoroughly outlined for him prior to his departure. He was to make a number of side trips throughout the Auvergne to attempt to find a setting or series of factors that might advantage the Maquis.

Russell understood the basic concepts, but was somewhat taken aback when the SOE-F briefing officer told him to, "Look at everything you can. When something strikes you as extraordinary, make note of what you see. You will know it when you see it, or at least that's our hope."

He had pedaled the better part of a week and had seen a good deal of the countryside but nothing out of the ordinary had popped into his mind. *Am I here on a wild goose chase? I am now bicycling my ass off and all I have to show for it is tired legs and an aching back. I am tired of eating ceppes (forest mushrooms) and whatever I am able to buy along the way. Even with money in my pocket, there is seldomly anything to buy. The people don't know me and are afraid I might be a Vichy spy or something. This isn't the most pleasant job I've had and I'm not really sure what I am looking for...*

His forged identity papers for this mission were in the name of Thierry Thibault, a deceased minor Vichy official from Toulon in the very southern reaches of Frances's so-called Free Zone. He also carried Vichy orders that allowed him to transgress the entire area of France that was under the Government at Vichy's actual control.

Russell recalled the Vichy checkpoints that had been given to him on a crude map drawn in the Maquis camp. He had committed them to memory and so far the map had proven quite accurate. *It's a good thing the Vichy police and Franc-Garde are lazy and don't change their checkpoints very often. If they did change the spots, I would really have to be careful. If I am correct, there is another checkpoint coming at this bridge ahead. It must be the Allier River again or one of its tributaries. This river runs throughout the entire Auvergne, or so it seems. I must have crossed it two dozen times or more on this ride.*

He braked for the checkpoint and removed his papers from inside his jacket. A youthful Franc-Garde *soldat 1e classe* waived him to a stop. Another young conscript stood in the background with a bored look on his face.

"*Bonjour,*" Russell said pleasantly to the youth.

"*Bonjour,*" the Franc-Garde soldier returned. He examined Russell's papers and asked. "What brings you all the way to the Auvergne when you are from Toulon?"

"I am temporarily assigned to Vichy itself. There is a pass included in my papers." He pointed to a piece of paper that the young soldier studied. "The wise ones at headquarters have assigned me to a silly job of touring the countryside to visit our forces in remote areas to ascertain their morale. In other words, are they happy with what they are doing? And, they have provided me with this miserable bicycle to get around the Auvergne."

The soldier regarded the bicycle and grinned as he handed the identity papers back to Russell. "We are all in the same situation Monsieur Thibault. Vichy makes my friend and I man this checkpoint all the time. There are very few people who cross the river here and we have never found anything suspicious. We think it is a waste of our time and have told our sergeant so. He says that 'orders are orders,' and that's that."

Russell smiled back and prepared to leave. "Always be prepared my young friend. You can never tell when a Resistance fighter might cross your path."

The Franc-Garde soldier nodded his head and grinned back. "They wouldn't

152

dare. We always have our rifles loaded and cocked."

"So be it. Maybe we will meet again one day." He waived as he began to pedal away.

The soldier waved back and turned to his cohort. "Nice sort of person, that one. His job is just as boring as ours. Only difference is that he gets to travel around and see the area. We just have to stand here and wait."

The second Franc-Garde soldier nodded his agreement. He then yawned deeply and took a seat on a wooden box that served as their only comfort.

The explosives thrown by the French Resistance partisan in Marseille onto the hood of SS Oberstrumbannfuhrer Ernst Dunker's Mercedes failed to kill the senior Gestapo officer. While Dunker's face and arm sustained multiple wounds, the quick action by the Wehrmacht doctors prevented the loss of too much blood and ultimately saved Dunker's life.

Dunker lost consciousness at the time of the blast and woke up two days later in a small hospital that had been taken over by the Wehrmacht when they first came to Marseille. The place was intended to meet the German military's direct needs and was staffed by German doctors and personnel. Dunker groaned and attempted to move in his bed.

"Here now, none of that," a heavyset frau krankenschwester warned in German. "The doctor says you must be still so that the new skin can grow on your face. You have been pretty badly wounded."

Dunker reached up and felt the bandages. Every part of his face burned as well as his right arm. He felt the arm and found that it too was heavily bandaged.

"What time is it?" he demanded. Where am I and how long have I been here?"

"This is the Wehrmacht Hospital in Marseille, and you have been here for the past two days."

Dunker tried to focus as his memory of the explosion returned to his mind.

"Yes, I saw something coming at the car and I started to duck behind the front seat. I remember that much."

"That probably saved your life, Herr Oberstrumbannfuhrer," another voice, this one masculine, answered back. "If you had not ducked, the explosion would certainly have blown your head off. Your driver was not as fortunate. What we could find of him wasn't very much, and that included his head. The explosion took care of that."

Dunker reflected on what he was hearing. *The French Resistance is behind all this. They simply won't give up. I don't know what it will take, or if we will ever gain an upper hand. We arrest and kill off a number of them and more seem to materialize to take their place. They are afraid of nothing and are determined to drive us out of their country. Don't they realize the Third Reich is here to stay no matter what they do to us?*

The krankenschwester came over and touched his uninjured arm. "I have some more medicine that will help with the pain," she offered. "I will give you this shot and you will fall right asleep."

Dunker felt the slight prick as the needle entered his skin. In a few moments he was again in the embrace of a restful sleep. By most accounts, he was considered by the hospital's doctors and staff to be a most lucky person. In their eyes, the fact that he was still alive was nothing short of a miracle.

The B24-D Liberator Bomber transporting Violette Szabo to her dropping point just off the French Coast was cold and windy as the young woman sat on the makeshift seat which she had been provided. She accepted a cup of to some hot tea that the American flight engineer Richard Thomas offered, and found it quite good according to British standards.

It was now two days after D-Day and this was the second time in two days that Violette and her team had boarded a B24 for the flight to France. Something had gone wrong with the initial flight and the bomber had turned back to England. Had the bomber crew informed them, Violette and her friends might well have seen the vast armada that stretched out across the English Channel. As it was, the return flight was conducted in silence along with a sense of disappointment by the SOE team.

This time the dropping zone was near the village of Sussac, some thirty miles or so southeast of Limoges. Conditions were almost perfect and the dropping of supplies along with the four SOE agents commenced just before 0200. Prior to leaving the aircraft, Violette kissed members of the crew including both the pilot and co-pilot. She felt it was her own personal way of thanking them for helping her get to France.

A jubilant band of about forty Maquis met the new arrivals. Word of the invasion had spread and the new supplies that accompanied the four agents were incredibly well received. SOE Agent Philippe Liewer, Violette's partner from her first mission to France, was also part of this team. Their job was to help strengthen the Salesman Network for the SOE.

Early the next morning, Violette set out on the first part of her assignment, which was to travel approximately 100 miles. She accepted the company of another young French agent, Jacques Dufour. Dufour was twenty-one years of age and a forceful sort who offered to strap her bicycle to the side of his Citroën that could take her half-way to her destination. She realized this would save her valuable time, so Violette quickly accepted.

As a precaution, Violette approached Liewer about taking along a STEN Mk II 9mm submachine gun and several 32-round magazines. Due to the proximity of the invasion, Liewer agreed to Violette's request.

As she rode along in the black Citroen Berline 11, Violette thought to herself. *If I am placed in a tough spot, I will take some Krauts with me. This time it's all for real. The invasion proves that we really mean business and the German bastards know it. I really hope we see some enemy troops so I can show them what I mean.*

Her spirits rose as the car passed through the countryside, now verdant with wildflowers and green grass. Violette looked over at Dufour who smiled back at her with genuine warmth.

Along the way, Dufour picked up another Maquis associate, a twenty-six-year-old named Jean Bariaud, who was to accompany him on his return trip. The trio talked freely, with Violette offering the lion's share of the conversation. She inquired as to their rationale for getting involved with the Maquis and also about their past experiences in fighting the Germans. She was happy to hear these accounts of actual Maquis actions in the area.

"You have both been quite successful for such young men," she observed. "It is good for you. The more we fight the bastards, the sooner we will win and drive them from France."

Both men agreed as the car rounded a curve in the road. The village of Salon-la-Tour was just ahead in the distance. A T junction crossroad preceded the town and some activity there caught their attention. The Germans had set up a roadblock and were waving for the oncoming car to stop.

Dufour began slowing the car and told Violette, "You prepare to jump out when we stop. I will start firing to give you a chance to get away."

Violette watched intently as the car finally came to a halt about thirty yards from the roadblock. As he promised, Dufour immediately jumped out and began firing his own gun. Violette was just a step behind followed by their passenger who was unarmed.

A steady flow of bullets from Dufour had already wounded several Wehrmacht soldiers who fell to the ground around the roadblock. Additional German soldiers took up firing at the car. Dufour looked to see Bariaud running for the nearby woods. Violette however, had assumed a firing position and was raking the Germans with her STEN.

"Get out of here!" he shouted at her. "I'll keep firing."

Violette obeyed Dufour's command and made her way to a high wheat field on the other side of the car. Upon reaching the cover, she started firing at the Germans again to allow Dufour to join her. When he reached Violette, the pair began making their way through the wheat to escape their pursuers. Violette reached down and felt her leg that had begun to ache. She saw blood from what appeared to be a bullet wound in the fleshy part of the leg. She tied a ribbon from around her hair to just below the wound to stop the bleeding. Satisfied she had stopped the bleeding, she returned her attention to the ongoing gun battle.

The Wehrmacht soldiers had called for reinforcements and in minutes armored vehicles arrived. They began spraying the field with machine guns. Both Dufour and Violette began crawling on their stomachs to escape the bullets, but the going was slow and fatiguing. At times, their progress came to a near stop but the pair trudged on as the Germans continued their fire. Dufour urged Violette along, but her wounded leg held her back. Every time she attempted to stretch out and crawl, the leg reacted with additional pain.

The hostile firing persisted for almost a quarter of an hour. More infantry soldiers began combing the field and additional armored cars encircled the meadow. Violette Szabo saw Dufour ahead of her and pleaded with him to go on as she was in a state of total exhaustion. She promised to give him whatever cover she could so that he could manage his escape.

She began firing again until the last bullet in her STEN was exhausted. Dufour finally made it through the wheat and into some woods. Minutes later he was able to hide in a haystack on a small nearby farm.

Thirty minutes later, he was witness to the Germans bringing Violette to the very farm where he was hiding. They began questioning the young woman as to where her companions were hiding.

He heard Violette laugh when she told them, "You can run after him, he is far away by now." It would be the last time Jacques Dufour would see Violette Szabo.

An odd-shaped, semi-circular building on Portland Place, in London, housed the studios of the British Broadcasting Company. Formally known as Broadcasting House, the location in northwest London was the transmission lifeline of all SOE agents working in France and other occupied countries.

News bulletins were aired five times daily. All were coded for special groups and helped the agents in the field on a regular basis. These bulletins allowed the field agents less frequent radio transmissions that were sure to be monitored by German direction- finding vehicles.

Each agent had a special code name that assured specific information for each individual. In Nancy Wake Fiocca's case, her code name was Hélène, and any specific message would always start 'Personal to Hélène' with details immediately following.

The BBC announcer would finish his broadcast and then follow with the words 'et maintenant, quelques messages personnels'. For the next half hour, a series of nonsensical phrases would follow such as 'Cock a doodle doo', 'Goosey Goosey Gander' or "Diddle, Diddle, Dumpling, My Son John' would follow. Key phrases were inserted for the benefit of agents who monitored the broadcasts with necessary meticulousness. Many of the messages were pure nonsense, intended to fool the Germans who also monitored each broadcast in an attempt to figure out what was happening throughout Europe.

The system worked particularly well for Nancy and her fellow agents, Hubert and Denden. The Maquisards began counting on her to deliver what she had promised and she soon became their *chef du parachutage*. Nancy took this role quite seriously and would only arm the Maquis when they agreed to follow her strict rules regarding secrecy and military planning. She also personally vetted each plausible dropping site and gave each of them the name of a particular fruit. She then took an old Michelin map and marked each field on the map. Only Denis Rake and Nancy knew which dropping spots were fruits designated for their operations.

She would also include the phrase, 'the cow jumped over the moon' along with a specific reference to a coded drop spot. When 'cow jumped over the moon' was received and was followed by a particular reference spot, blackberry fields for instance, Nancy knew that the following day whatever she had ordered would be dropped there.

But problems with Gaspard still thwarted her involvement with the Auvergne Maquisards. She decided to make a trip to Clermont-Ferrand to see a former French Colonial Army officer, Colonel Thomas, who had organized a group of soldiers to act after D-Day. She had been told that Colonel Thomas wasn't a huge fan of Gaspard and she hoped to talk the officer into coming to Chaudes-Aigues to persuade Gaspard into cooperating more with London's directives.

The road to Clermont-Ferrand was heavily guarded by the Germans at the time and was considered impassable by the Resistance. She decided on taking the train and was forced to board at Montluçon.

Nancy was also expecting an important message from London and decided to conceal her small receiving set in one coat pocket. Dressed in a navy blue suit and her favorite camel hair coat, she hid the various leads under her coat. The leads to the tiny microphones that plugged into her ears were hidden along her back and under her hair. The battery for the set occupied her other coat pocket.

As the train departed, Nancy found herself surrounded by German officers. She acknowledged her enemy's presence with a faint smile and calmly sat back and listened to the BBC during the entire ride. The expected BBC message never materialized and her meeting with Colonel Thomas fared even worse. Colonel Thomas was a stolid sort to deal with. After several exchanges, it was apparent he would not commit to coming to meet Gaspard. Frustrated and annoyed at his indifference, Nancy departed Clermont-Ferrand in an ill-tempered mood.

The unterofficer (sergeant) who was in charge of the roadblock around the village of Salon-la-Tour was a veteran of the 2nd SS Panzer Division Das Reich couldn't believe his eyes when his men finally brought Violette Szabo before him. The division was on their way to Normandy from their headquarters in Montauban north of Toulouse when elements of their division had been surrounded by Maquisards. A high ranking officer, SS Sturmbannfuhrer Helmut Kämpfe, had been captured by the Maquis and the division had set up roadblocks to help find him. Had the SS colonel not been captured, the roadblock that led to Violette Szabo's arrest might not have happened.

The Unterofficer was simply amazed at what had occurred. The fact that this particular adversary was a slightly built and incredibly beautiful young woman who could shoot as well as any man didn't matter.

When a young hauptman (captain) approached her at a nearby farm after her capture, she spat at him and refused his offer of a cigarette. A short while later, she shouted at her captors to leave her alone and free her hands so she could get her own cigarette.

The Unterofficer was thoroughly impressed with the entire scenario. *This is one brave young woman, maybe the bravest I have ever seen. She fights like a man and swears like one too. I would hate to get into an argument with her; there would be no way I could win.*

The initial questioning of Violette Szabo was relatively mild considering the fact she had wounded a number of German soldiers. She gave them no name and steadfastly refused to cooperate in the least. She provided menacing looks to anyone who approached her and attempted to stop the bleeding in her ankle that had been nicked by a German bullet.

The Germans waited at the farm for almost an hour before orders were received concerning their prisoner. She was to be taken to Gestapo headquarters in Limoges and then transferred on the following day to Limoges Prison in the Place du Cham de Foire. The unterofficer who had initially captured her gave her a military salute as Violette was taken away. The salute wasn't a typical Heil Hitler salute, but rather a traditional German military salute reserved for respected friends and foes.

At Gestapo headquarters she finally gave her name as Vicky Taylor, the actual name she had intended to use if she had ever needed to escape through Spain back to England. She had picked the name herself. The word Szabo means tailor in Hungarian, and was intended to be a play on her real name.

After an exhausting bike ride that consumed the better part of a week, US Army Captain Brian Russell decided he had had enough of the Auvergne to last him a good while. He wearily pedaled his bicycle up the steep incline that led him to Lieutadès and his SOE cohorts. As he came to a stop at the hotel where everyone was staying, he was greeted by Denis Rake who examined his wrinkled clothes and disheveled appearance.

Russell acknowledged his friend's expression and spoke first.

"What do you expect after a week in the forests? It was miserable out there, with little to eat and only a couple of small rivers to wash in. I feel like I am the dirtiest person in the world. I need a bath badly and my attitude won't improve until I have one."

"My, my, old chap," Denis replied. "Aren't we a bit over today?"

"I'd hate to see you in a similar position."

"I'm much too smart to accept duties riding about the forests. I made myself good with the radio set so I wouldn't have to do such things."

Russell considered Rake's reply and grinned. "Yes, my dear Denden, I guess you are right. Perhaps I should specialize in something other than bicycle riding myself."

Rake beamed back and patted Russell's shoulder. "Come inside you big sod and grab your bath. I happen to know this old place has a decent hot water boiler that is working at this moment. In no time you'll be back to yourself."

The pair headed toward the front door and was about to enter as Nancy Wake Fiocca appeared in the doorway.

"So you're back from your little adventure," she chided Russell. "I trust everything went smoothly on your ride."

"I didn't have any flats if that's what you mean. For the most part the going wasn't all that bad. Some of those inclines were too much for me. I had to stop and walk up to the crests. It's not the best way to see the sights."

"Well, I have some good news for you. I've managed to find an automobile to take us around from now on. It's much more efficient than riding bicycles and saves a great deal of time."

"*Now,* get a car for us. After I have sweated my way through the entire Auvergne, it will take my legs a week to recover."

"Just be happy we have a vehicle to ride in. There aren't many around here and we are quite lucky. I used some of our money to make a deal for the car."

"It looks like a nice one, a Citroën right?"

"Right. And, we can steal all the petrol we need from the Germans. The Maquis is quite slick about it. I'm not sure the Jerries even know we are stealing their gasoline."

Russell grinned at the confidant woman who beamed right back. "These Maquis are like something out of a novel. For years they have fought with nothing ---food, arms, ammunition or clothing, and they have held their own against a supposedly superior army. Now that they have the essentials, what's going to stop them?"

"If I have anything to say about it, not a damn thing," Nancy swore out loud. "We'll drive the buggers out of France then out of Europe, that's what. You can quote me on that my dear Captain."

"Thierry," Russell corrected. "You know the drill."

"Yes I do. I could have written the book on it."

"If you had written it, it would have to be censored."

Nancy laughed out loud. "No doubt about it. My mouth is what makes me who I am."

The two allies parted. Russell went directly to his room and turned on the hot water in the ancient bathtub in his room. A soaking bath was just what his aching muscles asked for in their pain.

Nancy hopped into her Citroën followed closely by her driver. She had scheduled a full day that included visits to three additional Maquis elements in the Auvergne. The driver utilized the back roads to reach their first destination that was about a two hour drive away. As they rounded a curve, smoke from a burning farmhouse almost obscured the road. As the car slowed, Nancy could see a number of burning bodies between the road and the farmhouse.

"What's all this?" she asked the driver.

"The German pricks did this," he explained. "The farmer was probably suspected of being in the Resistance so the Germans came and burned his farm. While they were at it, they killed his family and set their bodies on fire. They are sending a message to everyone that it is unwise to support the Resistance."

Nancy felt her stomach tighten as the smell of burning human flesh reached their car. She quickly put up her window but the smell lingered. *How can human beings be so brutal? She pondered. Such actions are certainly the low mark for the human race.*

She recalled a recent incident while visiting Henri Tardivat's group of Maquis to the west. Tardivat had set up an audacious plan to destroy an armaments store in Mount Mouchet that was being utilized by the Germans. The place was well guarded by the SS but Tardivat's daring plot called for the elimination of the guards, which then opened up the store for an assault. Nancy requested and was allowed to lead one of the four-man teams that would neutralize one of the two guards. All lights had been turned off and the entire area was pitch black.

It was determined that both squads would crawl up on their bellies to a point where they could engage the guards. A light rain had silenced the rustle of the leaves as the Maquis crawled closer to the guards. Nancy felt her throat dry up as the gravity of the situation encompassed her. This would be her first encounter with hand to hand combat, but she felt she was equal to the role.

The two sentries came together, about faced and began their return march. At the end of the sentries walk, when the SS soldiers could not really help each other, the Maquis plan was to be put into effect.

The time came and Nancy gave the signal. She stood and began running directly toward the sentry who was her target. As she neared the SS soldier, he began to turn toward her. He sought to bring his gun to bear with its bayonet slicing through the damp night air. Instinct took over and Nancy formed her right hand into an axe as she had been taught in the SOE's training course. The German's surprised look at the attacking woman turned to horror as her hand connected with his neck some two inches below the ear. He slumped to the ground as Nancy looked around to see the other group signaling that the other sentry had also been neutralized. It was the first time she had killed someone with her own hands, and that fact had not yet registered with the young woman. She felt a pain in her arm and saw a steady stream of blood oozing from a wound inflicted by the soldier's bayonet.

The other Maquis in her detail gathered around and wrapped Nancy's deep wound. They quickly set the charges around the building. The blasts that quickly followed caused severe damage to the armaments store.

Next, they immediately took Nancy to a friendly doctor nearby where the wound could be properly stitched. Nancy was near unconsciousness when she finally reached the doctor's home...

As the Citroën regained speed, Nancy remained in deep thought. The semblance of a plan had slowly begun to take shape in her mind that could possibly unite Gaspard and some of the other Maquis with whom she was working. She decided to continue to mull it over in her mind during the ride. She would then discuss it with Captain Russell on their next meeting. Nancy hoped ardently that he would agree to her idea.

René Alexander Dussaq was an extremely attractive, even-mustachioed United States Army 1st Lieutenant who enjoyed one of the most colorful pre-war careers of any infantry officer.

Born in Argentina to a Cuban diplomat, Dussaq was schooled in Geneva and became a star athlete as a young man. He captained the Swiss Olympic Rowing Team and was tennis champion of both Switzerland and Cuba.

He fled Cuba during a revolution and wound up in San Diego where he became a Hollywood stuntman. He was featured as a wing-walker, parachutist and stunt car driver. He was drafted into the US Army where he immediately attended Officer Candidate School. His skill in foreign languages made him an ideal candidate for the newly-formed Office of Strategic Services (OSS). He trained for his mission to France with members of the SOE-F and was a contemporary of a number of SOE-F agents including Nancy Wake Fiocca, Violette Szabo, Denis Rake and others. He was also with Fiocca at the Astor just prior to her leaving for France. The two danced together and were close friends.

Just over 30 years old, Dussaq's specialty was weapons. It was decided that he would be parachuted into the Auvergne where large numbers of new weapons were being dropped nightly to inexperienced members of Maquis and the FFI's.

He was dropped at a point southwest of the Village of Monton, almost directly south of Clermont-Ferrand. An action had already started with a German force in the area and Dussaq was placed in charge of a band of thirty young Maquis. The Maquis was surrounded in a wooded area by a force of about five hundred German Wehrmacht troops. Dussaq skillfully guided his band out of danger by using a river bed in the center of the woods that was divided by two German infantry groups. When the Germans opened fire a short time later, they succeeded in firing into each other, inflicting heavy casualties in the process.

But Dussaq's (code name Anselme) real mission was to link up with the SOE-F's Stationer Network and Major John Farmer (Hubert) in particular. After a near brush with the Gestapo in Chateauroux, he made his way to Montluçon where he awaited contact from the stationer Network.

He would not have long to wait.

The German Wehrmacht garrison at Vichy had waited patiently for just the right situation to arise. Generalmajor Curt von Jesser, a World War I veteran and senior Panzer commander decided the steady flow of information from his agents within the French Resistance and Maquis was genuine enough to start an action. His most recent intelligence placed the number of Maquis at nearby Mont Mouchet at between three and four thousand Maquis, the largest number of enemy fighters he would encounter in one place since the occupation of France.

He gathered his commanders together and outlined a plan. The feared Jesser Brigade of Panzers, all veterans of the eastern front, would occupy a position a mile and a half north of the suspected Maquis encampment. Other 9th Panzer Division units would be situated at another position southwest of Mount Mouchet. Some 1000 men from the Sicherungs Motorisierte Regiment and another 1000 men from the Aufklärungs Abteilung would be reinforced by a number of additional German military units. Included was an artillery battery of the 189th Reserve Division and three motorized reconnaissance platoons that had been ordered to the Auvergne from Paris.

A firm believer in air power and air superiority, Majorgeneral von Jesser also ordered help from two Luftwaffe squadrons from Luftwaffe Gruppe III~Schlachtgeschwader 4 at nearby Aulnat Airfield in Clermont-Ferrand.

The career military officer addressed his commanders. "For some reason the miserable Maquis have decided to gather themselves together in one wretched place. The site is around Mont Mouchet, and is at an elevation of around 4900 feet.

This particular place offers us an excellent opportunity to lob our artillery right upon them without any danger to our forces. I know there are few roads to work with but I want your Panzers deployed so that they have excellent line-of-sight to this area. The artillery battery of the 189th Reserve Division will be placed here." He pointed to a cross on the map, again within close proximity to the expected battlefield. "It's something of a high plateau and should be able to accommodate the artillery guns without a problem."

The assembled commanders nodded affirmatively to their leader.

"And, finally, gentlemen, for the best news. I have persuaded the Luftwaffe to give us a number of the new Fw 190's to cover our activities from the air. You must coordinate our attack with the Luftwaffe to prevent us from shooting down our own planes. If all goes well, we should catch the enemy by surprise and inflict heavy casualties. After all they have done to us recently; it is finally our chance for some real payback."

Chapter Thirteen

Her recent assignments for Gaspard's Maquis partisans had not set well with Christine Allard. She had been given several minor tasks to preform, but nothing like the important missions she had completed over the past two years.

Christine was sure Gaspard was repaying her for the incident where she took out the two German direction finding vehicles. *I know he was not happy with me after that episode, but that was a while ago. I realize I took some added chances that time, but I have learned my lesson. I think I will approach him and let him know how I feel. I'm sure he will relent and give me some more responsibility.*

It was mid-afternoon as she made her way to his guarded camp at Mont Mouchet to talk with him. The sentries waved her through the thick forest as she neared the site. She noticed an unusual number of Maquis gathered, more than she had ever seen at one time. *There must be thousands of youths here, but they are all strangely quiet, just standing around looking at each other. I wonder what is going on. I am not so comfortable with all these Maquis in one place. And it's so quiet, not much noise for so many men.*

Christine went directly to the part of the encampment area where she thought Gaspard could be found. The Maquis leader was there, surrounded by several of his men as they scrutinized a large map of the Auvergne. The men shook their heads in agreement as Gaspard looked up to see Christine.

"Ah, my dear Sofian. What brings you all the way out here? Are you here to see me? If so I am honored at the prospect."

He's being nice to me, I'm not sure how to take that, Christine thought. I'll just be myself and see what happens. He is so stubborn when he wants to be.

Gaspard finished his meeting and turned his attention to Christine.

"So, how are you Sofian? I hope you are well..."

Christine decided to forgo any pleasantries and get right to the point.

"Gaspard, I want to know when you are going to give me some more responsibilities. Let me do things that really make a difference."

Gaspard viewed the young woman whose face was deadly serious. *I thought as much. She's finally figured it out. This is what I wanted from her. She realizes she made a mistake and will not do the same thing again.*

"I am glad you came here Sofian. It's nice to see you."

"Please cut the niceties, Gaspard. I know you are disappointed in me. I want to do something about it."

"And you will, Sofian. That much I can promise you." The Maquis leader's face softened as he continued. "I just wanted you to understand what I was talking about, Sofian. It's not just your safety that is important; it is the safety of all those you might command. It is the same for me whenever I send out our heroes on dangerous missions. I must take into account their ultimate safety so that they may live to fight another day."

Christine remained silent, her eyes fixed on Gaspard.

"I believe you have learned a valuable lesson from all this. I think you will consider the consequences of your actions on the next task I assign you. I want..."

The sounds of a series of nearby explosions and shouting broke the relative silence of the camp. It was as if a series of thunderstorms were all breaking at the same moment.

"The Germans are attacking us!" one of Gaspard's men came through the door and shouted at his leader.

"What the hell ...?" Gaspard mumbled as he grabbed his STEN 9mm submachine gun. "Everyone get out of this as best you can. I have made plans for such an occurrence. It all depends on our outer defences. They are designed to make the Bosch pay for every yard they take. If we can hold them off till nightfall, we can all sneak out of here."

Christine looked around and finally located a Thompson M1 submachine gun.

She searched for some box magazines for the gun and finally located a pair. Scooping them up, she quickly made her way to a nearby group of partisans who were pinned down behind the corner of a small building. The group was unarmed and seemingly bewildered by the turn of events. She yelled at the group who turned to see a beautiful young woman approaching them.

"You must go back and get some weapons to defend yourselves. The guns are stored over there," she ordered roughly, pointing to the direction from which she had come. "You must be sure to get ammunition for the guns, and make sure it fits the gun before you leave. Do you know how to do that?"

One of the older men looked at her and shook his head. "Yes, mademoiselle. We have learned that much. Leave it to me."

"Good. I will cover you until you reach the guns. But be quick. I can only fire for a few seconds."

"Let's go!" the older partisan yelled. The small group started running with their heads lowered.

Christine stepped out from behind the corner and began firing small bursts from her gun. She looked back and saw the Maquis had made it safely to the area where the guns were stored.

I have to get out of here and find a spot where I can do some good with this Tommy gun. She glanced in several directions and decided to head back in the same direction she had just come from. She reached another corner of the small building and saw a thicket of trees about twenty yards from where she stood. *There. If I can only get there I will have some cover and possibly a way out of this mess.*

She started crawling on her stomach and finally reached the first of the large trees. Large explosions continued to rock the entire area. She pulled herself up and rested her back against one of the trees that offered protection from the firing. *Mortars, those are mortars exploding. I've heard enough of those sounds to identify them. We must be under attack by a large force if they are using mortars. I wonder how smart it was to have so many Maquis here at one time.*

The shelling continued for several hours. Christine was able to make her way deeper into the forest and eventually approached a clearing where a good deal of activity and loud noise was originating. She peered out from behind some foliage and was pleased to see a pair of Wehrmacht mortar teams busily loading and firing their weapons. Christine surveyed the area and saw that a position to her left would give her uninterrupted access to the enemy. Again she made her way quietly to the position directly behind the mortars. She cocked her Thompson and stepped out with the gun trained on the Germans.

Christine fired several bursts until all the enemy was down. She held her smoking weapon and surveyed the damage. She approached the dead soldiers and was startled when a voice called in her direction.

"*Viola, mademoiselle.* You have killed them all." A man materialized out of the woods and was soon followed by several others. The young Maquis gathered around Christine and patted her on the shoulders.

"Enough of that," Christine ranted. "They were already dead when I arrived. You take these mortars and as many rounds as you can carry and find a spot where you can train them on the Bosch. They are simple to operate, you just drop the rounds into the cylinders and they fire automatically."

"We can do it mademoiselle," one of the Maquis answered. "We were caught without any weapons when the enemy opened fire on the camp. We were fortunate to get to the forest and hide. We wanted to do something about the mortars but we didn't have any guns to fire at them."

"Pick up guns from any dead or wounded you come across. And, grab some ammunition if you can. It always comes in handy."

"Yes, of course. Let us get going now. Thank you again, mademoiselle."

"Call me Sofian," Christine answered. "And, may God's luck be with you."

"And you too, mademoiselle, er, Sofian. May we meet again…"

Christine watched as the Maquis drifted off into the woods. She glanced around and decided to take a path that appeared beyond the clearing. If she was lucky, she could hide herself until night came. Then she could escape along with her other Maquisard brethren.

Nancy Wake Fiocca returned to her hotel at Chaudes-Aigues the same evening that Russell had returned. She was exhausted from her travels but secure in the knowledge that several more Maquis bands had been financed and had received instructions from London. Her mission was all beginning to come together, she decided. She was well into improving the performance of the Auvergne Maquis bands.

She encountered Russell in the small chamber that served as the hotel's waiting room. He looked greatly refreshed and greeted her warmly. "I see you made it back safely, Madame Andrée. I trust you had a fruitful day?"

"Actually, it was quite rewarding. I was able to accomplish everything I set out to do and even a little more." She paused and continued. "I see you have been able to freshen up. You look a sight better."

"I was also able to grab a long nap this afternoon. Nothing like sleeping in a bed after being out in the wild for a while."

"I know how it is. We have had to rough it now and then ourselves."

"I'm sure Roland (Denis Rake) loves roughing it," Russell joked. "It is his nature."

Nancy laughed out loud at the obvious pun. "He certainly does. He doesn't stop squealing until it's finished."

"Nature of the beast," Russell added. "But he's such a good sod."

"That he is. I wouldn't trade him for anyone else."

The conversation drifted until Nancy asked him point blank, "Well, how did your mission fare? London wanted a report back as soon as possible. They even mentioned it on one of their transmissions to me."

Russell considered his options and replied, "I guess it would do no harm to let you see my report. After all the traveling around the Auvergne, I came to one simple conclusion."

"Oh?"

"Yes. The one almost perfect place for a real battle with anyone is the plateau right above here in Chaudes-Aigues. It's almost flawless for several reasons. It commands a view of the entire area and is easy to defend. A small force could keep a much larger force at bay if they had the right guns and equipment. It also offers some excellent escape routes if you know the area. The Maquis had the right idea when they set up their base camp here. Someone thought long and hard about the location.

Aside from some minor points, that's the gist of my report. I have a list in my room if you want it."

"We'll give it to Denden right away. He can send it off at the first chance. London will be interested in what you have to say."

"By the way, has Denden been a good boy while I was gone?"

"A perfect angel," Nancy replied. "He really can't get into much trouble up here, can he?"

"You have a point Madame Andrée. There aren't really many opportunities for anyone to get into trouble."

Just then a messenger walked in the sitting room. He identified himself as a member of Gaspard's Maquis and informed Nancy that Gaspard's force had been attacked by a large force of German soldiers. A number of Maquis had been killed and wounded and a number of survivors would be headed toward Chaudes-Aigues to join up with Laurent's Maquis. They could be expected within the next twenty-four hours."

Nancy thanked the man and told him to fetch himself something to eat at a house close by the hotel.

She turned to Russell and spoke. "Well now, our German cousins have finally decided to do something specific about the Maquis around here. I was wondering when they would get around to that. We must really be hurting them if they are compelled to send a large force to subdue us. That's really good news and London will be delighted to hear it. I will be sure to add it to the report Denden will send."

This is nice and peachy, or so it seems. Gaspard will now be forced to accept our help. I need to get him up here and spell it all out. After this incident with the Wehrmacht, he won't be so high and mighty. The German attack actually worked to our benefit. She returned her attention to Russell.

"I think it is time to have all the Maquis leaders assemble to develop a strategy in case we are attacked. And, our most difficult Gaspard must also attend. It will be necessary to get him to agree to our strategy if we are to succeed. He still commands most of the men in the Auvergne even if he isn't the smartest sod around." She paused a moment to think about her next remarks. She looked directly at Russell and continued.

"I also want your advice on something. If Gaspard balks as I think he will, I want to try something different."

Russell looked at the woman, a puzzled look on his face.

"I want to get him off to the side and tell him exactly who I am."

"You mean about the White Mouse?"

"Exactly. In London I was told that the White Mouse was the most famous SOE agent in France, and that everyone in the French Resistance knew about her and the five million franc reward the Germans had posted. If all that is true, then I must believe that even someone like Gaspard would bend in the face of a suggestion from the White Mouse. Why would London have sent such a person back to France if the job were not incredibly important?"

Russell considered Nancy's appeal. *She has a point all right. No Resistance leader in his right mind would say no to a true heroine of the Resistance. The Germans have seen to that, increasing her stature by placing such a high value on her life. I guess it's worth a try.*

"You see to your report," Russell directed, nodding his concurrence to her plan. "I'll go round up Laurent and have messengers sent to the other Maquis chiefs. We should gather them as soon as possible; we have no idea what the Germans are planning."

"Right. I'm off to find Denden. He might even be snoozing if I know him at all."

Russell watched her leave and started off to find Laurent. He was unsure of just how much time he had to act.

Rene Dussaq (Anselme) had teamed up with the semi-trained Maquis under the command of Colonel Thomas. He had tried to explain to the old colonial soldier that the weapons that were supplied to them by the British were for commando-style fighting, and not the classic military style of defending one's position from attack.

One aspect of Anselme's training had attracted the immediate attention of the leaders of the Auvergne Maquis. The M1 bazooka, an antitank rocket launcher, had been dropped to the Maquis courtesy of the United States Army. Dussaq loved the weapon and was an expert in its use. The Maquis admired his passion for the weapon and soon referred to him as Captain Bazooka.

Within ten days of his arrival in France, Dussaq had taught the better part of more than 7,000 Auvergne Maquis the subtle art of firing the stovepipe-looking weapon. He directed that these weapons and suitable rocket-charged warheads be dispersed to individual Maquis units so as to achieve greatest results.

The efficient US Army 1st Lieutenant than set about convincing the Maquis leaders that commando tactics were their best chance of defeating superior troops who were often better trained and better equipped. Anselme had some success with the more insightful leaders. Fournier (Laurent) readily agreed and so did a few others. Some disagreed strongly, among them Gaspard and the ageing Colonel Thomas.

"My men are brave and not afraid to die," Gaspard offered. "We will defeat the Bosch one way or another. We know these mountains better than the Germans and that will help us."

"Many will *die*," Anselme concurred. "If you don't use hit and run tactics. Get the enemy to break into small groups where you have superiority and in places that they are unfamiliar. That way you have all the advantage. It might take a while, but you will win in the end."

"We could win right now if the Allies would send us tanks and bigger guns!" Gaspard nearly shouted. "And, what about airplanes that could bomb the Jerries into submission? The Germans use their Junkers on us whenever they have a chance. Why can't the allies do something about that?"

Anselme saw that it was useless to argue with the Maquisard leader and went about his job of training the Maquis on their new equipment. Practically every clear night brought a new assortment of guns and equipment that were vital to the French Resistance. The US Army officer soon became familiar with the complexities of the Auvergne itself and its natural advantage for being able to wage the type of warfare that London considered so important.

Wherever he travelled, Captain Bazooka carried his signature weapon. He was the toast of the region and was warmly welcomed wherever he set foot.

Gaspard was totally shaken by the recent events that had forced him to abandon his encampment at Mont Mouchet. He had lost more than 150 of his Maquis troops along with another large number of wounded. His men had scattered as best they could and were now largely unaccounted for. He dispatched his lieutenants in different directions order his men to Chaudes-Aigues. He had no idea how many would respond to his call.

Worst of all, he blamed himself for everything that had happened. He pondered the situation as he headed toward the new headquarters. I grew too lackadaisical about the enemy and its ability to pursue us. That was simply stupid of me. Maybe I should designate some more responsibility to my officers instead of trying to do it all myself? And, the fact that I let so many men gather in one place, well, that was stupid also. The fact is we barely escaped with our lives, those of us that were lucky enough to get out of there? Why didn't I have a better escape route planned? That would have been the smart thing to do. *Another major blunder on the part of their leader. I can't make the same mistakes again or my men will wind up shooting me or something. I'll have to start all over again, from the beginning. And if we are lucky and the Germans don't attack again, well maybe this will work itself out. I wonder if London will continue sending us all those weapons and supplies after this, I wonder if they have lost confidence in me as a leader.*

The truck carrying the Maquis leader continued its steady climb toward Laurent's hideout. In another twenty minutes, Gaspard would have to face his men again. For the first time since he had assumed command, he felt a twinge of doubt creeping into his mind. He quickly dismissed the thought. He assured himself he would never allow the setbacks of Mont Mouchet to occur again while he was in command.

The following day found the leaders of the Auvergne Maquis seated around a table in the hotel that served as Laurent's headquarters. Gaspard presided over the gathering that included all his chief commanders, Madame Andrée, Anselme and Thierry. Gaspard had decided it would be wise to address his shortcomings and take whatever his group decided as to his role of continuing leadership.

"I must apologize to everyone here," he began in a low tone. "Because of my miscalculations, I allowed my forces to be attacked by the Wehrmacht at Mont

Mouchet. I felt our location was invulnerable and I allowed a large number of Maquis to gather there. We were taken by surprise and a large number of our compatriots were either killed or wounded."

"How many were killed, Gaspard?" Nancy asked. "Do you know for sure?"

"I am told that around 150 or more are dead and another larger number were wounded. I am not sure of the exact number."

A dead silence ensued, no one wishing to speak.

"Well, we cannot bring them back to life," Nancy finally declared. "What's important is what we do about it. I believe we all agree on that."

"Thank you my friends," Gaspard replied. "I was prepared to step down as your leader if you desired."

"No, no, Gaspard, the men look up to you too much," one of the men at the table said. "It would be bad for the entire movement for you to step down."

Gaspard waited a few moments, and then spoke. "Very well, I will remain. That is, if it is okay with London for me to stay."

Nancy spoke hesitantly, "There is too much to do for you to leave, Gaspard. You have already accomplished a great deal." *What I really mean is that this would be a great time to get rid of the uncooperative bastard. But, reorganization would be a bloody mess and we simply don't have time to do it.*

Gaspard regained control of the meeting. "I have given orders for as many of our Maquis to make their way up here to Chaudes-Aigues whenever they feel safe to do so. I know it will increase our numbers here, but there was little choice. This plateau can be well defended and I want to work on possible escape routes should they become necessary.

It seems obvious to me that we are doing some real harm to our enemies if they are willing to send such a large force to try and kill or capture us. We must continue to harass them at every turn and inflict as much damage as possible. We know that they are sending reinforcements to Normandy through the Auvergne and we must try and stop those reinforcements from reaching the coast.

I know it will be impossible to stop all the troops, but if we can delay them to some extent, we will have accomplished a great deal. I am going to assign certain key roads and railroads to each of you. You must develop a plan to have these roads watched and contingencies made to alert our Maquis to stop any major movements."

The hardened Maquis leaders nodded their heads in agreement.

Nancy spoke up once again. "As *chef du parachutage*, I am asking London to supply us with the largest guns they have available. I know the bazookas have become a favorite of the Maquis thanks to Captain Bazooka here."

Anselme smiled and graciously accepted Nancy's praise.

"There will be a large number of bazookas dropped in the near future; starting tonight if the weather holds. Your men have already been taught how to use them and not even Panzer Tiger tanks are immune to this weapon.

And, take my word; Gaspard is absolutely correct on having escape routes available at all times. I will see to it that the supply of weapons and arms stops if I observe there are no escape routes planned for each operation!"

The men muttered to themselves at the small woman's latest outburst. Even if she was the *chef du parachutage*, and a killer of Germans in hand-to-hand combat, she was still a woman, and an Englishwoman at that.

Gaspard spoke again. "Now, if you will all sit down with your officers and come up with some plans, I will show you your specific areas. Let me know if you have any reservations or questions, now is the time to express such opinions."

He proceeded to take out a large, detailed map of the Auvergne. "Laurent, since you are headquartered here in Chaudes-Aigues, your area of concentration will be from here to here." He pointed at the map and followed an area that had been circled. And, Colonel Thomas, here is your..."

Violette Szabo had been taken from Limoges Prison to the much larger Fresnes Prison located just southwest of Paris near Orly Airport. A day later, she was taken to Gestapo headquarters at 84 avenue Foch. The beautiful and elegant avenue was lined with trees that led from the Place de' l'Etoile towards the Bois de Boulougne.

The Sicherheitsdienst (SD) Headquarters was commanded by Waffen SS

Sturmbannfuhrer Joseph Kieffer, a professional police officer who had joined the SS in 1933. Kieffer was a professional in all aspects of the job and treated most prisoners at 84 avenue Foch with restraint and respect even though he was known to have struck male French prisoners during interrogation.

Clean shaven and looking the part of an Aryan in every respect, Kieffer was a feared man by everyone he faced. That is, with the exception of Violette Szabo.

When Kieffer first interviewed Violette, she looked down at him with disdain as she stood in front of his desk. She continued her charade as Vicky Taylor and actually demanded to be set free at once.

"But, mademoiselle," Kieffer explained, "that is impossible. Your record shows that you were caught in a gunfight with our soldiers. You had a STEN gun in your possession and it is believed you killed and wounded several of the Third Reich's panzer soldiers."

"They started shooting at us. Was I to stand around and get shot? Ask the others who were with me, your soldiers started shooting first."

"Unfortunately, you were the only person captured. The others managed to escape according to my report. To your credit, the panzer unterofficer thought you to be the bravest woman he has ever faced. He noted it in his report."

"I would have gotten away too if I hadn't been hit in my foot. It hurt so much! I couldn't go on any longer."

Kieffer regarded the young woman with such beautiful eyes and thought. *This is one resilient woman. The sergeant was right about her. She isn't afraid of me or anyone else. And, her demanding to be released when we first met was something else. That took some fortitude all right. I'm glad the French don't have a lot more like her; it would make this struggle even more difficult. I'm afraid there isn't much to do here but send her along. I don't think she would crack even if I gave her to the SD for some of their treatment. No need to waste such an attractive woman on those dogs.*

Three days later, Kieffer signed the papers that would ultimately send Violette Szabo to the Ravensbrück concentration camp in Germany. He knew it would not be a pleasant trip for the young woman.

A number of stories related to the German attack on Mont Mouchet had reached the camp at Chaudes-Aigues, told mostly by survivors of the sad events at the campsite. There were several accounts of bravery on the part of Maquis soldiers. US Army Captain Brian Adams Russell listened to the stories with particular interest. He wanted to learn from the mistakes made by the Maquis, and in particular their lack of escape routes for their partisans. One of the stories was about Nancy's treatment of the SS sentry, possibly embellished by the hero-starved young Maquis. Even though it had not occurred during the pitched battle at Mont Mouchet, it somehow became part of the lore than accompanied the battle.

He questioned a number of Maquis who were at Mont Mouchet and decided that over confidence by the Maquis leadership was to blame for so many dead. The fact that Gaspard and his officers thought the camp impenetrable was bad enough, but the fact that so many Maquis had been allowed to gather in such a small area was inexcusable. He fired off a report to London that outlined his feelings and included suggestions to fix the problem. He proposed breaking the Maquis down into smaller units and fixing exact areas of responsibility for each. He also implied a scenario where one unit could contact another unit if it ran into trouble, a sort of buddy system for the units involved. He stated he would be happy to improvise such a system if London thought it necessary. He did not, however, call directly for Gaspard to be replaced as head of the Auvergne Maquis. He felt the established boss of the Maquisards had learned from his mistakes and would not be prone to such bad decisions in the future.

As to the story concerning Nancy, it seemed her beauty and fearlessness increased with each telling. *She is something else. I realize she is a good fighter and good for our mission. She is perfect for the Auvergne Maquis right now; they desperately need someone or something to feel good about.*

Russell continued his interviews with additional Maquis survivors. Any parcel of information that he could glean from these men would prove helpful to London.

Chapter Fourteen

Nancy had attempted to get Gaspard alone several times but had always found the Maquis leader surrounded by underlings and too busy to see her. She bided her time and finally found a moment when he seemed unoccupied. She approached him and patted him on the back.

Gaspard looked up at the young woman and half-smiled. "Madame Andrée, just what can I do for you this morning?"

"I want to talk with you a minute, Gaspard. It's important, just you and I."

"This *sounds* important, Madame Andrée. Of course you can." He motioned to one of his Maquis that was standing guard to keep anyone out. The guard acknowledged and moved outside the room. The two were now alone.

"Gaspard," Nancy began, "I didn't want to have to resort to this, but your lack of cooperation in important matters forces me to tell you ..."

"But, I am cooperating of late..."

"Please let me finish, Gaspard." She paused and continued. "We need your full cooperation on what we are doing, not just when it is convenient for you. London had been very specific as to what we should be doing here in the l'Auvergne, and they are planning for the entirety of France, not just one part. If everyone doesn't cooperate fully, the whole process is put in danger."

Gaspard listened attentively but did not interrupt her.

"The next few weeks and months are imperative to what we are doing. I don't want to have to plead with you about my orders, there simply isn't enough time for all that bullshit. You know what I mean. The other commanders agree and you

181

choose to disagree. It doesn't make sense."

Gaspard felt his blood pressure rising and started to reply, but chose to hold his tongue.

"I suppose you have heard of the White Mouse," Nancy continued.

Gaspard nodded and spoke. "But, of course. She is the Resistance heroine of Marseille and has a five million Franc reward on her head. The Gestapo has her on the top of their list of most wanted persons."

"Correct. That is all correct."

"Why do you ask me about the White Mouse?"

"Because I am the White Mouse, Gaspard. I wanted you to know who you are dealing with on these matters."

"How can you be the White Mouse, Madame Andrée? You cannot be in two places at the same time."

"You are correct again, Gaspard. I was compelled to leave Marseille when the Gestapo got too close and forced to flee this country through Spain. When I reached England, the SOE decided to continue sending information to the Gestapo to make them believe I was still operating in France. I think the bastards still believe I am somewhere around Marseille."

Gaspard considered her words but said nothing.

"I wanted you to know this because I want you to see just how important your cooperation is to what we are doing. If London didn't believe this was among the most important missions in France do you think they would have taken a chance of sending me back to help you?"

Gaspard looked directly into the eyes of the fiery woman as the revelation of her declaration sunk in. He knew she was telling the truth.

"So you are the White Mouse, Madame Andrée. I would never have believed it, but what you say makes some sense."

"You can check with your FFF sources. They can query London and London will confirm my identity."

"I don't need to do that," Gaspard lied. His intention, however, was to do just that as soon as possible. After all, anyone could walk in and say they were the White Mouse, right?

"I will try and cooperate more fully, Madame Andrée. You have my word on that."

"Good. And by the way, I would prefer that no one else know the part about the White Mouse. No point shaking up the can as it were."

"As you wish. It will be our secret."

"Thank you for your time, Gaspard. I hope all this proves fruitful."

She rose and left the room. Gaspard called his guard back and gave him some instructions. The wheels were already turning to check on Madame Andrée's story. Gaspard thought Nancy's story was probably true, but decided to check it out anyway. One could never be too careful in matters like this.

The large number of incoming Maquis at Chaudes-Aigues had swelled the fighting force to many thousands. Most of these fighters were unfed and only partially uniformed. They presented a multitude of logistical problems to Laurent and his unit that were in effect, the host entity for the Auvergne Maquisards.

In her role as *chef du parachutage*, Nancy had been able to provide additional supplies with more frequent airdrops whenever the weather cooperated. Practically all the useable dropping sites were pinpointed, with multiple drops occurring each allowable night. The amount of weapons and ammunition increased to more than acceptable levels but the problem of fresh food and sanitary conditions were particularly alarming.

The German Wehrmacht soldiers that were garrisoned in and around the Auvergne were also aware of the increased activity in the area. Vichy sympathizers and spies were dispatched to gather information from food stores and bakeries as to any suspicious activity. Anything out of the ordinary was to be reported to the authorities at once for fear of arrest and imprisonment.

Along with the successful dropping of weapons and ammunition, additional amounts of Franc notes were also included, a fact that allowed the Maquis to buy food supplies directly from farmers. Eggs, hams, homemade breads, vegetables and other basic items were readily available from the farmers who were delighted to be paid for their goods. Since, by necessity, the Maquis had formerly stolen such items, these payments were a welcome relief to the farmers of the area.

Nancy Wake Fiocca was busy attending to some upcoming drops when US Army Captain Brian Russell approached her. She nodded to him as she kept on counting from a list she was handling.

"Madame Andrée, if I could have a minute," Russell opened. "I think it's quite important that I speak to you."

"Of course, Thierry. I *always* have time for you…"

Russell smiled. He was used to her flirtatious ways. "I am becoming anxious about the large number of Maquis we have here," he began. "I estimate there are more than six thousand or so partisans here. I cannot tell exactly how many as they tend to move around a lot."

"I think it is closer to seven or perhaps a bit more," Nancy replied. "I had a couple of the officers go out and count and that's what they came back with."

"That's even worse. I am beginning to see a parallel between Chaudes-Aigues and Mont Mouchet. Too many soldiers gathered in one place at one time. The Germans aren't exactly stupid and if I were them I'd allow as many fighters to join us here as possible. Then they could surprise us with an all-out attack. If they were successful, it would disrupt Maquis operations here in l'Auvergne for some time. Maybe even forever."

"I, too, have concerns about our numbers, Thierry. I spoke to Gaspard and he doesn't believe it to be serious as of yet. He said that this plateau is much larger than Mont Mouchet and that he has developed a number of escape routes in case we are attacked. He has also set out a large number of sentries to report on any movement of German troops or equipment."

"What about the Stukas? Much of this area is uncovered. If the Luftwaffe sends out a large number of planes, many of our men would be sitting ducks. There are few places to hide around here, don't you agree?"

"Yes, I agree completely. But Gaspard is stubborn as hell. Once he sets his mind, there is little that can change it."

"Did you tell him about the White Mouse?"

"Yes, but I'm not sure he truly believed me. I have a feeling he's having my story checked. His attitude hasn't changed much, at least not on the surface."

"He's something of an idiot, that's what. He should never been in command of so many partisans."

"Well, for better or worse, he is in command. We simply have to work through him if we want to get anything accomplished."

"I know that, but I don't have to like it."

"Neither do I, Thierry. Neither do I."

Christine Allard was on her way to join the Maquis units at Chaudes-Aigues.

She had confiscated an old bicycle and begun her journey to the south. If nothing stopped her, she would be in Chaudes-Aigues the following day. As she continued pedaling, a sudden early summer shower covered the area. Christine quickly pulled off the road and sought shelter under a clump of tall trees. She would wait until it stopped raining to continue her ride. She was pleased that she was able to remain completely dry under the thick branches of the forest.

I used to do this as a young girl she remembered. *Whenever it rained my friends and I would take shelter under some branches and tell stories to each other. The time would pass by quickly and soon the rain would stop. I guess a lot has happened since then. I am no longer a young girl. Not with all that I have already gone through...*

As the shower abated, Christine rolled her bicycle onto the wet road. She would take her time on the slippery surface until the road dried out.

It was evident to Rene Dussaq (Anselme) that the biggest problem the Auvergne Maquis faced was the inability of its officers to make correct decisions. Since the Normandy invasion, Maquis number had grown to huge proportions and the Maquis leaders had not grown along with their swelling numbers.

Anselme continued his mission from London---training the Maquis in use of guns and captured artillery and doing whatever he could to aid the Maquis' struggle against the Milice and Gestapo. He was thwarted in most situations that involved military planning and following the course of guerilla warfare. Maquis leaders, sensing a change in the direction of the war, suddenly became bolder in their missions, decisions that frequently lead to destruction and deaths of their Maquis troops.

Even the fact that he was Captain Bazooka and universally recognized by even the lowest Maquis had little effect. *These idiots will simply not listen to an outsider about tactics. They feel they have been doing it so long and with such success, they have the right to make their own decisions without help. That might be okay to think like that, only so many young Maquis are being slaughtered due to inefficient planning and the like.*

He presented his case to US Army Captain Brian Russell when he returned to Chaudes-Aigues.

After listening to his fellow agent's plight, Russell replied. "I agree with you Anselme, I am facing a lot of the same shit. We can see the big picture but our Maquis commanders, with the exception of Laurent, simply cannot. The problem starts with Gaspard and when the commanders see him doing what he wants, they follow suit. I have radioed London, but there is little we can do. His officers seem to have confidence in him, no matter what has happened."

"We are letting ourselves get into the same problem here," Anselme countered. "Too many of our people in one place. The Germans will know all about this huge plateau and they will figure out how to attack us. It is just a matter of time."

"I fear sooner than later, The Krauts won't want to miss out on this chance. We have been hurting them too much lately."

"This is crap, Thierry. We will all get killed if we don't do something about it."

"Perhaps. I just don't happen to have a spare plan handy. Do you?"

Anselme shook his head in disgust. "I think I will head to somewhere else where I can do some real good. Perhaps I'll head over to the Allier. I hear that Tardivat's group has done some real good."

"That's your decision Anselme. My orders say to stay here and help the partisans. That's what I intend to do."

"God bless, Thierry. I have enjoyed working with you."

"Same for me, Anselme. You have been an excellent teacher. I wish you well."

The older American officer stood and started making his way down the terrain around Chaudes-Aigues. After a few minutes, he was completely out of sight.

Russell looked around and saw little signs of movement among those gathered at the large camp sight. *Anselme is right about certain things. If the Germans mount an all-out attack, many here will be killed and wounded. I guess that's just how it has to be.*

The lack of noise and near stillness at the camp also caught the attention of Nancy Fiocca and Denis Rake. At length, Nancy turned and spoke to her radio operator.

"This silence certainly speaks to the fact that there isn't much to do around here, don't you think, Denden?"

"It's a bit eerie, all right. With this many fighters gathered, you'd think there was at least a loud hum. "

"I agree, Denden. I wonder is Gaspard has noticed. He isn't particularly aware of those sorts of things these days. I guess Gaspard feels that time is on his side. People forget things soon enough anyway, and for him later is certainly better."

"He really hasn't had much to say lately. His mood and presence have been rather subdued."

"I can't really blame him. Until the heat is off I think he will maintain a low profile."

"Invisible is more like it. I really haven't seen him around much."

"He has been in meetings a great deal, making plans or something. It took me two days to see him alone when I really needed to talk to him."

"Sometimes I think he does too much planning. Maybe it is the effect of what happened on Mont Mouchet. Now he pays attention to every little detail."

"He is determined not to let the same thing happen again, that's all."

"But you can see that more and more Maquis arrive here each day. There are thousands of young men all milling around with little to do."

"I am aware of that Denden. I had a conversation with Thierry about that earlier today. Thierry doesn't think there is anything we can do. As long as Gaspard's mind is made up, the numbers here will continue swelling."

"Can we get enough supplies to feed and equip them all?"

"Denden, you know I have queried London for additional airdrops and more money. I'm sure they will acquiesce to our needs. We'll be in really poor shape if they don't."

"I'm not sure they are satisfied with Gaspard's leadership anymore. That might influence their decision."

Nancy paused, reflecting on Rake's statement. "You might be right, but we have so much already invested here. It wouldn't make sense to stop supplying us at this time."

"Do the decisions from London always make sense? I'm not always sure…"

"We are not in a position to question *any* decisions, Denden. We are here to follow orders and follow we will."

"I didn't mean…"

"Forget it, Denden. I know what you meant."

Denis Rake looked at his watch and announced, "It's almost time for us to receive London's transmission. I hope it's all good news."

"It better be. We are in a serious situation here. And, it seems to be getting worse by the day."

Denis stood and moved toward the door. "See you in a few minutes. I hope this won't take too long."

Nancy watched her assistant leave and pondered the situation. *London had better agree to what I asked for or we will be in the shitter with no way out. Damn that stupid bastard Gaspard for being so stubborn. He's only hurting himself with all this foolishness, but he can't see that.* She returned to the present and glanced at her watch. Only three minutes had passed since Denis Rake had departed.

Back in London, Colonel Maurice Buckmaster had finally approved Nancy Fiocca's request for additional airdrops of supplies and money. Since there was no assurance the money would fall directly into her hands, a simple switch had been made in cartons labeled Sanitary Napkins. No self-respecting Frenchman would consider opening such a package and Nancy would be on the lookout for just such a carton. As an added precaution, a layer of napkins was also placed on top of the stacks of French francs.

Buckmaster passed the orders on to Vera Atkins who channeled them to the proper departments. Within minutes, Lorries were dispatched to several warehouses where the supplies destined for France were stored. Two hours later, several United States Army Air Force B-24's were readied for their important mission.

Crews were briefed on specific dropping areas and coded messages were sent to Maquis units on the next scheduled BBC broadcasts. At 2120 hours, these same B-24's accelerated down the RAF Station Tempsford runway and slowly transitioned to flight.

In less than two hours, they would deliver their precious cargoes to the needy inhabitants of the Chaudes-Aigues plateau. Due to the seriousness of the situation, it was decided to drop the supplies directly over the assembled partisans. Instructions were sent to France to be prepared for such an eventuality. Maquis commanders on the ground designated a number of special squads to retrieve the supplies and distribute them to the correct units. For so large an accumulation of Maquis fighters, this was no easy task to accomplish. Special fires were readied for the upcoming drops. The final elements of the operation were in place for but ten minutes when the first sounds of approaching aircraft were detected.

Orders were quickly given and a series of bonfires were lit to guide the B-24's.

In another ten minutes, parachutes could be seen floating toward the earth. The squads that had been assigned to collect the supplies quickly went about their business and even conscripted some other Maquis to help carry the cartons back to a central storage point in the camp.

Nancy Wake Fiocca was also part of the operation. As *chef du parachutage*, she was unofficially in charge of the entire drop. In reality, Nancy was discreetly searching for the carton that contained the French francs that were so necessary for the maquis' continued operations.

At one point, a bearded Maquis approached her and sheepishly handed her a carton. Nancy looked at the package and accepted it with a knowing nod of her head. Her courageous Maquisards would be able to buy their food as soon as she could disburse the money. She made her way back to the building that served as the camp's headquarters. The wise agent had designed a safe hiding place for her valuable shipment when she first started receiving the additional monies. Nancy made sure no one was looking and carefully slid the package under a pair of wooden floorboards that were conveniently loose and moveable. Satisfied that the money was now safe, she replaced the boards and left the room. Moments later, she was back in the fields directing the deployment of the newly arrived supplies.

The miserable conditions for prisoners at Ravensbrück Concentration Camp were worse than Violette Szabo could have ever imagined. The camp itself was situated some fifty miles north of Berlin, on the banks of Lake Fürstenberg. The land was rumored to be the property of SS Reichsführer Heinrich Himmler or of a company of which he held ownership.

Violette was one of about 60,000 women prisoners that were being held at Ravensbrück. The camp's commandant was SS Hauptstrumführer Fritz Sühren, an iron-fisted veteran of German concentration camps.

Prisoners were identified by different colored patches on their arms. Green triangles identified common criminals and red triangles were for political prisoners of all nationalities, including German citizens. Black triangles were reserved for prostitutes and gypsies, while Jews were forced to wear yellow stars. Women accused of having sex with non-Aryans wore yellow and red stars while prisoners jailed for religious beliefs wore purple triangles. The main work of the women at the camp consisted of making uniforms for the Waffen SS. Some prisoners also became forced labor for companies such as BMW, Siemens, Krupp and aircraft producer Heinkel.

The effects of the long journey took its toll on Violette Szabo. She was now quite pale, and much thinner than when she was first arrested. Violette had two close friends at the camp, both SOE-F agents. The two women were wireless operators Denise Bloch and Lilian Rolfe.

Life at the camp was a page from the Book of Hell. Rows of triple bunks that were covered with straw mattresses held at least two prisoners to each bunk. A shrill siren sounded at 0300 and all prisoners had to be dressed and standing outside by 0345. Since their wardrobes consisted of only one thin dress, no one ever undressed for bed. All prisoners were forced to stand outdoors under the glaring illumination of Ravensbrück's numerous searchlights. No one, not even the sick or dying, was excused from the roll call.

Violette decided that she wanted to plan an escape from the camp and began talking with other prisoners she trusted about such an idea. Before anything was finalized, she was sent to Torgau, seventy-five miles south of Berlin, to work in a munitions factory on the Elbe River.

Conditions at Torgau were only slightly better than at Ravensbrück. Food was of better quality but still limited in quantity. And for Violette Szabo, Torgau represented a chance to renew a friendship begun at Fresnes Prison after her capture during the summer.

Marie Lecomte was 40 at the time, and more than fifteen years older than Violette. She had been imprisoned for her Resistance work around her home in Morlaix in Brittany. Marie was French and had been badly beaten when arrested. She bore signs of the brutal treatment on her face and body. Violette looked at Marie as something of a surrogate mother and always referred to her as Madame Marie. The pair became close and took care of each other during hard times, which was just about always.

A dispute among prisoners about producing munitions for the German Army brought SS Hauptstrumführer Fritz Sühren to Torgau to settle the matter. Sühren indiscriminately picked out half the women prisoners and ordered them sent to an even harder work camp located at Königsberg. Situated more than 300 miles away in East Prussia, the camp was among the most horrible in Germany.

Violette, Marie, Denise and Lilian were among the unfortunates sent to Königsberg. They found the place absolutely deplorable, left so by Russian prisoners from before. The place had little heating, was infested with vermin and had terrible food. A single loaf of bread would feed the fourteen women assigned to each hut. Soup made from water and mixed with unwashed scraps of beet and potato peelings was the only other nourishment available.

Königsberg broke the spirits of most of the women, even that of Violette Szabo. The once cheerful, bright eyed young woman was suddenly a disheartened soul. Any thoughts of escape from these impossible conditions were now gone.

Christine Allard was completely taken back by the huge number of Maquis fighters lingering around as she approached the main buildings of the Maquis camp at Chaudes-Aigues. At the same time, Gaspard emerged from the main building and spotted the young woman.

"Sofian, I am glad that you ave made your way here. Did you have any problems along the way?"

"Not really, Gaspard. I took my time and traveled on the back roads. I really didn't encounter any Bosch on my trip."

Gaspard looked at the woman with understanding, but Christine sensed he was far away in his thoughts.

"You don't seem yourself, Gaspard. Is everything okay around here?"

Gaspard paused for a moment. *Should I tell her about my failures?* His face tightened noticeably as he began. "It is quite simple, Sofian. I made a huge mistake in underestimating the facts at Mont Mouchet. I allowed the Germans to have an advantage that should never have happened. We lost a lot of brave young men who should still be alive and fighting with us."

"But it was not entirely your fault. How could you have known about the attack?"

"It was the precautions I did not take that were my fault. I allowed too many Maquis to gather and gave no thought as to escape routes if we were attacked. I was their leader. It was entirely my fault they were killed." Gaspard's head hung as he sunk down in despair.

Christine looked at Gaspard and felt instant empathy for the man. *I know he has his faults, but lack of caring is not one of them. I think he is overburdened with all the responsibility he carries and that has caused him such anguish. I wish there was something I could do to help.*

Christine finally broke the silence. "What do you want me to do, Gaspard? I'll do anything you feel is good for our cause. Just tell me and it's done."

Gaspard raised his head and started speaking. "You can do whatever I assign you, at least for the immediate future. That's what will help right now. I will attempt to correct the entire incident of Mont Mouchet sometime in the future. You have my word on that."

She thought for a moment and nodded her head. "Consider it done, Gaspard. I want to do what is best for our movement."

"I know that, Sofian. Thank you for your support."

"You are welcome," she replied solemnly.

"Now, go and put some food in your stomach. I can't believe you have eaten much on your journey up here."

"You are right. I'm quite famished."

"The food is over there," he pointed to another smaller building. "They will find you something warm and filling."

Christine left her leader's side and walked toward the nearby building. A good hot meal was something she could really use right now. She realized that she hadn't eaten in two days and was prepared to do something about it.

Chapter Fifteen

The futility of attempting to influence the Maquisard leadership lasted all of about thirty minutes for René Dussaq, code name Anselme. As he left the camp at Chaudes-Aigues, a feeling of disloyalty on his part formed in his mind and he immediately turned back toward the camp.

I have too much invested in all these men to simply leave, no matter what happens. I will see this through to its blasted end. No more feeling sorry for myself that I can't make these commanders see the errors of their ways. It's really not their fault anyway. Only one of two is an actually trained military officer, and he is among the most difficult to convince. I must find Thierry and tell him that I have decided to stay after all. I wouldn't want him telling anyone I was about to leave.

Anselme followed the same route back to where he had left Russell almost an hour before. He hoped his friend hadn't moved far from his last location.

US Army Captain Brian Russell witnessed the Maquis' new perception of Nancy Fiocca as she walked toward the main building of the Chaudes-Aigues camp.

They certainly seem to follow her every movement, he thought. *I guess it comes with killing a person with one's bare hands. It is good for Nancy, and has gained her a good deal of respect from the Maquis soldiers.*

He observed Nancy nod to several groups she passed and then stop to talk to another woman she encountered. The second woman's back was to him and Russell was unable to identify the other woman, a rarity in the Maquisard encampment.

Fifty yards away, Nancy spoke to Christine. "It's good to see you Sofian, have you eaten?"

"I've just finished, Madame Andrée. The food was just what I needed."

Nancy reached and took her hand. "Come with me, young lady. I have a place for you to take a bath if you wish."

Sofian acknowledged Nancy's offer and followed her toward the village and the hotel where the SOE agents were staying. They passed in front of hundreds of tired faces that smiled appreciatively as the two women walked by. Nancy acknowledged the smiles and proceeded forward. The pair entered the hotel and headed directly for Nancy's room.

"I'll try and arrange something specific for you tomorrow," Nancy said pointing to the hotel room. "For the present, you can consider this your room too."

"You are very kind," Christine returned. She squeezed Nancy's hand with genuine warmth. She had already sensed a warm affection with this remarkable woman.

The German Officer who commanded the Wehrmacht forces in the Auvergne could not believe the reports he was receiving. Generalmajor Curt von Jesser continued to finger the pieces of paper that his staff had assembled. He called his aide to confirm the accuracy of the reports.

"Are all these correct?" he asked abruptly. "The Resistance cannot be so stupid. Their Maquis are using the national highway to gather in Chaudes-Aigues and not trying to conceal the fact from us?"

"Jawohl, Herr Generalmajor. Such is the case. We arrested several of these filthy people and they confessed that they had just joined the Maquis and that they had been told to gather in Chaudes-Aigues."

"We are either extremely lucky or they are extremely reckless. They are inviting another attack." He thought for a moment and continued. "Have my staff gather here in one hour and plan for an attack. We must take advantage of this situation. With any luck, we will deal the Maquis a death blow once and for all."

"Jawohl, Herr Generalmajor. In one hour." He clicked his heels and saluted smartly.

The generalmajor turned his chair and studied a large map that had been pinned to the wall of his office. *This area is similar to Mont Mouchet but a great deal larger. I will need more troops if we are to contain these Maquis. There is only one national road in and out of here, but these fellows know the back roads better than we do. We must plan this carefully and then strike quickly. I will also need the help of the Luftwaffe again, even though it pains me to ask for help from those flying pricks who make it seem like a favor to actually help us bomb something.*

He stood and backed away from the map, but continued to study its intricateness. The experienced panzer leader was convinced this could be a great victory for the Third Reich if he did his job properly.

Nancy Wake Fiocca greeted her new guest with a smile and a sweet croissant when Sofian finally woke up the next morning. "I thought you could use the rest so I let you sleep," she remarked pleasantly. "All that hiking to get up here must have taken a lot out of you."

"I feel better today. I had my first decent sleep in more than a week."

"Enjoy it while you can, I'm sure Gaspard will find something for you to do right away."

"I certainly hope so. He seemed somewhat distant when we talked yesterday. I felt his mind was somewhere else. He paid attention to me but I don't think he really heard what I was saying."

"Gaspard has important matters to deal with at present. All these Maquis gathered here at Chaudes-Aigues present an inviting opportunity to the Germans. I can't believe they will wait very long to attack us."

"But surely Gaspard is aware of such things. At Mont Mouchet..."

"Gaspard is a stubborn man, Sofian. You must surely know that since you have worked with him for so long."

"Yes, he is stubborn," Sofian conceded. "But he is also a good leader. We have accomplished much here in the Auvergne. The Germans have put a high price on his head and he hasn't backed off one bit."

"I agree about his leadership qualities. What I don't care for is his inability to follow orders from higher sources. London, for one. He simply won't do what London asks. He is willing to take their arms and supplies. And, oh yes, their money. But when London tells him that he should distribute his forces out into guerilla units that have been so successful, he refuses. He wants to fight pitched battles against a better trained army. Such misconceptions will always end in defeat."

Christine did not answer and digested what Nancy had said. She finally raised her head and replied. "What you say makes sense. What can we do about it? It seems rather hopeless if he won't cooperate."

"We will do the best we can. I am supposed to go on a little trip tomorrow to talk to other Maquis commanders in another part of the country. I'm not sure it will do any good, but London wants me to try."

Sofian did not reply but took a bite of her *croissant* instead. She savored the flavor and spoke softly. "I haven't had one of these in a long time. I'm surprised you have them here."

"Money can buy almost anything, Sofian. And London is supplying us with loads of money at present. It certainly makes our job a bit easier."

"I agree, Madame Andrée, and it's nice to have some little pleasantries to enjoy. It sort of reminds me of what I have been missing."

"Yes, yes, Sofian. All of our men fight better with their stomachs full. I believe it has been that way throughout history."

"And it is mostly because of your efforts, Madame Andrée. I see the way the men have taken to you."

"All in a day's work, my dear. All in a day's work."

The German plan for the attack on Chaudes-Aigues called for a combined force of more than 10,000 men and equipment. Artillery points were set up some three miles from various targets and an agreement with the Luftwaffe was concluded that would supply the ground troops with at least ten Ju88's for air cover. Jesser's Panzers would again lead the German advance up the national road to the Maquis' suspected camp located on the large plateau.

The actual timetable for the attack was thirty-six hours from the time of his staff meeting, the time Jesser's staff felt was necessary for amassing the various components for the assault.

The generalmajor finally found time to relax in his quarters with a bottle of Obster Schnaps. His favorite flavor was a blend of apples and pears and was called an Obstwasser. He took a sip of the exquisite nectar and rolled it in his mouth. Satisfied he had extracted its wonderful pleasantness, he indulged himself with anther sip. He closed his eyes and contemplated. I had better make this stuff last, there's no telling when I will get another bottle. This one is half finished and I don't even remember the last time I had some. War is like that, some things you remember, some you don't.

His mind drifted and he returned to the present. *I have a good staff and they have made a good plan for our attack. If the Maquis want to fight it out with us, all the better. I'll take our crack troops and Panzers against an ill-trained and ill-equipped band of rag tail soldiers any day.*

He eyed the bottle of Obstwasser again but decided against another swig. *It is better for me to be of a clear mind when the attack begins. I'm already feeling the stuff a little and another shot would make things more difficult.*

Before she could leave the following day, Nancy was called by an alarmed member of the Maquis.

"Madame Andrée, you must come right away. Something terrible has happened. Roland is in trouble."

Nancy gathered her pistol and hurried after the man. She arrived at a location down the road from the camp where she confronted a singular Frenchman who was holding a gun to Denis Rake's (Roland) throat. The man, a local farmer, was totally irate and spoke in heated tones.

"*This espécé de merde* (piece of shit) who calls himself a soldier is indeed *un pedé,* (homosexual) has made a sexual advance at my son. I am ready to kill the bastard and no one will think badly of me for doing it."

Nancy was perplexed as to what to do. She tried comforting the farmer but her words had little effect. She explained that Denden was a British agent and was very critical to the Maquis' war against the Bosch. Killing him would help the Germans and not the Maquis. She also described Rake as very theatrical in his manners, actions that could sometimes be misconstrued. Nancy finally promised to look after the matter personally and the farmer finally relented.

Nancy grabbed Rake's arm and literally pulled him back toward the village and the hotel. "You are a fool, Denden," she reproached the now contrite radio operator. "One of these stupid escapades is going to get you killed."

Rake shook his head in disgust, and whimpered. "I know, I know. It's just that the young man was so attractive and he seemed to like me…"

Nancy threw up her hands in abhorrence and walked ahead of her compatriot. Right now, she wanted nothing to do with the man and his absolutely inappropriate behavior.

An order was received at Königsberg that would send Violette Szabo, Lilian Rolfe, and Denise Bloch back to the dreadfulness of Ravensbrück. The three agents were told to be ready by 0500. New clothes, shoes, some soap and a comb were issued and they were allowed to wash themselves with the soap. Violette asked Madame Marie to wash her back and help rid her hair of the lice that were there.

Violette questioned the sudden niceness of her captors in her mind. *Why are they doing this now? Nothing has changed to alter our situation, so all this doesn't seem to be a good omen. At least I feel like I'm human again, with these new clothes and shoes. I wish my little Nadia could see me now, she would think I look pretty nice after all I've been through. I wonder how she is faring through all this. I know she is in good hands and will be well looked after. I have made a really stupid choice with my life and now I am paying for it. I just hope we all survive this insanity and can one day return to our families…that would be more than I could hope for.*

Violette kissed Marie seven times as she left, one for each member of her family. She made her friend promise to tell her family what had happened to her if her friend should survive.

The trip back to Ravensbrück was uneventful. Upon arrival, the British women were placed into solitary confinement where they remained for several days. Even with the new clothes, their conditions could only be described as dreadful.

On a particular evening, the three were summoned and taken to a narrow alley that existed between the isolation block of the camp and the camp's inner wall.

Once there, the Ravensbrück Commandant, SS Hauptstrumführer Fritz Süh-ren, read an order that for their execution.

Both Denise Bloch and Lilian Rolfe were unable to walk and were carried by SS soldiers to a spot where they were made to kneel. Violette walked by herself and knelt beside her close friends. An SS corporal then took a position behind the three women and fired a single shot into the back of each woman's head. As was the German custom at the camp, the women's clothes were immediately removed and the dead bodies were then taken to be cremated.

When Nancy Fiocca broke the news to US Army Captain Brian Russell about Denis Rake's abhorrent behavior in the matter of the young Frenchman, Russell took the news personally. He confided in Nancy.

"I'm afraid he's done it this time, Madame Andrée. The main reason I was sent here was to look after him and he promised me that nothing like this would happen while we were in the field. I'm afraid he lets himself go whenever he wishes. I'm not sure he can help himself anymore. It's like a sickness…"

"It certainly seems so, Thierry. I wish there was something we could do about it."

"There is one thing we can do. We can send him back to England as soon as possible. I will ask London for a replacement on our next transmission."

"But Denden must make that transmission, right? It will kill him to know that he has been a failure. It will ruin his career."

"Right now I'm not too interested in his career, Madame Andrée. I can't fault his work here, but he was told he had a short leash when he was first sent over."

"You are certainly right, Thierry. I just wish there was something else we could do about it. I do adore the poor chap."

"I like him a great deal, too. We were friends at Beaulieu and I wouldn't want to hurt him for anything."

"Can't you reconsider your decision? Have a really heated talk with him and lay down the law. If he does anything else naughty, then throw the book at him."

Russell considered Nancy's entreaty. *Should I give him another chance? Does he deserve another chance? Do his actions really endanger our mission?*

After a few moments, the American captain again addressed Nancy. "All right. I will give him one more chance. But, we should both be there when I kick his butt. Maybe that will have some effect on him."

"I think you are making a wise decision, Thierry, for all of us here. After all, he is the best SOE radio operator in France."

"Yes, that he is," Russell added, not totally convinced he was doing the correct thing. "That he is."

The command to begin the attack on the Maquisards positions at Chaudes-Aigues had been briefly postponed pending the positioning of a number of Panzerkampfwagen IV tanks. A number of rough mountain country roads that were nearly impassible caused the Panzers to be late for the start of the attack.

Since Generalmajor Curt von Jesser was himself a veteran Panzer officer, he chose to wait for his tanks to be in proper position before ordering the attack to begin.

This did not sit well with the area Luftwaffe command at Clermont-Ferrand.

"Are we supposed to fly around until the generalmajor decides to begin his attack?" an exasperated Junker squadron operations officer asked. "We are low on petrol as it is, and this doesn't help matters." He immediately ordered the 10 Ju88's that were airborne to return to base and top off their fuel supply.

On the ground, the lead units of the attack force were reporting only sporadic contact with the French Maquis. One or two sightings resulted in the Maquis immediately vanishing into the forests, with the German columns continuing their steady advance.

Finally, a signal was received at Jesser's command post signaling everyone was in place.

"Alert the Luftwaffe, again!" he ordered. "And tell them this time we mean it."

Jesser consulted his watch and contemplated, *We must wait to give the Luft-*

waffe a chance to get down here. Ten minutes should be sufficient. I want the attack started before they actually fly over. No sense in alerting the Maquis for no reason.

He waited patiently as the minutes ticked away. A nod of his head started the attack.

"Beginnen Sie den Angriff" one of his officers barked. "Alle Einheiten vorwärts!"

The huge force lumbered into action from a number of positions surrounding the plateau that housed Chaudes-Aigues. The sounds of motors starting spread through the valleys quickly and alerted some of the Maquis that had been stationed as lookouts.

At one such post, Jean-Paul de la Houssaye quickly figured out what was happening. He immediately dispatched his fastest runner, his son, Georges, to go back to the main camp and inform Gaspard of the news. He hoped his son would make it back in time to warn the partisans.

At a position on the national road leading to Chaudes-Aigues, two Maquis fighters were crouched behind a large tree that had been strewn across the motorway. At the sounds of approaching engines, the Frenchmen loaded their bazooka as they had been taught by Anselme some weeks before. The men had only fired the weapon on one prior occasion, but were confident they could stop on oncoming tank.

"Remember Gaston, we must aim at the treads of the tank. That's where we can do the most damage."

"I know, I know, my friend. You have told me that several times already."

"I guess I am just scared," Gaston replied. "This is the first time we have used this bazooka for real."

"Captain Bazooka said it was capable of many things, and I have faith in him," the other Maquis replied. "We will wait and see."

Seconds later, a huge Panzer rounded a curve in the road and came into their view.

"*Mon Dieu,* it's so large. Are we sure this will work? Our bazooka is so small in comparison."

"Quiet, Gaston. I want to let it get closer before I shoot. As close as possible."

"What if we miss or do it no harm. Surely it will fire back at us."

"We will leave as soon as we shoot. Head for that thicket back there." He pointed to a line of trees some thirty yards away. "We'll be safe if we can make it to there."

Gaston said nothing more as the tank steadily approached. His partner lined up the sight and waited another few seconds. When he was satisfied the tank was near enough, he pulled the trigger and the missile exploded toward the Panzer.

"Let's go," the Maquis shouted, grabbing Gaston by the arm. "We don't have much time."

Behind them, the US M6 warhead found its way between the fourth and fifth wheels of the oncoming vehicle and exploded, causing the tank to stop. A column of smoke quickly engulfed the panzer. The tank turned slightly to its left and stopped.

Another panzer in the column behind the lead tank moved up to push the stricken vehicle off the road. Once done, the next panzer fired directly at the tree that blocked its path across the road. The tree splintered and fell into two large pieces. The panzer continued forward and pushed the tree part. As subsequent panzers passed through the opening, each one pushed the tree further apart until it presented no problem to the remaining vehicles.

Meanwhile, the two maquis responsible for the bazooka attack were well on their way to safety. Gaston had even remembered to bring the second warhead with him on his flight. After all, rounds for the bazooka were scarce enough, and he wasn't about to leave such a valuable round for the Germans to find.

Chapter Sixteen

Their meeting with **Denis Rake** went smoothly enough for Russell and Nancy Fiocca. Rake was completely contrite and hung his head sheepishly as Russell spelled out the facts of his continued work in France. The SOE-F operative realized this was his last chance and thanked Russell for the second time in as many minutes.

"You will not regret giving me this chance," Rake said assuredly. "I won't make the same mistake again."

Russell looked at Nancy who quickly looked away. *She isn't sure about him either. I think she let her feelings cloud her judgment about him. Oh, well, it's done and I can't take back my promise to let him stay. I truly hope he can keep his word this time...*

The meeting broke and Denis Rake left the room.

"I hope he makes it this time," Nancy said. "I believe he will really try this time."

"I'm sure he will," Russell replied. "I just don't know if he has the intestinal fortitude necessary. I am pulling for him."

"By the way," Nancy inserted, attempting to change the subject. "Have you seen the other woman that is here with us, yet? Her code name is Sofian and she is one of Gaspard's best operatives. I understand that she has proven herself on many occasions. I find her quite attractive and seemingly at home in practically any situation. I only had the chance to speak with her on two minor occasions but she seemed well informed. She actually seemed quite dear to me."

"No, I haven't had the chance. I noticed you talking to her yesterday, but you two left quite abruptly; I haven't seen her again to be able to meet her."

"Well, don't take too long to do it. No telling what's going to happen up here if you get my drift."

"I think I'll mosey over there right now. I don't have much to do now anyway."

"I wish I was so lucky," Nancy confessed. "There are three more drops scheduled tonight and I want to be sure everything is ready."

"*Semper paratus*" Russell added. "Just like the United States Coast Guard. Always prepared."

"Always, my friend. There's no better way to be." She laughed and proceeded to leave the room.

Russell gestured to her as she left and closed the door behind him. *Now, for the woman that Nancy feels is an absolute dear...I believe her name was Sofian...*

A large number of Maquis had congregated at one area of the camp and Russell correctly surmised that the young woman might be part of the gathering. He was entirely correct.

Sofian was standing next to a large tree among fifteen or so Maquis. Her back was to Russell as he approached. The crowd was on the verge of breaking up and had just started to scatter. Russell stepped behind the young woman and spoke.

"So you are Sofian. I have heard about you from Nancy."

The woman turned and stared at Brian Russell for a second. A gleam of recognition swept through her eyes. Russell's reaction wasn't as swift but suddenly everything became clear to him too.

He was standing in front of Christine Allard!

The black Citroën carrying Nancy Wake Fiocca southward to her scheduled appointments with other Maquisard units was followed by some heavy artillery sounds coming from the direction they had just left.

"It sounds like it's coming from where the camp is located," the Maquis driver offered his lone passenger.

"I would guess the Germans are attacking Chaudes-Aigues," Nancy responded. "We all knew it was coming sooner or later. Gaspard simply would not listen to me or anyone."

"He is like that, Madame. Once he sets his mind, he can be quite stubborn."

"Yes, that he can." *I hope we don't lose our entire force of Maquis in this. It would be such a waste. It would set us back months or even years. I hope Thierry and Denden can get out of there safely, I don't know what I would do without Denden. He's such a fool but he has been absolutely wonderful for me. I guess I am lucky to have escaped. This road to the south might be the only road the Germans haven't sealed off yet. I pray that everyone back at Chaudes-Aigues will make it through this difficult time. I must find Laurent and his band. They were smart enough to leave Chaudes-Aigues before the shelling started. Now, where did Laurent tell me they were headed? I think it was Fidefront. Yes, Fidefront...*

She quickly motioned to her driver who immediately turned the car in the opposite direction.

Sounds of artillery in the distance heralded the arrival at the Maquis camp of Georges de la Houssaye with his important news. Gaspard received the young soldier who blurted out his message.

"The Bosch are attacking with mortars and artillery from a number of positions around the valley. It seems as if there are a great many of them. My father wanted to alert you as soon as possible."

"Thank your father, for his help. I will disperse all my units as soon as possible to contain this attack. You have been a great help today, and, to France."

The youth bowed and started back to his father's position.

Gaspard gave orders for all commanders to put his plan into effect that would thwart the Germans offensive. *We will meet them now and stop them once and for all. My brave Maquis have been waiting for this chance for some time. We will now show our enemies what we are made of.*

The artillery fire seemed to be getting closer as the Maquis leader consulted his map of the Auvergne. He studied the map for a few minutes and shook his head affirmatively. *This time I have made provisions for my men to get through all this. Our defenses should hold back the Germans for the time being, that is what they were designed to do. As soon as night comes, our men can utilize the escape routes we have designated and get the hell out of here. Our losses should be minimal and we should be able to take out a number of the Bosch in the process. This will not be another Mont Mouchet, I am sure of that.*

Christine and Brian had held each other closely for what seemed like an eternity. They then kissed lightly and then more intensely. Russell saw that Christine was crying softly and wiped the tears from her cheeks.

"Why are you crying, my darling?"

"I'm just so happy. These are tears of joy. I have waited so long."

"We have waited so long," Russell added. "Much too long if you ask me."

"I just knew you were alive and that I would see you again one day. I prayed to the Blessed Virgin and she has finally answered my prayers. We need to pray to her again and give thanks for her wonderful gift to us."

"Of course, my darling. Whatever you say…"

"How did you get to the Auvergne and to Chaudes-Aigues? Did the British send you again?"

"Yes, they did. I have been here several weeks and am helping some other SOE-F agents and Gaspard get supplies and arms to the Maquis."

"But, I work for Gaspard. How is it we have never run into each other?"

"Fate has that answer, Christine. I have heard of Sofian, but I thought your code name was Jeanne."

"That was my old code name when I worked for Victor a couple of years ago. The Gestapo learned about me from an informant and I was forced to leave my home in Saint Flour and come here to join Gaspard's Maquis. He decided to give me a new code name, Sofian, and that's what I've been ever since."

"You look terrific, whatever name you go by these days. A little thinner than I like but beautiful nonetheless."

"You are most prejudiced, my dear heart. Of that I am quite sure."

"I give up. I'll admit I'm prejudiced when it comes to you."

The looked into each other's eyes again and continued their kiss. Neither wanted to part, so the kiss lingered.

Russell leaned back and spoke softly. "I'll never let you get away from me again, so help me God."

"I won't leave you for anything. I promise you that much. Even for the Resistance. I have thought about you so often."

They couple held each other warmly, until the sounds of incoming artillery boomed in the distance.

"What is that?" Christine exclaimed. "It sounds like big guns to me."

"I would think it is artillery and tank fire. I would imagine we are in the process of being attacked by the Jerries."

"They can't attack right now. We've just found each other again. They have no right..."

"Hush, my darling. I figured it would come any day now. We have too many Maquis gathered here. We are an inviting target."

"I want you to go back to the headquarters building and wait for me there. A chap named Roland (Rake) should be there. He's one of our agents. Stick with him for a short while. I need to check on two specific places where our defenses are set. If everything is in order, I'll be right back to get you."

"I can come with you. I can take care of myself, you know that."

"That's not the point. You would just slow me up. I'll be back in no time at all."

"I don't like leaving you again. Remember what we just said."

"This will only be for a short while. You will see."

Christine grudgingly agreed. "If you insist. But, you better make it back here fast, there's no telling what will happen."

She kissed Russell lightly on the lips and turned to leave. Another set of tears were already forming on her face. She started away and began to leave, but turned to see Russell one more time. She looked for a moment at her love and waved a good bye. In another second she was headed toward the headquarters building.

Denis Rake (Roland) heard the first artillery blasts and immediately went to the headquarters building. He was aware that Nancy had departed prior to the start of the shelling but was unsure of what he should do next. He found Gaspard who immediately enlisted his help.

"Can you radio London that we are under attack?" the Maquis leader hollered.

"What good would that do, Gaspard? They are in London and we are here. I probably couldn't get through right now; it isn't my scheduled time to broadcast. No one will be monitoring my frequency."

Gaspard shook his head, realizing his request was futile. He dismissed Roland with a flick of his eyes and returned to his map and runners who were waiting.

Rake surveyed the scene and knew that there was little he could do. Runners were coming in and out and an endless stream of subordinates was reporting situational updates to the Maquis leader.

"We seem to be holding our own," Gaspard shouted in his direction. Denis Rake considered the situation. *But for how long and at what cost? This isn't going to be pretty. Maybe I should think of making myself scarce around here. I'll need my radio and equipment, but I can't see the Maquis here holding out for very long.*

Rake's attention was diverted as an amazingly attractive young woman entered the headquarters building. She talked to several of the Maquis. One pointed in his direction and she started toward him.

"I'm called Sofian, monsieur. I understand you are Roland."

"That's what everyone calls me, my dear," he said, looking her over from head to toe. "Nice to meet you… Yes, I'm Roland. How can I help you?"

"Captain Russell of the US Army told me to come here and find you. We are old friends from years ago. He will be along in a while. I'm to stay with you until he arrives."

"That's perfectly okay with me. I could stand the company if…" His speech was broken by the sound of airplane engines and the falling of nearby bombs.

"That would be the Luftwaffe, ready to bomb us into oblivion," Rake offered. "We must get out of this building. This place is like a sitting duck."

"But, Brian said I was not to leave you for any reason."

"You can stay if you wish but I would suggest we leave if you want to stay alive. Everyone should leave this place!" he screamed in the direction of Gaspard.

The Maquis leader shook his head in concurrence and ordered everyone out. Rake grabbed Christine and pulled her along with him. "We can catch up with your captain sometime later, but let's go. They won't miss a second time."

The pair made their way out of the building and headed for some trees about a hundred yards away. The Ju88's swept through on another pass and the building behind them exploded with a resounding force. The blast knocked both Rake and Christine to the ground. He got up first and helped her to her feet.

"Just in time," he smiled. "The Jerries still haven't got my number. The pigs never will…"

"Let's get to safety," Christine warned. "We are still out in the open if they happen to come back."

Christine and Rake hurried to the edge of the forest and started into the growth of large trees. They traveled for almost a half-hour on a simple trail until Rake finally called for Christine to stop.

"I am completely out of breath," he panted. "I need to stop for a bit. I also have some small rocks in my shoes that are driving me crazy. I need to get them out."

"We should not stop for anything, Roland. It is too dangerous to stop. There are probably many Germans in these woods."

"You go ahead if you wish. This trail should bring you out somewhere above the camp. There will be other Maquis out here and we can join up with them. I'll be right behind you as soon as I can get my shoes fixed up."

"I will go ahead and scout the trail. If I come to a clearing, I will wait for you there."

"As you wish, Sofian. I'll be right along."

Christine departed and Rake began the task of taking off his boots. The large number of laces involved made the task tedious. He finished with the first, and took the second boot. He shook it heartily and began retying the bootlaces. A short while later, he was finished.

He started off up the trail and walked for about ten minutes. He was turning a corner when he heard voices in the front of him. Cautiously, he dropped to a low position and continued forward. He peered from behind a thicket and saw Christine standing in the middle of a squad of armed Wehrmacht soldiers. Her hands were raised and the Germans were raucously shouting instructions at her. Rake stepped back and tried to find another way that would give him an advantage if he were to open fire with his Thompson. His route took him several minutes to complete. When he emerged again, both the German soldiers and Christine were already gone. A sinking feeling engulfed Denis Rake as he pondered his next move. He realized one thing for certain. It was suddenly imperative he find US Army Captain Brian Russell and apprise him of the situation.

The arrival of the Luftwaffe bombers was icing on the cake for Generalmajor Curt von Jesser and his staff. The aircraft began dive bombing the Maquis positions producing an effect of near bedlam. Many of the young Maquis recruits had never seen a German airplane and the idea of one bearing down on them spitting bullets and bombs was more than they could handle.

Large numbers of Maquis broke and ran, throwing down their new weapons. Some more experienced Maquis fighters attempted to calm them, but it was of little use. Many were mowed down in the open areas of the plateau before they could reach the safety of the woods.

Still, Gaspard's Maquis were giving the Germans a good fight. Bazookas had taken out or disabled a number of the huge Panzers and the German attack was stunted in certain spots. Jesser's commanders quickly changed their plans of attack to compensate for these unforeseen problems.

German ground troops encountered few real pockets of resistance until they neared the actual camp where Gaspard had set up several lines of defence. The Maquis manning these positions stood firm in the face of enemy fire that was continuous.

"This might take longer than I expected," Jesser remarked to his adjutant. "These Frenchmen are good fighters even if they are outnumbered. I want the Luftwaffe to continue their bombing as long as possible; I think their presence gives us a great advantage."

"Jawohl, Herr Generalmajor. Consider it done."

We have a great advantage and must make the most of it as soon as possible. I don't want these people holding us off until dark. They might easily escape if that happens. I must see to it that they do not escape. This will be a great victory for the Third Reich.

Russell's visits to the outposts took a little longer than he had anticipated. When he finally made his way back to the camp, he was troubled to see the headquarters building completely destroyed. He looked about the wreckage for any sign of life but found nothing. The ruined building was empty, and Russell silently thanked heaven for that.

They were able to get out, and for that I am grateful. The question is where would they go? Most of the trails from here head either north or east, but those are the directions the Germans seem to be attacking from. I wonder where Gaspard is right now. Christine and Denis might be with him but I don't think so. Everyone here probably scattered to look out for themselves. I'm not sure what I should do...

For some reason, his instinct led him away from the camp site. He picked a trail that he knew and began following it. Minutes later, Russell recognized a Maquis commander ahead who had stopped to consult a map. The Maquis had several fighters with him who raised their guns as Russell approached. The Maquis ordered them to lower their weapons.

Russell spoke to the leader. "I am looking for Roland and the woman called Sofian. Have you seen them?"

The leader replied and pointed. "I saw them just after our building was attacked.

I'm not completely certain, but I believe they went in that direction." He pointed north by northwest.

"Thank you, my friend. It is imperative I find them as soon as possible."

"We are all supposed to meet at Saint-Santin, a village near Aurillac. Gaspard will meet us there. He pointed to a spot on his map for Russell to see. Russell looked at the map and guessed it was nearly 75 miles to Saint-Santin.

"Good luck to you all," Russell said. "But first, I need to find these people."

"There is a path just around the next curve that will take you in that direction, friend," the Maquis leader declared. "Good luck to you, too."

Russell started off and quickly came to the trail that branched off to his right. It was less used than the one he was on but he took it nonetheless. *I simply must find them; I can't afford to lose her again.* He continued along but his pace was slower. The brush was becoming thicker and the trail became hard to follow.

Christine was marched to a Catholic church in the small commune of Neuvéglise, not far from Chaudes-Aigues. While the Wehrmacht troops that had captured her took her Thompson from her, they had failed to search her any further. Christine had kept a small Beretta Model 1934 in a crude holder that she had designed that fit around her lower abdomen. She had found the gun early in her association with the French Resistance, but had never fired the weapon except in practice. Moreover, not even the heartiest German soldier would ever think of searching a woman around her abdomen, a fact Christine hoped would hold true on this occasion.

The church was obviously a holding place for captured Maquis. Christine was among the first to arrive and watched as the church slowly began to fill with captured and wounded Maquis. A few of the prisoners recognized her from her brief time at the camp, but no one made any attempt to talk to her. A guard was situated at the back of the church and another at the front.

Merde. What a stupid thing to do. Get caught without firing a single shot. I guess that's what I get for not being careful enough. Now I must get myself out of this mess. I still have my Beretta but I'm not sure that will be enough to get us all out of here. I must consider taking everyone with me; it will give us all a better chance to escape.

Christine pondered the situation for almost an hour and made eye contact with one of the older Maquis in the church. She nodded her head for him to come over. The Maquis looked around him and slowly made his way to where she stood.

Christine whispered to the Maquis who turned his back to her. "We need a distraction to divert the attention of the guards. Can you start an argument with someone that would make the guards come to break it up? I have a pistol but it only has seven shots in it."

"I probably can, mademoiselle. But I think we should wait until the place is more crowded. The more Maquis that are in here, the easier it will be to overpower the guards."

"You might be right. I also need to go to the toilettes before we act. I'm sure you understand."

The Frenchman had no idea what she was referring to but readily agreed. "After I see you come back, I'll start a commotion. You take it from there. But, we must wait for more prisoners to arrive."

Christine moved away from the man and casually sauntered to a spot underneath a stained glass window. The glass was thick and would not allow anyone to see out. She looked around the small church for any advantage she might find. There was nothing apparent there that could help her. She would have to get out of the incarceration on her own.

Chapter Seventeen

The route that Nancy instructed her driver to take finally brought her Citroën to the tiny village of Fidefront, some five miles away from Chaudes-Aigues. It was here that Laurent's Maquis were located, not far from the Lanau Reservoir. Nancy had always been able to count on Laurent. In her eyes, Laurent was the most dependable Maquis commander in the entire Auvergne.

She arrived to find Laurent surrounded by a number of his men and additional Maquis that had traveled to Fidefront.

"Madame Andrée," Laurent greeted her cordially. "It has happened again. The Germans attacked in force all those who had gathered at Chaudes-Aigues. They had Luftwaffe support again plus a large number of tanks. These men," he pointed at some of the Maquis, "are just getting here from the battle. I think we have lost a large number of Maquis if their reports are at all accurate."

"But, you and your men were not there. Am I correct Laurent?"

"No, Madame Andrée. I became worried that there were too many Maquis in one place so I moved my men here to Fidefront. The Germans have not bothered us at all."

"You are very smart, Laurent. I wish all the Maquis commanders were as smart as you. What else have you learned?"

"Not much else. One of the men saw the Germans leading prisoners to the old Catholic church at Neuvéglise. Other than that, there are Maquis scattered all over the Auvergne."

"Neuvéglise, huh?" Nancy thought. "I believe that's only four or five miles from

217

here. We might just be able to help out there. If we are lucky and they haven't yet moved the prisoners."

Her attention was diverted as Denis Rake pushed his way into the group. Rake was disheveled to say the least and completely out of breath. He looked imploringly at Nancy and spoke.

"Madame Andrée, something terrible has happened. Sofian and I were leaving the camp and we got separated. I caught up to her just as she was captured by the Bosch. I tried to find a better vantage point but by the time I got back to where she was they had all left. Thierry had sent her to stay with me. I think she knows Thierry from sometime before. I must let him know what has happened."

"Take your time, Roland," Nancy cautioned." I was just thinking about a plan that might be the answer. If she has been taken to the church at Neuvéglise with the other Maquis prisoners, we just might be able to get her out."

"We have an old truck, a *gazogène*, here, Laurent offered. It's not fast but it is very dependable."

"It seems there is a road through Lavastrie that leads to Neuvéglise," Nancy said again pointing at the map. I only want four or five of your best marksmen to come with me. You must stay here and reorganize the Maquis."

Laurent shook his head, knowing that Nancy's recommendation was correct.

"Bring plenty of ammunition with you," Nancy instructed the Maquis that Laurent selected for the mission. Roland and I are going to really need your help."

Rake was nearing exhaustion but summoned up what strength he had left.

"I'm as ready as I will be," he shrugged. "Let's get going."

The small group of Maquis piled into the old truck that was already burning wood. It lurched to a start and began its journey around the reservoir.

The path that Russell was following finally led to a larger trail that seemed to head northeast. He followed the trail until it came to a large body of water that seemed to stretch forever. *I might as well follow this until I come to somewhere that*

I can get my bearings, he deliberated. *It can't go on forever and it looks as if it is man-made. This must be one of the big reservoirs around here, but which one?*

He continued moving eastward, and made good progress along the well-used trail. *There don't seem to be any Germans around here; at least I haven't seen any. I'd better be careful, no need to find myself in trouble when I can help it.*

Russell continued his walk and passed next to a pair of oxbows in the reservoir. *This is a pretty place; I wouldn't mind taking a holiday around here.*

He continued for another hour and finally approached a spot where the water narrowed. On his right side was what appeared to be a lake that was intersected by what Russell perceived was some sort of a paved road.

At last, a real road. Now I can find out exactly where I am.

He started up the road and had gone about a mile when the sound of a motor approached from his rear. He turned just in time to see an old *gazogène* truck making its way toward him.

Could these be Maquis? No German would ever ride around in a gazogène.

He waited until the truck pulled up. A friendly face leaned out the front window and a familiar voice asked, "Hey sailor. Need a lift?"

Russell squeezed Nancy's arm and planted a kiss on her cheek.

"You are absolutely wonderful, Madame Andrée. I don't mind if I do? Is that Denden riding next to you?"

Rake leaned over and looked Russell right in the eyes. "Yes, it me, or what's left of me. Thierry, I have some bad news for you."

Christine. My God, she's been killed or something...

"Sofian has been taken prisoner by the Jerries. We believe she might be being held in a church at Neuvéglise. We are on our way there now."

Russell handed his weapon to one of the Maquis riding in the back of the truck and hopped up on the truck's running board. Nancy gave the order to start up again and the old truck belched appropriately and lumbered up the road. Russell was now filled with a new sense of determination and resolve. His long lost love was again in trouble and he determined to do something about it. He would not have long to wait.

The Maquis fighter that Christine has spoken with earlier in the afternoon glanced in her direction and nodded that all was set with the other Maquis that were being held as prisoners in the old church at Neuvéglise. Christine glanced at her watch and saw that it was almost six o'clock.

We must wait a bit longer, she decided. *It will be almost dark in about two hours. We will have a better chance of escaping if it is night time. I will wait until the time is right. No point in lessening our chances by being too impatient.* She nodded to the Maquis to wait some more.

Christine looked about the sanctuary and estimated that there were about forty or so Maquis standing and sitting around the church. New arrivals had slowed to a trickle and she was only aware of two new arrivals during the past two or three hours.

She contemplated her situation and thought about what had happened to Roland. *He was right behind me when I was captured. I made it a point to put my hands up to warn him, I just hope he saw me. He probably tried to do something to help me, but there was little he could do. I hope he was able to get back to Brian and let him know what has happened. Brian. My poor, brave darling. Here I am in trouble and he is so close. I must get myself out of this church and free all these wonderful Maquis.*

As the old *gazogène* truck approached the outskirts of Neuvéglise, Nancy tapped the driver to bring the vehicle to a halt. She alighted as did all the Maquis who were riding in the rear of the truck. She instructed the driver to turn the truck around and hide it in a nearby grove.

"If you hear any shooting, start the engine and wait for us. We might need to get out of here quickly, so be prepared." The driver nodded his agreement.

"We must be very careful from this point on," Nancy cautioned. "We have no idea if the prisoners are still here and just how many Germans are on guard. I will go forward with Thierry and scout the area around the church. You follow us at a safe distance and wait for us to return. Does everyone understand? There will be no shooting until we have developed a plan."

The Maquis from Laurent's group were seasoned veterans and understood her instructions. Nancy was now a revered member of their group who had earned her own reputation for toughness. They fanned out and waited for Nancy and Thierry to start.

"Well, here we go," Nancy remarked to her American friend. "With a bit of luck we'll find the place lightly guarded. I can't believe the Germans would waste a lot of their troops on guard duty."

"I hope you are correct, Madame Andrée. What you say makes good sense to me."

The pair started down the road but kept to the side between the trees that lined the road. In about ten minutes, they began approaching some buildings. So far there was no sign of life apparent from the small village.

Russell took the point and checked his Thompson. Satisfied it was cocked and ready, he crouched down as he approached the first building. The edifice was more of a shed and Russell took advantage of the fact that it shielded him from the rest of the commune. He motioned for Nancy to join him. He moved silently from one building to another, followed closely by his female accomplice.

As he neared the center of the village, a building with a high steeple appeared on the left side of the main road. A pair of armed guards could be seen standing outside the main entrance of the building. Russell decided to get closer in order to better identify the guards at the church.

He signaled Nancy to wait as he made his way closer. He finally reached a point some thirty yards and studied the guards. These were not regular German troops but looked to be almost oriental in appearance.

Of course, these could easily be Azerbaijanis, Russian volunteers in the Wehrmacht. I had a couple of documents cross my desk that mentioned them and their involvement with the German military. So they are part of the German attempt to control the Auvergne. Interesting...

Russell made his way back to where Nancy was waiting. "We are in luck. It appears there are only two of 'em, and they didn't seem to be all that attentive. They were standing and talking while smoking, so I can't believe they will be much of an obstacle. Let's get the men and work up a plan. You stay here and I'll bring our guys back with me."

Nancy nodded and turned her attention to the front of the church. No movement was apparent at present. The trained SOE veteran took that as a good sign.

It took Russell a little over fifteen minutes to return with Laurent's Maquis fighters. Three were designated to make their way to the rear of the church and storm the back door when the firing was initiated.

Russell took the remaining Maquis along with Nancy and Rake and slowly made their way to the front of the edifice.

He pointed to Rake. "You and Nancy go around and come in from the left of the church. I will come from this side. Make sure we take out the guards right away; we don't want them sending out an alarm. You should be able to get pretty close without being seen. There are plenty of bushes around for cover on that side. Go slow and don't get spotted."

The pair departed and Russell followed their movement until they were out of his view. He moved forward and crouched behind a small fence that was his last spot of cover before the church itself. It was becoming darker now, and the darkness was definitely his friend.

Nancy and Rake should be in place by now, and the other Maquis should also be around the back. It's just about time...

Inside the church, Christine had already given the signal for the Maquis to start a disruption to distract the German guards. A series of rifle shots from outside the church caught the attention of the prisoners. The Maquis began shouting and the confusion startled the Azerbaijanis that were guarding the prisoners.

A number of captured Maquis quickly moved toward each of the soldiers who leveled their rifles at the oncoming Maquis. Two Maquis near the back door and a single Maquis fighter near the front guard went down as the shots resounded through the ironstone church. The remaining Maquis grabbed the guards and turned the weapons on their captors.

A sudden splintering noise came from the rear of the church as the Maquis from Laurent's group entered the back door. A cheer went up from the prisoners as they recognized their countrymen.

A few seconds later, the front door opened as Nancy, Russell and Rake also entered the church.

Christine saw Russell at once and rushed to meet him. She flung herself toward him and hugged him passionately.

"I can't be doing this on a regular basis," Russell joked. "It takes way too much energy."

"Shut up you crazy person," Christine answered. "Just kiss me and never let me get away from you again."

They kissed until the applause from the now liberated Maquis filled the church. The couple looked sheepishly around and blushed accordingly.

"This is a great day for France," Christine finally shouted. *Vive la France!*

"*Vive la France, Vive la France,*" resonated from the rafters of the old church.

End

Afterword

The heroics of Nancy Wake Fiocca, Dennis Rake, René Dussaq and hundreds of other SOE operatives in France and Europe did not end at the conclusion of this novel. Historical accounts of these brave individuals detail numerous courageous events that literally changed the tide of war in France and elsewhere.

Nancy Fiocca did not learn of her husband Henri's death until the liberation of the town of Vichy where she encountered an old friend from Marseille. After the war, she returned to her old city to investigate the details of his death and then left the place for good. It simply had too many bad memories for her to stand.

As far as the specific time period around the allied invasion of France, a major fact emerged. The German attempt to reinforce its troops around Normandy was severely impaired by the brave actions of SOE operatives in France and England along with the courageous members of French Resistance. Many military strategists recognized the interruption of German participation and the successful impeding of German supplies as deciding factors in the eventual Allied victory.

France, England, the United States and many other countries have honored these heroes in their own manner. Numerous plaques and monuments have been erected to their memories.

It was my intention to focus on a few of these memorable events in *The White Mouse*. I have attempted to be historically accurate in every sense.

Heroes, Heroines and Their Adversaries

Nancy Wake Fiocca — survived the war and became Great Britain's most decorated SOE operative. Her British decorations included the George Medal. France awarded her two *Croix de Guerre* with Palm and a third Croix de Guerre with Star. An additional honor, the Resistance Medal, was given to her, a rare honor that was almost never awarded to foreigners. The United States awarded her the Medal of Freedom with Bronze Palm, another medal rarely given to foreigners. Immediately after the war, she returned to Marseille and was reunited with her faithful terrier, Picon, who had been cared for by neighbors after Henri's arrest. She died in London on August 7, 2011 just prior to her 99th birthday. Nancy asked that her ashes "be scattered over the hills where I fought alongside all those men."

Henri Fiocca — arrested by the Gestapo after Nancy's departure from France, Fiocca was tortured to give up his wife's whereabouts. The son of a prominent shipping family from Marseille refused to comply with the Germans and was executed in 1943. As tribute to his loyalty, a street in Marseille's 1st *Arrondissement* is named rue Henri FIOCCA.

Colonel Maurice Buckmaster — was awarded the French *Croix de Guerre* to go along with his OBE. After the war, he became an executive with Ford Motor Company in France. He is believed to the inspiration for the character 'M' in the 007 James Bond series. Bond creator Ian Fleming also worked in the SOE office with Buckmaster and Vera Atkins.

Vera Atkins — (born Vera Maria Rosenberg in Bucharest, Romania) was Buckmaster's principal assistant. She is believed to have seen each of the SOE agents off as they boarded their flights for jump offs in France. It is widely held that she was the inspiration for the character Miss Moneypenny in the James Bond 007 movies.

Violette Szabo — (born Violette Reine Elizabeth Bushell) joined the SOE after her husband Etienne Szabo was killed just south of El Alamein. Fiery and fearless, she was the best female shot in the SOE. She was captured in a gun battle with the Germans near Limoges and later transferred to the Ravensbruck concentration camp. She was shot along with two other female SOE Agents on 5 February 1945. The book and film, *Carve Her Name With Pride*, chronicled her daring exploits and is considered one of the exemplary war films, which recounted the efforts of women during WWII.

Virginia Hall — joined the Central Intelligence Agency postwar. In September 1945, General William "Wild Bill" Donovan presented Hall with the Distinguished Service Cross; the only such honor awarded a civilian woman during WWII. She died at age 66, on July 8, 1982, at Shady Grove Adventist Hospital, Rockville, MD. She is buried in Druid Ridge Cemetery, Pikesville, MD.

René Alexander Dussaq — American Army officer played a key role in the major battle of the Auvergne. Was awarded the Distinguished Service Cross for his efforts and became the oldest person (age 83) to reenact the original parachute drop in June of 1994. He passed away in 1996.

Patrick Albert O'Leary — (real name Major General Comte Albert-Marie Edmond Guerisse). For his valiant efforts, the Belgian-born Guerisse received some 35 decorations from a number of different nations. After the war, he assumed his real name and joined the Belgian Army. For his lifetime services, the King of Belgium granted him a peerage with the rank of count. He died in Waterloo, Belgium, on March 26, 1989 at the age of 77. He claimed the name Pat O'Leary was Canadian in an attempt to explain his not-quite British accent in English, and his not-quite French accent in French.

Henri Tardivat — leader of the Allier Maquis lost his leg in the fighting at Belfort Gap where he had joined Free French forces mopping up remnants of the German Army fleeing France. He remained close friends with Nancy and later christened his daughter in her name as well as choosing her as the baby's godmother. He became a successful businessman in Paris where the two visited for many years.

Gaspard — (real name Émile Coulaudon) always referred to as Colonel Gaspard; he formed one of the first resistance groups in the Auvergne that eventually numbered 10,000 men. Highly decorated for his work by four countries, he was featured in the 1969 film *The Sorrow and the Pity*. Gaspard died of cardiac arrest in June of 1977 and is buried in Pontgibaud (Puy-de-Dome).

Maurice Southgate — survived the horrors of Buchenwald Concentration Camp and later testified at the American war crimes trials at Dachau in 1947. He lived out his life in France and retired near Sarlat. Southgate was always private about his experiences during the war with the SOE-F. He finally died in February 1990 at the age of 77. He was awarded a DSO for his work by the British Government.

Denis Rake — supposedly born in Brussels in 1901, Rake's early childhood was spent as a member of a troupe of child acrobats in a circus. He enjoyed a brief career on the stage prior to the war and became a translator for the Royal Army Service Corps. An expert wireless operator and fluent in French, Rake was in high demand. An openly gay man, the forty-year-old was considered highly effeminate and even a drug user due to the high number of sedatives he consumed to help him sleep. Post war, he eventually became Douglas Fairbanks, Jr.'s valet. Several books have been published that chronicled his life. He died in September, 1976.

SS Obersturmbannfuhrer Ernst Dunker — was a racketeer and thug in Berlin before the war. He became head of KDS Office IV in Marseille in 1943. Captured after the war, he was found guilty of war crimes and shot on June 6, 1950, exactly six years to the day after the D-Day invasion of Normandy.

SS Sturmbannführer Rolf Muhler — was Chief of Gestapo in Marseille from 1943 to 1944. Even though he eventually transferred into the Wehrmacht with great discretion, he was recognized and captured. Sentenced to death, his sentence was commuted to a prison term. He died in 1967 in the German city of Wuppertal.

SS Sturmbannführer Hans Joseph Kieffer — was chief intelligence officer for the Gestapo in Paris. Captured shortly after the war, he was questioned by none other than Vera Atkins. He began to cry during the interrogation and Atkins told him, "Kieffer, if one of us is going to cry it is going to be me. You will please stop this comedy." Found guilty of war crimes, he was sentenced to death by hanging at Hemelin Prison on June 26, 1947.

Generalmajor Curt von Jesser — was born in Poland to an Austrian family. He was decorated in World War I and commanded numerous fighting units during World War II. He was awarded the Knight's Cross of the Iron Cross for bravery as an Oberst (Colonel) of Panzer-Regiment 36. He was captured by Allied troops in 1945 and spent four years in prison. He was released in poor health in 1949. He died on August 18th, 1950.

SS Sturmbannführer Fritz Sühren — was born in 1908 in Varel. He was captured after the war and was sentenced to death for the atrocities committed while he was Commandant of the Ravensbruck Concentration Camp. He was hanged on June 12, 1950 in Sandweier, Baden Baden.

Also by Jack DuArte

The Resistance (Revised)

SINGAPORE (Revised)

Spitfire

MALTA

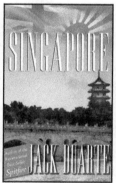

Preview and order all three at:

www.jackduarte.com

The White Mouse is the fifth installment of Jack DuArte's best-selling World War II series that includes *The Resistance, Singapore, Spitfire* and *Malta.*

DuArte is a decorated Vietnam Veteran who resides in Lexington, KY with his wife Susan, their basset hound Tucker and miniature horse Darleigh.

He can be reached at jackduarte41@gmail.com.

CPSIA information can be obtained
at www.ICGtesting.com
Printed in the USA
BVHW060927080720
583176BV00004B/411